Until Every Animal is Free

By Saryta Rodriguez

Vegan Publishers™

Published by:
Vegan Publishers, Danvers, MA, www.veganpublishers.com

Cover and text design: Nicola May Design
Cover Photo: Jo-Anne McArthur / Save the Chimps

♻ Printed in the United States of America on 100% recycled paper

ISBN: 978-1-940184-19-7

Table of Contents

Dedication

For my mother, who taught me by example the resilience of the human spirit. All that I am and all that I do can be traced back to Iris Rodriguez, a truly remarkable woman.

For Alex Ludlum, who has provided me with limitless love and support while I pursue my passions.

For Joy Tutela, who showed me the ropes and always believed in me.

For David Black, who inspired me not to see the wall.

For my PALS, Phoenix Animal Liberation Squad, who motivated me to stop talking and start doing.

For everyone at DxE, for the wisdom, knowledge, and experience they lent to the development of this work.

For all of those who helped support the production of this book, with special thanks to Dawn Moncrief, Georgie Cooper, Diane Gandee Sorbie, Nicholas Shaw-McMinn, and Christy Marsh-Trombelli.

Last but not least, this book is dedicated to animal liberationists everywhere. Keep fighting the good fight. The animals need us.

Prologue

A Brief History and a Call to Arms

We can see quite plainly that our present civilization is built on the exploitation of animals, just as past civilizations were built on the exploitation of slaves, and we believe the spiritual destiny of man is such that in time he will view with abhorrence the idea that men once fed on the products of animals' bodies.

–Donald Watson
First-ever Vegan Society newsletter, 1944

It is difficult to pinpoint the exact "beginning" of the Animal Liberation Movement, as vegetarian, and to a lesser extent vegan, diets have been practiced for centuries— and the reasons for adhering to said diets were not always necessarily aligned with liberationist philosophy. In addition to the myriad religious traditions that uphold one of these diets, such notable philosophers and scholars as Socrates, Plato, Pythagoras, Leonardo da Vinci, Benjamin Franklin, Gandhi, and Albert Einstein were vegetarian. One place some modern animal liberation scholars like to start is with the founding of the Vegan Society in 1944 by Donald Watson. To keep a long story short, after being a member of the Vegetarian Society in England for many years, Watson and others felt there needed to be another term to distinguish people who not only abstain from animal flesh, but also from dairy, eggs, and other products that are acquired via animal exploitation.

The first Vegan Society newsletter, *The Vegan News*, published in 1944, declared the new society's commitment to abstaining from all animal byproducts—not for any health or economic reasons such as abound today, but simply for the sake of not engaging in or contributing to animal cruelty. These vegans were true liberationists, motivated strictly by the Moral Imperative: That every sentient being has a right to autonomy over his or her own body.

The first vegan cookbook, *The Hygeian Home Cookbook*, was published in New York in 1874—seventy years before the term "vegan" was coined—but the focus of this book was primarily human health. In 1910, *No Animal Food: Two Essays and 100 Recipes* came along, with a much more obvious focus on animal ethics (as evidenced by both the title and the inclusion of essays). This serves as a strong indication that sentiments against animal exploitation were growing, at least in the UK, as early as the mid-to-late nineteenth century.

The Animal Liberation Movement now stretches far beyond food. While this was understandably the primary concern of the Vegan Society when it was founded, technological advances coupled with mass media and the development of the "consumer-society" have presented new challenges to the movement. Today, animal exploitation is evident in our clothing, our toiletries, our cosmetics, our cleaning products—you name it—and if you didn't read the back label carefully (or, better yet, research the company thoroughly prior to making the purchase), odds are there's either part of an animal in it or an animal suffered needlessly in order to "test" the product before it hit the shelves.

The history of *human* liberation in America is itself a work in progress. Sadly, for much of our nation's history, African Americans were not given the status of white men; in 1787, our government decided that an African American constituted only "three-fifths" of a white person. The Jim Crow laws forcing African Americans to use separate—and unequal—facilities in the

US remained in place until 1965. That's right—a mere fifty years ago, African Americans were not legally recognized as equals to their white counterparts in America.

The Nineteenth Amendment, which granted women the right to vote in the United States, was not passed until 1920; in light of the racist legislation that persisted thereafter, one might be tempted to say, in terms of achieving "equality," that women have a lead on African Americans. Unfortunately, women in the US *today* make an average of seventy-seven cents to every dollar men make, depending on industry as well as state—and that's just *white* women. The numbers for women of color are even worse. Men are still being paid more than women to complete the same tasks, regardless of experience or education—why?

There remains work to be done with respect to both of these movements; still, the strides that have been made in both arenas in the past century are encouraging. Minority rights aim to put an end to the Myth of White Supremacy. Feminist initiatives aim to put an end to the Myth of Male Supremacy. The Animal Liberation Movement proudly joins these traditions, aiming to put an end to the Myth of Human Supremacy.

The Animal Liberation Movement aims to liberate all animals—not just those used for food, although this is perhaps the most common reason for animal abuse. The movement includes ending the use of animals for fashion, in scientific research, for entertainment (such as circuses and rodeos), and all other forms of animal oppression. The end goal is to eschew the consideration of nonhumans as commodities—items to be bought and sold, and tools for our knowledge and entertainment—and respect their autonomy over their bodies, families, and lives.

Animals need not be tested on for product safety, as many companies forgo such testing and nevertheless create effective products (anything from shampoo to counter cleaner to lipstick). We don't need animals to research disease or test medications; laboratories such as Pharmagene (based in Royston, England) and

Merck (headquartered in New Jersey) have made great strides without using animals, while the use of spare or synthetic human tissue provides a more ethical as well as more accurate alternative. In his June 2013 speech at the National Institutes of Health campus in Bethesda, Maryland, Dr. Elias Zerhouni, who served as America's National Institutes of Health Director from the years 2002–2008, said of animal testing, "We all drank the Kool-Aid on that one, myself included."

We don't need animals for food. It is written on our bodies—the length of our intestines, for example, or our obvious lack of claws—as well as in our instincts. When was the last time you saw a squirrel or a rabbit pass by and had to suppress the urge to pounce? Our nutritional needs can be met readily using plants such as nuts, legumes, and leafy greens. Not only do scores of strong, powerful animals such as bison illustrate this, but millions of human vegans also exist as living proof!

We don't need animals to teach college kids; universities such as Harvard, Stanford, and Yale have eschewed this barbaric practice in favor of cruelty-free teaching methods. I highly doubt this will make the next generation of surgeons from Stanford University School of Medicine any less efficient than that which preceded it.

It's time for a societal shift in perspective. Animals were not put on Earth to serve us. Neither our ability to speak nor our dexterous hands give us the right to exploit other creatures for food, fashion, or even in the name of Science. We must shift the dialogue away from *how* animals are being raised and toward *why* they are being raised—for exploitation and slaughter. We must remember how to live in the world and be part of it, without destroying it.

Chapter One

How This Became My Life

It is no use walking anywhere to preach unless our walking is our preaching.

−St. Francis of Assisi

A Goat Named Pepa

When I was roughly five years old, my mother related to me the story of Pepa, a young female goat who was also her best childhood friend. My mother's grandparents, by whom she was raised, murdered Pepa one day while she was visiting an aunt—and served her for dinner that night, to celebrate the arrival of my mother's uncle. I'm not sure whether or not my mother cried while telling me this story. I do recall distinctly that her voice cracked, and her brow furrowed ever so slightly. This is the first memory I have of ever seeing her in pain.

Years later, my mother was kind enough to send me an email recounting the story to me in her own words, as memory is unreliable at best and I wanted to do justice to Pepa by sharing her story on Direct Action Everywhere's blog, *The Liberationist.* Direct Action Everywhere is an international animal liberation coalition of which I am a part, having first encountered them in Phoenix, Arizona in 2013 and having joined their now independently-run Phoenix branch, PALS (Phoenix Animal Liberation Squad) that May. Upon moving to Oakland in March 2014, I joined the Bay Area branch of the organization; in October 2014, I became the group's Blog Manager.

Here is Pepa's story, in my mother's own words:

Pepa was a baby goat that grew to be my one and only companion after school and on lonely weekends. How did I acquire Pepa? A neighbor was looking for someone to take care of his goat: Pepa's mom. In return for taking care of the senior goat, I was given baby Pepa to keep as my own.

I was super excited! I was finally coming home to a friend who would listen to me talk about my day at school! I accepted the neighbor's offer and started looking forward to coming home from school to do all of my chores on time and take care of the goats—especially mine. I made sure that her mother was always well-fed and clean. I then would take my goat to the hill and sit in front of her, talking about my day at school...the day of a twelve-year-old lonely girl who was left without brothers and sisters and in the care of her old grandma and grandpa. I was happy to have that time alone with Pepa; she looked at me as though she understood my life better than I did!

Years passed, and Pepa grew to be a beautiful, healthy goat that everybody wanted to buy. Everybody congratulated me on a job well done in raising her, but one unfortunate Mother's Day, my long-lost older uncle decided to come visit us. Hours of house-cleaning and organization.... Rehearsing what to say and what not to say....After all, he was coming from The City—and that was A BIG DEAL!

My grandmother asked me to visit my aunt, who lived about two miles from our home. I looked to my grandfather for permission, and he granted it. None of this was strange to me; he always did what she wanted. I hesitated to ask them why. I think deep inside, I knew something bad was going to happen, but I never thought that they were going to kill Pepa as a present to celebrate my uncle's visit.

They did—without any regard for my feelings, or hers. Somehow, after days of quietly crying and feeling sad, I forgave my grandparents. My uncle, on the other hand, was impossible for me to forgive; he was the first one to die in the family, and he was the only one for whom I did not cry!

Pepa's story is, I believe, one of many reasons that I became an animal advocate. Rather than emulating her caregivers and suppressing my empathy, I choose to emulate my mother and acknowledge the individuality of all sentient beings—not just cats and dogs.

The switch was not immediate. I did not eschew my carnivorous ways the moment I heard the story; truth be told, while I was sad upon hearing it, I doubt I gave it much thought in the days and weeks that followed. I was young and imaginative; I spent more time in my own head than I spent focusing on matters of even local, let alone global, justice. I had more imaginary friends than anyone could count, and each had particular likes and dislikes, which I kept carefully catalogued on folded-up sheets of printer paper, under my bed and in my underwear drawer.

If I didn't like what was being served for dinner one night, I'd go up to my room and imagine myself a yummier dinner: chocolate cake topped with cookie dough ice cream, French fries, and, yes, chicken nuggets. When I didn't like how my mother dressed me for school, I'd spend the day envisioning that I was wearing something entirely different—something *über-cool*.

My family actually thought, for the first two or three years of my life, that I might be deaf or severely hearing-impaired, because whenever someone called out to me I did not answer. A doctor would eventually reveal that the problem was not that I couldn't *hear* my name being called; it was that I wasn't *listening*. I was lost in my own thoughts, and the Real World was miles away.

Besides, my family didn't eat goats; we ate cows, chickens, and pigs—just like everybody else. What could be so bad about *that*?

An Animated Activist

The first animal advocate I ever met was Lisa Simpson. I was around eight years old when I first saw *The Simpsons* episode "Lisa the Vegetarian" (Season Seven, Episode Five), in which Lisa becomes a vegetarian after visiting a petting zoo and realizing that the lambs she petted earlier that day were just like the lamb whose "chops" were being served for dinner that night. Later in the episode, Homer hosts a barbecue at which he roasts an entire pig, the corpse of whom Lisa "liberates" by pushing it off of a slope while aboard a lawnmower.

The image of the entire pig is important; I'm not sure I would have connected with the episode as strongly as I did without it. Almost annually while I was growing up, pig roasts were hosted at my home, a relative's home, or Belmont Park on Long Island, where my large family would celebrate birthdays, graduations, and the like. I had seen many a whole pig roasted by age eight, but I'd always thought that the corpse was *scarier* than it was *sad*. I didn't take the time to feel sorry for the pig; I just avoided it—and when someone cut a piece off of the corpse, put it on a plate, and gave the plate to me, I ate with gusto. I don't know that I ever watched the actual slicing happen; if I did, those memories are tucked away somewhere beyond my reach. I only remember the plate.

The "food" on my plate tasted good, and it wasn't attached to anyone's body. On my plate, it just looked like a brown mound. It wasn't cute. It didn't have any personality. I had completely divorced the product from the process—a skill at which we as a society have excelled, much to our own detriment as well as that of nonhumans. Part of what made it so easy for me, I think, is that I didn't know all of the details about the process that I know now; for instance, I didn't have a clue about *castration*.

The Simpsons episode brought to light something I had never before considered. It seems like an obvious enough fact, but it simply had never occurred to me before then that lamb chops came from lambs, pork chops from pigs, etc. I was deeply entrenched in the speciesist mentality, though I lacked the theoretical knowledge with which to ascertain this about myself. I suppose some part of me imagined that the animals I ate had died natural deaths, or that there were special "food animals" out there who were somehow distinct from the few live farmed animals I'd encountered at that point. When I looked at the pigs roasted at family parties, I didn't think of pigs I'd met anywhere else; perhaps I *hadn't* met any other pigs just yet. Sadly, I can't recall with any certainty the very first time I met a pig.

With respect to dairy, I always imagined that there were special cows that simply *always* produced milk. I had no knowledge whatsoever of bovine reproductive goings-on, and had no idea that a female cow—like a human woman—could only produce milk if she were pregnant. Perhaps this had something to do with my Hispanic, quasi-Catholic upbringing; we didn't talk about things like sex or reproduction at my house. It would be many more years before I fully understood the atrocity that is dairy production. At this point, post-*Simpsons*, I was only just becoming aware of the atrocity that is meat.

I became increasingly aware of other atrocities in the years that followed: world hunger, religious wars, and global warming, to name a few. One night, when I was roughly ten years old, I stayed up all night crying (quietly, so as not to wake anyone) because I couldn't stop thinking about all of the hungry children all over the world who were going to bed with empty tummies. I couldn't help them, and I felt guilty that my own tummy was full. I knew it wasn't fair; I wasn't any better than any of those kids. Why did I get to eat while they starved? Why did I get a warm bed while so many other kids had to sleep in crowded shelters or on the streets?

I didn't want anyone to wake up and know that I was crying, because I didn't know how to explain why I was doing so. Nothing was "happening" to me; I wasn't sick, I wasn't in any physical pain, and for once, no one in particular was picking on me at school. (I wouldn't say I was "bullied," necessarily, but I was occasionally teased—first for being nerdy or a "teacher's pet," then, once I started crying, for being a crybaby.) I was coming to the painful realization that the world is not as it should be; I was overwhelmed, and felt helpless.

Unfortunately, awareness of the atrocity that is meat wasn't enough for my picky, particular self to give it up just yet. The thing is, I was actually a *very* enthusiastic "carnivore" as a child and in my early teens. I didn't just *like* meat; I *loved* it—and, like most children, I *hated* vegetables. At family parties, while everyone else walked around with plates of meat, rice, veggies, and beans, my plate would be piled high exclusively with body parts. On our semi-annual drives to Florida from Long Island, we would often stop at Waffle House, where almost everyone else ate waffles. I ordered steak—for breakfast. Every. Single. Time.

So it was that I spent roughly the next decade eating meat while feeling guilty about it. In high school, I started challenging myself to become a vegetarian. My friends mocked me on the rare occasion that I visited the school cafeteria and did not return to my seat with a stack of chicken fingers. "*OOH*, I guess you're vegetarian this week, huh?" they'd tease. No one expected it to stick—least of all, me.

I kept trying; by age seventeen, I'd finally succeeded. My family took the news relatively well, though they lamented that I would no longer be indulging in some of my childhood favorites, including Cornish game hen and our family's traditional Easter ham. I remember my sister chiding me once, "Just *please* don't become one of those crazy vegan chicks. That shit just ain't healthy. Vegans look like they're dying."

I could see where she was coming from; I had encountered a few girls who called themselves "vegan" and who did look patently unhealthy, and as we attended the same high school, I imagine my sister had those same or similar individuals in mind. I later discovered that these girls weren't true vegans or liberationists at all; they were suffering from eating disorders, hiding behind veganism as an excuse to abstain from eating in social settings. They knew next to nothing about animal liberation; continued to wear leather, fur, and cosmetics tested on animals; and often cheated on their diets—because that's all veganism was to them: a diet.

Even after this revelation, I remained hesitant to go vegan. For starters, I loved cheese, and like many new vegetarians, I relied on cheese all the more heavily after I'd given up meat. I still hadn't developed a taste for fresh, natural foods, and I replaced chicken and steak with pizza and grilled cheese sandwiches. I also loved—still love—baked goods, and the notion of vegan baking was entirely foreign to me.

Furthermore, from an ethical standpoint, I still just "didn't get" veganism. Embarrassingly enough, even in my late teens, I *still* didn't realize that cows needed to be pregnant in order to produce milk. I had also heard several times throughout childhood that milking cows does them a favor; they get uncomfortable when their udders are too full, so they "need" us humans to milk them. It hadn't occurred to me that this problem already had a solution, completely independent of human involvement: let the calf stay by his or her mama and drink the milk to which the calf—and the calf alone—is naturally entitled.

I did always find it odd that of all animals in the Animal Kingdom, humans are the only ones who choose to drink the milk of other animals. I thought to myself often, though casually and not through any social justice lens whatsoever: *Cows drink cow's milk, goats drink goat's milk, and puppies drink dog's milk... Why don't humans just drink human milk?* Later, I would come to question the duration of our milk consumption as well, as the more I learned about other species, the more evident it became to me that most milk-drinking species stop drinking milk anywhere from a few months to a few years after birth. Only humans seemed to "need" milk in adulthood—why?

It wasn't until I did some homework in my early twenties that veganism started to make sense. The first item that caught my attention was the Rape Rack: the machine to which cows are strapped while they are "artificially inseminated" repeatedly until conception. I learned that calves are stolen from their mothers so as not to interfere with the milk supply resulting from their mothers' rapes. My feminist inclinations rebelled against both the sexual violation and the family disruption inherent in these practices. I no longer looked at cheese as food; to this day, when I see cheese, I think of one thing and one thing only: *rape.*

I use the term *rape* here because cows are tied to the Rape Rack and then, without their consent, an item is forcefully inserted through their genital region. In my mind, any such instance qualifies as rape—whether the victim is human or bovine. For this to happen to someone even once is a grave injustice; considering that it happens to many individuals several times throughout their lives, what we have here is an atrocity of epic proportions.

Yes, cheese is also terrible for human health in a variety of ways. One such way is that, like milk itself, cheese contains addictive casomorphins—protein fragments derived from casein that have an opioid effect, instilling drowsiness and euphoria, but cheese has a much higher concentration of these than milk does.[1] It takes roughly ten pounds of milk to make a pound of cheese; ergo, every pound of cheese contains roughly ten pounds' worth of milk—and all of the casomorphins that go along with it. So, unbeknownst to me for most of my life, I didn't just "love" cheese because it's so very delicious; I was chemically addicted to it.

For me, this chemical addiction was merely an afterthought, a reaffirmation of my stance; I learned of it *after* learning about the Rape Rack, and the Rape Rack alone had been enough to compel me to kick the habit. Once I'd learned what happens to cows in order for cheese to be produced, I couldn't be persuaded to eat it if it gave me superpowers. I wouldn't eat cheese if it enabled me to fly or granted me immortality; I wouldn't eat it if it caused me to lose weight, be prettier, win the lottery, *and* be awarded a Nobel Prize. There is no temptation great enough to compel me to participate in sexual violence of any kind—independent of the species to which the victim belongs.

While learning about the atrocity that is dairy, I remembered Lisa Simpson. I wondered how she would react to this information. I wondered how an episode in which this was revealed would play out; perhaps that would simply be too much for children? It's easy enough to explain to a child that killing is wrong, and thus eating corpses is wrong. How can one explain to a child a thing like *rape*? Especially one so young that he or she doesn't even quite know what *sex* is yet?

One pressing challenge for the Animal Liberation Movement today is: How do we move beyond vegetarian children and increase the number of vegan children? Yes, a vegan parent can simply impose his or her will on the child, but ethical choices only stick if their reasons are thoroughly understood. With imposing, the threat persists that your child will choose to eat meat and dairy the minute he or she leaves your home. In fact, one could easily argue that forcing your children to be vegan, rather than explaining the matter to them in a compelling manner, *increases* the likelihood that they will eat meat as an adult, if only to defy you.

Thankfully, there has been an emergence in recent years of children's literature regarding veganism, such as Ruby Roth's *That's Why We Don't Eat Animals* and Sybil Severin's *Lena of Vegitopia and the Mystery of the Missing Animals*. Hopefully, as the years progress and the movement gains traction, we as a society can continue to develop effective methods of explaining veganism to young children.

Hats off to *The Simpsons* for giving us a place to start.

A Wolf from Gubbio and a Conference with the Birds

While I do not prescribe to any organized religion, both of my parents were raised Catholic. As a result, I was taught certain Bible stories and facts about Catholic saints as a child, by my mother and a Puerto Rican cousin of hers named Mary in particular. I was most captivated by stories of Saint Francis, the Catholic patron saint of animals, born around 1181 in Assisi, Italy. Among the most famous fables concerning Saint Francis are one in which he preaches to birds and another in which he defends a wolf. Both can be found in *The Little Flowers of Saint Francis*,[2] a collection of stories that emerged shortly after Saint Francis's death in 1226, which I picked up sometime in my late teens or early twenties and is still one of my favorite "religious-y" books.

In the bird fable, Saint Francis is walking with some companions when suddenly they come to a spot surrounded by birds on either side of their path. Saint Francis tells his fellows, "Wait for me while I go to preach to my sisters, the birds." Legend has it that the birds were all quite still while he spoke; not a single one flew away or caused any kind of disruption.

In the second tale, Saint Francis visits the city of Gubbio, where he discovers that the townsfolk are terrified of a wolf who has been attacking and eating some of their number. Saint Francis determines to make peace between the wolf and the people, and so tells them, the wolf docile at his side, that the wolf had "done evil out of hunger" and that they ought to feed him regularly.

To me, the first story indicates that, while birds might not *literally* comprehend the human tongue, they are perceptive enough to know when they are being addressed, and will endeavor to listen. Let us not get carried away though; these are mere legends, and no one knows with certainty if these events even took place—let alone if they unfolded precisely as described in *Little Flowers.*

Still, where do legends come from? *Ideas. Observations. Instinct.* One or all of these surely must have prompted Saint Francis's disciples to write these stories, and one general idea we can draw from the bird fable is that to Saint Francis and his followers, birds and other nonhuman animals merited *respect.* One would not bother to preach to someone he did not respect, and his followers would not dare to claim that he had done so falsely if they suspected he would not approve of the claim—or might even be *insulted* by it.

The wolf fable, which I find even less likely to have actually occurred than the bird fable, nevertheless highlights the running theme in various Christian writings (including the Bible) that humans are to be the *stewards* of other animals, not their oppressors. The modern-day gut reaction to a wolf attack, in most places, is, "Kill it!" This thought never once entered Saint Francis's mind—at least, not according to the texts that sustain his memory. The wolf wasn't killing humans because he hated them or because he felt superior to them; he was simply hungry. It became the task of the Gubbian community to protect the animal from hunger in order to protect itself from attack.

This is what I mean when I attend animal liberation actions or group meetings and proclaim, "Animal liberation is human liberation." (Not that I invented the phrase; I'm just a fan of it.) In fact, that is just one of several things the phrase means to me:

- If we take better care of nonhuman animals, they will cease to be our enemies and become, as they once were, our friends. This basic premise is highlighted by the wolf fable.

- Since humans are themselves animals, animal liberation must, by definition, consist of human liberation.

- If we provide a strong, healthy planet for nonhuman animals to live on, this in turn provides a strong, healthy planet on which *we* and *our children* can live.

Animal liberation will free up farm land that is currently being used to raise cattle and grow crops with which to feed them, cut down on pollution caused and energy used by meat-producing facilities, and much more. In the long run, these changes have the potential to liberate numerous humans from hunger in addition to toxic air and water. They would also free the human victims of the Animal Holocaust currently working in slaughterhouses and other such facilities from their torturous daily cycle of killing.

A glaring example of the practicality behind this philosophy is the severe drought currently plaguing the state of California. In March 2015, Governor Jerry Brown imposed a host of water conservation rules, including a ban on restaurants serving water unless patrons specifically request it.[3] A far more effective conservation effort would have been to insist that the state of California go vegan; 132 gallons of water are used every time an animal is slaughtered, while the amount of water required to produce a gallon of dairy milk is equivalent to approximately one month's worth of showers.[4] In this case, animal liberation would quite literally liberate millions of humans from fear of running out of water and, ultimately, premature death. Both human and nonhuman animal lives are now at stake, owing to the former's ancient decision to dominate and oppress the latter.

A Personal Compulsion toward Universal Justice

How did all of these events shape who I am today? I'm reminded of Shrek's onion analogy: "Ogres are like onions—we have *layers!*" The Pepa story marked the first instance in which I heard of a human having a close relationship with an animal that was neither a dog nor a cat. Before that, I thought of dogs and cats as *friends*, and farmed animals as *food*. Pepa showed me that a goat could also be a friend, and, by extension, that so could any other animal. (This story also taught me the valuable lesson that our parents are not invincible; they, too, can experience pain and loss.)

Lisa Simpson helped drive home the notion that it's wrong to eat animals. Pepa's story did not quite achieve this, as I was a) too young when I heard it to synthesize what I was hearing, and b) my family didn't eat goats. Saint Francis taught me not only that religion doesn't have to be boring, but also, more importantly, that there are ancient traditions and fables honoring nonhuman animals. Human solidarity with nonhumans isn't a new, modern idea. It isn't a "fad." It is a deep, longstanding universal truth, and those stories were only the beginning. In college, like many Western students, I explored Eastern religions and philosophies—not to convert to any of them, as some lost young people eagerly do without really knowing much about them, but simply to *learn*. Buddhists, Jains, Confucians, and Taoists—just to name a few—all spoke of respect and compassion for nonhumans.

I came to understand Oneness. I understood that hurting others hurts me, not just in the practical sense (i.e., the meat and dairy industries are destroying our environment, jeopardizing the air I need to breathe and the soil from which the crops I eat are grown), but also in the spiritual sense. I knew I would never truly be at peace so long as I contributed to injustice. Having battled depression on and off throughout my teens and twenties, I suspected that if I could not find inner peace—through campaigning for outer, or global, peace—I would self-destruct in spectacular fashion. I would never be able to have a steady job or a fruitful interpersonal relationship. I would wallow in self-pity and world-pity indefinitely.

I was compelled to pull myself up by my pleather boot-straps and *do* something.

These feelings persisted long after I went vegan. I wish I could say I wore the vegan message like a badge of honor, spouting my newfound understanding of how we all must coexist to anyone who'd listen (and even some who wouldn't). That simply was not the case for many years. I was a "closeted vegan." I spoke about it only when I absolutely had to, and even then only in the most vague terms. I cited multiple reasons for my choice—environmental, health, and moral—without truly focusing on the Moral Imperative, my primary motivation for it all. I was afraid my ideals would be dismissed as "hippie college bullshit," and so endeavored to downplay the ethical element of the matter in favor of the practical, intellectually validated reasons behind my "lifestyle."

I was embarrassed, and yet I resented myself for feeling that way. *Why should I be embarrassed by the fact that I'm NOT eating a corpse right now? Shouldn't everybody else be embarrassed that they ARE eating a corpse?* Still, I just didn't like to draw attention to myself, and I had no real community on which to rely. I encountered some vegans at Columbia through CSAP (Columbia Students for Animal Protection)—which I joined near the end of my sophomore year—and at parties I attended in Brooklyn, but there was no one around me with any consistency to whom I could speak freely about the plight of nonhuman animals.

I was also afraid such talk would offend my family and my many friends who *did*—and still do—consume meat and dairy. I thought they wouldn't like me anymore if they felt "preached at." I thought, *It's one thing for me to make my own choice about this issue, but I can't force everybody else to see things my way.*

To an extent, I still agree with that statement. I can't *force* anyone to see things my way. Where I was wrong was with respect to considering veganism a matter of *choice*. I failed to see at the time that the choice I was making was part of a larger movement—a movement that needed *my help* to succeed. It's all well and good to stop engaging in cruelty yourself, pat yourself on the back, and say, "I'm a good person, because I no longer directly contribute to these violent industries." But what happens when everyone around you continues to fund these industries? Do you really expect them all to just disappear because *you* stopped supporting them?

I was ignoring the victims' perspective entirely. The nonhuman victims of meat, dairy, fur, leather et al. don't care if I personally go vegan or not. They care about being saved, and my personal "choice" might save some of them, but it doesn't save them all. Tigers enslaved by the circus industry don't care what anyone is having for dinner. A hen whose housing has been upgraded from a battery cage to a filthy, crowded shed—or even beautiful, sunlit hillside—isn't any more inclined to die than a hen in a battery cage. These animals want to live, and to be with their families—just like we do.

Joining CSAP helped. This was probably the first means through which I began engaging in nonviolent direct action on behalf of nonhumans. Before that, I had attended several protests against the war in Iraq as well as on behalf of the rights of immigrants—but none whatsoever concerning nonhuman animals. As a CSAP member, I helped organize vegan meals and lectures, including a Vegan Thanksgiving event at which guests from Farm Sanctuary in Woodstock, New York spoke about the work they were doing and the help that was needed. I wrote a puppet show with a few fellow activists about factory farming, though I was too shy to actually participate in putting on the show. I merely wrote the script.

Later, I co-authored an article with a guy named Eric about the plight of nonhumans, but I let him take the lead on that one. I was *still* fundamentally embarrassed about my beliefs. Writing, as usual, gave me a place to hide; I could say what I wanted without having to look anyone in the eye. Co-writing gave me an extra out, as I could always pretend any part of the article that someone didn't like or challenged me on had been written by Eric and not me.

It wasn't until I moved to Phoenix, Arizona briefly in 2012 that I was finally inspired to take my message to the streets. In Phoenix I encountered Phoenix Animal Liberation Squad, a group of dedicated activists from the surrounding suburbs who marched at Phoenix's monthly First Friday art crawl.

Initially, I kept my nerdy writer's cap on, contributing to the group by helping it start a newsletter, getting a blog up, and running and creating business cards for everyone. This group protested and demonstrated regularly, and with each successive protest I felt my embarrassment waning. Perhaps it was due to the new environment; I didn't have friends or family here around whom I'd feel embarrassed. Why should I care what a bunch of strangers thought about what I had to say? I'd probably never see them again!

As time wore on, questions I received from passersby inspired me to keep at it. For every hostile, aggressive naysayer spouting stereotypes at us (a popular one was to shout at us to get jobs, assuming that we didn't have any, when in fact every member of Phoenix Animal Liberation Squad was employed at the time I joined), there was a genuinely concerned and curious citizen with a burning question about the movement. I was always happy to answer—happy to know that my actions, alongside the actions of others, had prompted at least one person to *really think* about the Animal Problem. By the time I arrived in Oakland and joined Direct Action Everywhere's East Bay chapter, I was giving speak-outs (brief speeches on a megaphone) in both English and Spanish.

One thing I hadn't expected while becoming an animal activist was that it would positively influence my behavior in other aspects of my life. I became more confident not just in expressing my beliefs about animals, but also in expressing my beliefs about pretty much anything. I was less anxious, less timid. I felt an inner sense of resolve. I had a newfound sense of purpose and direction, and this did more than make me a better foot soldier for the animals; it made me a more effective and positive person in general.

Those of us interested in matters of social justice often battle depression, anxiety, and other emotional ills. When you're only worried about yourself, life, though not always easy, is at least simple. You only have to think about having enough to eat, having shelter, and having fun and interesting things to do. Once you've gotten everything on your checklist, you can come up for air. You can be happy, or at least optimistic. It's a lot harder to maintain a positive attitude when you are socially conscious—when you are constantly aware, regardless of how things are going for you personally, that every minute, every *second*, innocent lives are being extinguished and humans and nonhumans alike face discrimination. People are being removed from their homes, denied jobs, or even shot in the streets because of their ethnicity or religion. Atrocity is everywhere, and to call it overwhelming is an understatement.

There is no cure for the anxiety that results from knowing that there is so much suffering in the world, but there is medicine. That medicine is called Action. Action can take a variety of forms. It can be anything from writing to a politician, to demonstrating in public, to editing a video or writing a song. Whatever you choose to do, taking action against injustice is the only surefire way to crawl out of the pit of despair in which we often find ourselves when we realize that the world can be a cruel and unforgiving place. Complaining and hiding won't enact positive change. Only Action can do that.

If you are truly anti-cruelty—if you really want to put an end to violence and injustice, rather than just abstain from it personally—you have to spread the word. Participate in peaceful demonstrations, create multimedia, write, and conduct outreach to raise public awareness of the issues. Pressure the powers that be to halt their sinister practices, using both your social and your political might.

One of America's most prominent faces of nonviolent direct action, Martin Luther King Jr., wrote in his *Letter from Birmingham Jail*:

> Nonviolent direct action seeks to create such a crisis and foster such a tension that a community which has constantly refused to negotiate is forced to confront the issue. It seeks so to dramatize the issue that it can no longer be ignored.[5]

By being a closeted vegan, I was effectively continuing to ignore the issue—while allowing those around me to do so as well. Now, even when those around me don't agree with my ethics, my mere presence serves as a reminder to them of the Animal Liberation Movement—and that's *before* I even open my mouth.

My presence and my words compel those around me who consume animal byproducts to examine their actions from the victim's perspective. They are forced to think, at least for a moment: *this isn't just my dinner—it is the body of someone who did not want to die.*

With respect to my impact on nonhuman animals themselves, this is hard to measure. Sure, statistics abound about how many animals I won't be consuming for the rest of my life since I went vegan years ago; still, the fact that I personally won't be eating or wearing them doesn't necessarily mean I "saved" them. One tangible success occurred while I was in Phoenix, as PALS managed to halt Ringling Brothers Elephant Walk by chanting about a statute the company would violate if it chose to proceed:

> Marching elephants down the street
> On hot asphalt, in the blistering heat
> While knowing the sensitivity
> Of these beautiful animals' feet—
> Is a crime: Violation of Statute 13-2910 Section 9

This was a rare instance in which direct action produced an immediate result, but most of what activists do lays the groundwork for future liberation rather than resulting in imminent liberation. This ever-elusive immediate impact is a testament to the group's cleverness and commitment; it was hard-won, occurring only after days in which PALS made an appearance at every single circus event—whether in groups of four or five, or, as was the case that fateful Monday morning, only two.

Open investigation and rescue, which we will discuss in Chapter Four, provide an exciting opportunity to change this. However, the problem is too big, not just for any individual, but also for any one organization. It will take the collaboration of activists, scholars, philosophers, social scientists, lawyers, and others to institute true animal liberation worldwide.

It will, in short, take a movement—and it starts with *you*.

Chapter Two

Speciesism: The Final Frontier

The animals of the world exist for their own reasons.
They were not made for humans any more than
black people were made for white, or women created
for men.

—Alice Walker, Introduction to
The Dreaded Comparison: Human and Animal Slavery
By Marjorie Spiegel, 1996

We've all heard of racism, sexism, and a host of other evil –isms that have held our society back since its inception. Here's one you may be less familiar with: *speciesism.* Speciesism is the belief that one species—namely, homo sapiens—is superior to all other species and therefore has a right to enslave them. While most (though certainly not all) modern Americans have a relatively easy time understanding that white men are no better than black men and that men are no better than women, this last hurdle seems to be the hardest for us to overcome as a culture.

In his classic volume, *Animal Liberation*, originally published in the seventies and re-issued by Harper in 2009, Peter Singer defines speciesism as "a prejudice or attitude of bias in favor of the interests of members of one's own species and against those of members of other species."[1]

We have been trained for so long to believe that humans are "better" than other animals that we easily forget that we ARE, in fact, animals. There is no separate human kingdom among the classical scientific kingdoms. In case you need a refresher from junior high biology class, the six kingdoms currently taught in American schools are: **Animalia, Plantae, Fungi** (such as mushrooms), **Protista** (such as algae), **Archaea** (such as Methanococcales and other tiny, long-named creatures—typically aquatic), and **Bacteria** (such as the numerous bacteria occupying your body at this very moment). We belong to the same kingdom as the cows, horses, sheep, and other animals we allow to be exploited and murdered on a daily basis: Animalia.

The excuses perpetuating the Myth of Human Supremacy are vast, ranging in scope from historical to biological and beyond. Herein, I will endeavor to clear the air and address some of these issues; first, I'd like to walk you down the path of social progress our culture has so far traveled, and upon which animal liberation is the next logical step.

White Supremacy is a Myth

The roots of slavery, from a global perspective, are complex. One driving force in almost all instances of slavery is economics: Free labor naturally leads to greater profit margins. This is not a mere consequence of capitalism, but has been true for centuries before that term was even coined.

The apparent "need" for slavery being thus summarized, the question across communities, nations, and eras has been: *Who will be the slaves?* Herein lies the development of many of the –isms that have, and continue to, cripple us. This question has been answered in many ways; among the most common are religion and race.

The history of the Jews provides a fine example of the former, as Jews were enslaved in Egypt simply for being Jews; more recently, in the 1930s and '40s, they were slaughtered in droves throughout Europe for the same reason. American history provides us with an obvious example of race-based enslavement: the enslavement of African Americans prior to the Thirteenth Amendment, ratified in the US in 1865. While the Thirteen Amendment forbade the outright enslavement of African Americans in this country, it actually achieved quite little with respect to racial equality. The Jim Crow laws forcing African Americans to use separate—and un-equal—facilities in the US remained in place until 1965. (Let us not forget that we also engaged in race-based oppression by forcing over 100,000 Japanese-Americans into internment camps in 1942.)

Thankfully, brave souls such as Martin Luther King Jr. and Rosa Parks had the courage to stand up to the powers that were and fight for racial equality, at great personal risk. Today, while there are still racists to be found in America (such as exist in any country), they form a minority. Those who may still believe that white people are superior to Africans, Hispanics, Asians, or other people of color are usually ashamed to admit it—as well they should be.

Any racial minority living in America can tell you that all is not yet perfect. Systemic racism, unfortunately, is alive and well here. There are still more African American people in jail than there are members of any other race, according to The Sentencing Project, a national nonprofit organization devoted to reforming the American Criminal Justice System. In its August 2013 report to the United Nations Human Rights Committee, The Sentencing Project states:

> African American males are six times more likely to be incarcerated than white males and 2.5 times more likely than Hispanic males. If current trends continue, one of every three black American males born today can expect to go to prison in his life-time, as can one of every six Latino males—compared to one of every seventeen white males. Racial and ethnic disparities among women are less substantial than among men, but remain prevalent.[2]

African Americans also remain less likely than Hispanic students, and *far* less likely than white students, to graduate from high school. The National Center for Education Statistics reported than in the 2009-2010 school year, 5.5% of African American students dropped out of high school. This is more than double the rate for white students (2.3%), and half a percent higher than the rate for Hispanic students (5%).[3] Are we to believe that African American boys are just naturally criminal-minded? Or that African Americans, across the board, are either stupid or lazy?

Finally, the Michael Brown and Eric Garner court decisions of late 2014 confirm that racism is alive and well in the US. In both cases, the victim was an African American male, killed by a white, male police officer. In the case of unarmed black teenager Michael Brown, from Ferguson, MI, it was decided in November 2014 that the officer who had killed him three months prior—Darren Wilson—would not face charges. At all. For killing an unarmed teenage boy.

Officer Daniel Pantaleo, who illegally employed a chokehold on Eric Garner—causing his fatal suffocation—after catching Garner selling "loosies" (individual cigarettes) on Staten Island, NY, escaped indictment by a grand jury on December 3, 2014.

These two cases sparked waves of protest throughout the United States, namely in Ferguson, MI; Oakland and Los Angeles, CA; and New York, NY. The Twitter hashtag #BlackLivesMatter was created, and massive demonstrations were organized via social media. At an Oakland City Council meeting in December 2014, one citizen belted out the names of African Americans shot and killed by white police officers in Oakland, such as Oscar Grant.

While there is still a long road ahead of us with respect to achieving *true* racial equality—wherein people of all races have equal opportunities for advancement and are safe from racial profiling and police brutality—we have at least, finally, come to accept as a society that WHITE SUPREMACY IS A MYTH. Those who still uphold the Myth of White Supremacy know better than to say so out loud; those who reject it are allowed to demonstrate freely and openly against it. Racism may yet live in this country, but it is the underdog position, the outcast position; it is no longer in the mainstream. It is not "cool" to be racist nowadays in the way that it may have been "cool" in the 1800s to own slaves, or even "cool" in the 1950s and '60s to use the N-Word.

Male Supremacy is a Myth

Another evil –ism that has pervaded so much of the world for so long is sexism: the belief that one sex (typically male—although there are some women who argue that it is female) is superior to the other.

I personally have always found it rather odd that some women condemn the Myth of Male Supremacy while perpetuating a Myth of Female Supremacy. I believe the sexes, like the races and the species, should work in cooperation with one another rather than wasting valuable time, energy, and intellect trying to prove that one is "better" than the other—which is ultimately impossible. After all, has anyone even bothered to pinpoint what "better" is supposed to *mean?* Does it mean smarter? Stronger? More morally righteous? More attractive? More creative? More responsible? More athletic?

Before we go any further in discussing human women, I must interject: to all of you dairy-consuming feminists out there, *J'ACCUSE!* Feminists purport to be fighting for equality among the sexes and *condemn sexual exploitation* of women in various forms—including *rape.* What some fail to realize is that every time they drink a glass of milk or eat anything with cheese on it, they are financing and visually demonstrating their support of raping cows, goats, and other nonhuman mammals.

It bears repeating that, like human women and females of other mammalian species, in order for a dairy cow to produce milk, she must be pregnant. Therefore, dairy cows are consistently impregnated against their will—i.e., *raped*—in order to produce the milk we drink and the cheese to which we are so addicted. The industry term for the rack against which dairy cows are chained in factory farms is "Rape Rack." Not an activist term, mind you—the *industry's* term. What happens to the calf the cow ultimately births? He or she is stolen from his or her mother immediately, so as to prevent the calf from decreasing the supply of milk produced by the mother, which we've decided ought to be ours and not theirs.

Imagine being constantly raped AND constantly pregnant, without ever being allowed to raise any of your children. Not exactly the feminist ideal, is it?

A prime example of how women have been oppressed in the US lies in their inability to vote prior to the Nineteenth Amendment, which granted women suffrage in 1920. As is the case with racism, however, it will take more than a constitutional amendment passed nearly a century ago to close the gap between men's and women's liberties.

In spite of the passing of the Equal Pay Act by John F. Kennedy in 1963, which endeavored to enforce equal pay among the sexes, data from the U.S. Census Bureau's annual survey released in September 2013 asserts that white women in the United States today make approximately seventy-seven cents to every dollar men make in the same positions, with slight variations according to industry as well as to state.[4] Black women only make sixty-four cents to every dollar white men make in the same position. Native American women make sixty cents, while I, as a Hispanic woman, am only entitled to fifty-three cents of a white man's dollar.[5]

These unfortunate truths notwithstanding, I think most women would agree that they are better off now—or at least more liberated—than they were a century ago. Not only are they allowed to vote, but it has also become common for women to work outside of the home, whereas in the early-to-mid-twentieth century, women were expected to stay at home, clean house, and make babies.

Women who do so today do so by choice, not for lack of options. This makes a significant difference, with respect not only to women's liberation, but also to our nation's economy *and* the quality of care our nation's children are receiving. Economically, this is beneficial in that companies now stand to gain valuable insights from an entirely new segment of the population. It is also a well-documented fact that people perform higher on tasks about which they are passionate than on tasks that are forced upon them by a sense of obligation. Therefore, it stands to reason that mothers who presently *choose* to be mothers are more supportive and loving to their children than those scores of mothers who felt *forced* to become mothers were decades ago.

Today, there are even such things as "stay-at-home *dads*." I'm sure the typical American fifties wife never saw *that* coming, yet, less than a century later, here we are! In addition, more and more companies in the US are offering paternity leave, allowing men to take time away from work to help their female counterparts care for their new babies. This not only provides tremendous relief to new mothers, but also allows the modern American Dad to be present for those crucial milestones that occur early in a human's life, such as Baby's First Words and Baby's First Steps—special moments which, in the recent past, would have been shared exclusively between mother and child.

While we still have our work cut out for us, we've come a long way already in accepting the fact that MALE SUPREMACY IS A MYTH.

Human Supremacy is a Myth

Before we move on, I would just like to emphasize that the fights for racial equality and equality among the sexes are *not* the only struggles against oppression to occur in the US and elsewhere. I have chosen these two examples in the interest of time and clarity, but other forms of social oppression abound, including but not limited to:

- *heterosexism* (the belief that straight people are better than people of any other sexual orientation);

- *ableism* (the belief that people with full use of their faculties—sight, hearing, mobility, mental stability, and so forth—are better than people who are blind, deaf, or otherwise stray from the "norm"); and

- *cissexism* (the belief that gender is binary—everyone is either a man or a woman—and that people who adhere to the gender roles imposed upon them due to their sex at birth are better than people who are transgender, agender, gender-fluid, etc.).

Now that you have a bit of context under your belt, let's address the Final Frontier of social justice: the end of speciesism. Below is a list of common excuses people use for upholding the belief that humans are better than other animals, as well as evidence of our equality:

We're better because we are conscious. Nonhumans are not.

Why this is false:

In July 2012, an international group of scientists signed *The Cambridge Declaration on Consciousness*, proclaiming their belief—based on decades of research—that animals are not only conscious (aware of themselves and their environment), but are also capable of experiencing emotions previously believed to be exclusively human.[6]

While this may seem obvious to anyone who owns a pet or is a big fan of the monkey, there are two Big Reveals here. For starters, there has never before been such an open declaration by so many notable scientists about this issue. Individual studies have alluded to it, within the context of specific animals—but no document prior to this one asserted outright the consciousness of multiple species other than human. The implications with respect to both factory farming and animal testing remain to be seen, but are expected to escalate as the years progress and this information reaches a wider audience.

The second Big Reveal concerns the scope of the animals named in the article. It isn't just apes, who we've known for ages are similar to us in many ways; and it's not just dogs and cats—the cute, cuddly animals we adopt when they're young and raise "as if they were our own." *The Cambridge Declaration on Consciousness* names a wide variety of animals, including many that are patently dissimilar to us, such as birds and even certain cephalopods (the squid, the octopus, the cuttlefish, etc.).

Why this is irrelevant:

Of late, I've come to understand that this matter of consciousness really isn't all that important. After all, we are defining consciousness in *human* terms; when we say that, for instance, apes or birds are *conscious*, what we really mean is *they have a conscious experience that is similar to that of humans, and so we understand it and respect it.* This does not necessarily mean that other animals are *unconscious,* but simply that they are *differently conscious*—conscious in a way that we find more challenging to understand and, therefore, to respect.

…So what?

Who are we to decide what type of consciousness is superior to all others? Moreover, even supposing we are right—that our form of consciousness is the best and puts all other types to shame—does this really give us the right to abuse, confine, or murder everyone else?

Internationally renowned writer and lecturer J.M. Coetzee's novel *The Lives of Animals* is a poignant and resonant work in which Coetzee addresses The Animal Problem using fictional septuagenarian novelist Elizabeth Costello as his vehicle. Costello is invited to Appleton College in Waltham, Massachusetts to give a brief lecture series on the subject of her choice. Much to the academy's chagrin, rather than focusing on her vast body of fiction, Costello chooses to use her lecture time to appeal to the masses on behalf of nonhuman animals.

After Elizabeth delivers her first lecture, a dinner party is held in her honor at Appleton, attended by the university's president and his wife, among other bigwigs. A debate ensues, with various members of the dining party chiming in with this or that bit of information about religion, history, morality, and so forth.

Eventually, one attendee who had been silent throughout the entire evening—cleverly named Dean Arendt—offers the following:

> I am prepared to accept that dietary taboos do not have to be mere customs. I will accept that underlying them are genuine moral concerns. But at the same time, one must say that our whole superstructure of concern and belief is a closed book to animals themselves. You can't explain to a steer that its life is going to be spared, any more than you can explain to a bug that you are not going to step on it. In the lives of animals, things—good and bad—just happen. So vegetarianism is a very odd transaction, when you come to think of it, with the beneficiaries unaware that they are being benefited. And with no hope of ever becoming aware. Because they live in a vacuum of consciousness.[7]

The anticipated "vegan response" to such a claim is one of outrage. Of *course* they don't live in a vacuum! They are just as conscious as we are, and in the very same way! How speciesist of you to presume that we are the only ones who are conscious! All of this may well be valid, but much to my delight, Elizabeth's reply is not so affronted as all that. It is honest, heartfelt, and far more accurate than any claim about animal consciousness can ever hope to be:

> That is a good point you raise. No consciousness that we would recognize as consciousness. No awareness, as far as we can make out, of a self with a history.
>
> What I mind is what tends to come next. They have no consciousness therefore. Therefore what? Therefore we are free to use them for our own ends? Therefore we are free to kill them? Why? What is so special about the form of consciousness we recognize that makes killing a bearer of it a crime while killing an animal goes unpunished? There are moments—

Elizabeth is interrupted by another guest, Wunderlich:

> To say nothing of babies. Babies have no self-consciousness, yet we think it a more heinous crime to kill a baby than an adult.

> Therefore? Arendt prods.

> Therefore all this discussion of consciousness and whether animals have it is just a smoke screen. At bottom, we protect our own kind. Thumbs up to human babies, thumbs down to veal calves.

We're better because we have strong familial ties. Nonhumans don't have families, so they don't care when you take their babies away.

Anyone who truly believes this has never been in the presence of, or watched a video of, a nonhuman mother whose child is being taken away from her. There is a powerful YouTube video called "The Real Price of Dairy," in which an agricultural worker of some kind walks up to a cow and her calf in a field, and steers the calf away from the mother, into a van. The mother follows them both, watches while her child is loaded into the van, and mother and child stare at each other through the rear windows. As the worker drives away, the grieving mother chases the van for as long as she can (watching this video was the first time I've ever seen a cow *run*). Inside the van, her lonely, frightened baby cries.[8]

In the insightful yet misleadingly dubbed documentary *Blackfish*, directed and produced by Gabriela Cowperthwaite, one can see what happens to an *entire pod* of whales when just *one* calf is hauled away in a net.[9] I extend my gratitude to my sister, Denise Nuñez, for sharing this documentary with me.

Even fish—which we'll talk specifically about later, because it's just *so hard* for people to care about them given how quiet and "boring" they can be—swim in shoals (it is only when the group is moving in the same direction, in a coordinated manner, that they are called *schools* of fish rather than *shoals*). Fish who become isolated from their shoal experience palpable anxiety, which results in increased respiratory activity.

We're better because we have language. Nonhumans don't.

FALSE. Scores of animals have language; in fact, some even have *dialects!*

Take whales, for example. Whales have certain tones, lengths of tones, etc. that they use to communicate within their own pod; passing pods cannot understand these tones, and so do not register or react to them at all. It's like the Castilian Spanish language originating in Spain versus the Dominirican Spanglish dialect that originated at my mother's house. To most non-Spanish-speaking Americans, Spanish just sounds like Spanish, no matter who is speaking it. Similarly, to us humans, whale sounds just sound like whale sounds. To the whales, they are not only a means of communicating thought, but also of distinguishing members of their pod—their *family*—from other, foreign whales. For whales, as for humans, language serves as more than a mere tool with which to facilitate cooperation; it is an expression of *identity*.

There are also non-vocal forms of communication exhibited by, among others, bees. Bees have a sophisticated system for alerting others in their hive as to where nectar can be found. A "scout honeybee" will leave the hive and buzz around for however long it takes until he or she locates a source of food. Then, the bee returns to the hive, where many of the other bees anxiously crowd around him or her. Since beehives tend to be dark inside, rather than watching, bees will often reach out to touch the scout bee and *feel* the dance that ensues. Scout bees can perform a number of different "dances" to alert members of their hive as to a) how far away the nectar is, and b) in which direction the community must travel, using the sun as a point of reference. The details of the dances were worked out by Karl von Frisch and his colleagues, and are detailed in von Frisch's book, ***The Dance Language and Orientation of Bees*** (1967).[10]

I have a confession to make. I HATE bees. I've had it out for them ever since I sat on one when I was about four and, shortly thereafter, stepped on one while playing outside, barefoot. I know, I know; I hurt them just as badly as, if not worse than, they hurt me. The one I sat on may have been killed—I didn't stick around to check—while the one I stepped on, if it was a honeybee, may have died shortly after stinging my foot. When confronted with a bee, I flee, which is actually the exact opposite of what you're supposed to do. You're supposed to stay still, but I just can't.

I feel that it would be misleading to identify myself as an "animal-lover," because bees are animals and I certainly do NOT love them. Hell, I don't even *like* them, but you don't have to like someone in order to *respect* them. Being an animal liberationist isn't about loving all sentient beings; it's about respecting their rights to both life and freedom.

In the March 2004 article in *Scientific American,* "Birds Share 'Language' Gene with Humans," Sarah Graham reports that birds, like humans, possess the FoxP2 gene. We're still not 100% sure that this is *the* language gene—or that such a gene even exists. What we do know is that mutation of the FoxP2 gene in humans results in a severe developmental disorder that hinders speech and language skills.[11]

What the article calls "vocal learning" (and what some argue is a form or component of *language*) "is characteristic of a number of animals, including humans, dolphins, whales and birds." Genetic specialists Sebastian Haesler and Kazuhiro Wada led their team in analyzing the expression of FoxP2 in various bird species (including those considered "non-vocal learners," such as ring doves and chickens), as well as in a crocodile—the closest living relative of birds (Who knew?!).

In June 2011, Dr. Constance Scharff and Jana Petri of Freie Universität Berlin delved deeply into the question of nonhuman language. They sum up the general position of the scientific community, as it has progressed in the twentieth and twenty-first centuries, thus:

> In the 1960s, some linguists considered human language and animal communication to be so categorically different that they were essentially incomparable. Hockett postulated a continuum of complexity among animal communication systems—including human language. Those positions still mark the two ends of the spectrum, but concomitant with the emergence of biolinguistics as a research field, the abyss between the two camps is slowly being bridged.[12]

In other words, no one is ready to openly admit it just yet, but the scientific community is growing closer by the day to accepting that animals *do* have language. It just prefers to use phrases like "communication systems"—just as, regrettably, many Americans prefer to use the terms "civil union" and "domestic partnership" when talking about homosexual couples who are, in fact, *married*. This reluctance to use the same rhetoric to describe human and nonhuman languages is symptomatic of speciesism. It is an effort to "otherize" nonhumans and avoid admitting to yet another commonality between Us and Them.

We're better because we produce art. A pig didn't paint the Mona Lisa.

There is a plethora of mediums through which art can be expressed. There is visual art (paintings, sculptures, etc.), auditory art (music), locomotive art (dancing), and several others besides. With respect to these three types, birds provide us with the clearest evidence that yes, animals *do* in fact produce art. In an article published in Volume 20 of *Communicative and Integrative Biology*, ethologist and evolutionary biologist John A. Endler explores visual aesthetics among male bowerbirds. These birds "create and decorate a structure called a bower, which serves only to attract females for mating, and females visit and choose one among many bowers before deciding which male to mate with."[13]

Endler explains that in order for the male bird to produce the bower, he must have some idea of which attributes are more likely to impress a mate and which are less likely to do so. In choosing a bower, the female must decide which of the bowers displayed before her is the most attractive. This confirms that these animals are not "accidentally" creating art—doing something instinct tells them to do, that just happens to look pretty on occasion—but are both *intentionally* creating art and *actively passing judgment* on art.

Neither of these acts would be possible without the possession of an *aesthetic sense*—aesthetic being defined by *Oxford Dictionaries* as "concerned with beauty or the appreciation of beauty."[14] Beauty is a pretty highbrow concept that many humans believe can only be examined and appreciated by other humans. The bowerbird presents us with just one example to the contrary.

Is their behavior not also, to an extent, how we humans conduct ourselves with respect to mating? Do you not clean up your house extra-tidy before a potential new lover arrives? I can't resist sharing with you here that not one but two former lovers of mine (both male) have confided in me that: "The only reason men bother to paint/write/play guitar/etc. is to attract chicks."

Thrushes, warblers, and finches are among the many songbirds who sing intricate songs for mate attraction.[15] There are also nonhuman animals who rely on dance to attract mates, such as the comically named and equally comic-looking blue-footed booby (an aquatic bird similar to a penguin); as well as those who will dance *with* a potential mate prior to mating, such as the great crested grebe (an aquatic bird similar to a duck) and White's seahorse (a breed of seahorse unique to the coast of southeastern Australia).[16]

Do these songs not constitute music, a form of art? Do these dances disqualify as dances simply because the dancers have webbed feet?

The distinction between *song* and ordinary *sound* (or even *speech)* is as difficult to make among humans as it is among other animals. Consider the question from a human angle. How do we know when someone has stopped talking and started singing?

One answer lies in *auditory aesthetics:* certain sounds and combinations of sounds are more pleasing to our ears than others. Another distinction lies with *intent:* when someone intends to speak to us, it is only to communicate a particular thought, whereas when someone *sings* to us, the intent is also to entertain and/or to impress. The same can be said of those species that choose a mate via song; what makes it a song and not just language is that

a) the singer *intends* to seduce the audience with carefully selected sounds, and b) the audience *enjoys* the song more than it would ordinary speech.

How many times, as a teenager, did you hear your mother pound on your bedroom door, demanding that you "turn off that noise"? To you, that was probably music; to her, it obviously wasn't. Scores of musicologists have developed ample definitions of what music is and is not—for humans. In nature, at large, music need not be so complex as all that. We make it complex because we have tools at our disposal with which to do so: metronomes, sound-wave-measuring devices, machines that can monitor our brains and our eardrums, and so forth. We've divided notes into scales, and within scales we've developed arpeggios. This does not at all impugn the legitimacy of music produced by the world around us. Any true musician will tell you as much.

With respect to *dance* versus *movement*, a similar argument can be made. The former relies on *repeated, intentional movements*, strung together in an attempt to *please*. Movement is merely a means to an end—it gets you closer to or farther away from something. When you're walking alone to a grocery store to buy food, you are *moving*. When you notice a real hottie walking not two feet behind you and start swaying your hips side-to-side as a result, you begin to cross the bridge over to *dancing*. You are no longer merely traveling from Point A to Point B; you are now consciously employing your tush to impress the hottie.

Finally, we must bear in mind when discussing matters such as art that we are attempting to measure nonhuman animals using human yardsticks. Yes, birds did not build the Eiffel Tower; humans did. However, to a bowerbird, a bower is a brilliant feat of architecture. So too is an anthill, to an ant. To bowerbirds and ants alike, the Eiffel Tower is nothing. They are as equally unimpressed by our feats as we often are by their feats.

We're better because the goal of creation was US. After us, creation ceased.

While some religious texts arguably contribute to this point of view, they are not the only source of this notion. This notion exists independently of any organized religion; it is a notion that in fact *precedes* many of today's religions, and may have inspired them rather than vice-versa.

Consider the secular model of creation. First there was nothing and then there was the Big Bang or some other strange event, which is still hotly debated today and ultimately un-provable anyway; and planets were made. Then, on our planet, there was land in some areas and water in others, as temperature changes caused ice to melt. Tiny, single-celled organisms appeared (initially, in the water). They became more complex, and some of them made it out of the water, where they continued to increase in complexity. New species sprung up here, there, everywhere... And then there was Human. A monkey became a subhuman, which became a slightly "better" or more advanced subhuman, and eventually this creature became *Human*.

That's it. That's where the story *ends*. All of this other stuff came first, and it got more intelligent, more creative, bigger, with more organs, more nerves, and the fur fell off, and it started walking, and it was harder, better, faster, stronger...and one day it was Human. The End.

What's wrong with the story? Nothing specific with respect to its content; it's no more or less as credible as any of the faith-based creation myths that abound in the world today. The problem is that the story *ends*. In reality, creation never ceased; it's still going on today, all around us. New species appear every day, while old (or exploited) species disappear. The world was not created for us alone; if that were true, then presumably, creation *would* have ended with us.

I do not presume to know why the world was created, and would laugh heartily at anyone who claimed to have such knowledge. My goal here is not to answer the question, but to highlight the falsehood of the answer we've been given: The world was created for us, and we were meant to rule it. Since this is our destiny, there will be no consequences—at least, none with which we need concern ourselves. If anyone or anything else suffers at our hands, it's okay, because it was meant to be so. All of creation took place for the sole purpose of putting us here.

The evidence that this is false abounds. We clearly *have* caused problems with which we need concern ourselves. We've caused famine. We've caused environmental devastation. We've caused numerous extinctions and reduced a plethora of once-abundant species to the distinction of "endangered." If we were, in fact, not just choosing to dominate the world but had been destined to do so by design, I imagine we'd be doing a much better job at it.

People will point to humanity's inherent flaws—greed, ignorance, jealousy, and general emotional recklessness—but these were not born of modernity. By definition, an *inherent* quality is one someone *comes to the table with*—not something that can be bestowed or learned. Are we to assume that "primitive" or tribal societies such as existed prior to the Agricultural Revolution (and exist in some parts of the world to this day) were somehow exempt from these inherent human qualities? Is the whole "noble savage" thing really true? How so, if these humans are of the same genetic makeup, woven from the same universal cloth as we are? Tribal humans and modern humans are both nevertheless human, yet the former managed to survive for ages without wreaking the havoc that the latter have wrought on the world.

Perhaps we were simply meant to be Human, the way that Dog was meant to be Dog, and Dolphin was meant to be Dolphin. Why do we find this notion so offensive? I've found that people become considerably affronted when this subject is broached. They're with you when you tell them that animals have feelings; anyone who has ever lived with a nonhuman cannot object to this truth. They're even with you when you speak of animal intelligence, particularly with respect to apes and dolphins (animals that display intelligences remarkably similar to our own)… But to suggest that we might be meant to do precisely what they were meant to do, and nothing more? Surely this is blasphemy!

I think part of the problem is that when people hear, "Human was meant to do what Turtle and Snail and Raccoon were meant to do," they interpret this as, "Human was meant to do *what Turtle and Snail and Raccoon do.*" In other words, they assume that people of this position want humans to live as though they were not humans at all, but as though they were squirrels or pigs or baboons. We—or at least, I—mean nothing of the sort. It would be no more natural for Human to live as Antelope than it would be for Antelope to endeavor to live as Human. The point is for humans to live as one of many forms of life on this richly diverse planet. Humans must remember how to live *among* our nonhuman brethren—not on top of them, and not as though we are identical to them.

Yes, all humans are animals—but not all animals are humans. It is entirely natural for humans to exhibit certain distinctions, even while living amongst nonhuman animals. This has always been the case. Lions exhibit distinctions from earthworms, and eagles exhibit distinctions from otters. The world is no more ours than it is theirs. A sunnier way to put it would be: the world is *as much* ours as it is theirs.

Adopting this mentality would ultimately redefine what constitutes Us, resulting in this simple yet breathtakingly beautiful truth: the world is *ours.*

Intersectionality: Tying it All Together

"They are a damned set of jackasses..."
"It can be of no benefit commensurate with the additional expense involved."
"It is unwise to risk the good we already have for the evil which may occur."
"Every lover of his country should desire to vindicate its institutions, of which this is one."
"You are requested to attend and unite in putting down and silencing by peaceable means this tool of evil and fanaticism."

What do these quotes mean to you? Can you guess what they are about? To me, the first sounds like a popular sentiment amongst meat-eaters against animal liberationists. The second two refer to common concerns about the Animal Liberation Movement: that it will be costly, and risk the economic and social stability America holds so dear. It will disrupt the existing state of affairs, and who knows what might result? Why risk it, when everything is fine as-is?

The fourth quote implies that to challenge any American institution is to reveal oneself as patently un-American (one resultant implication being that liberationists, by challenging American meat and dairy industries, lack patriotism), while the final quote beseeches the public to use nonviolent means to disrupt a meeting that could serve as a "tool of evil and fanaticism." The person making the statement is presumably on the side of the Goodies, beseeching the public to help check the Badies using "peaceable means"—i.e., nonviolent direct action.

Here's what these quotes are *really* about:

"They are a damned set of jackasses..."
—Rioter during the Farren Riots, a series of anti-abolition

riots in New York, 1834. He was referring to Yankees and abolitionists. [17]

"It can be of no benefit commensurate with the additional expense involved."
"It is unwise to risk the good we already have for the evil which may occur."
—Pamphlet encouraging women not to fight for suffrage, published in the 1910s. [18]

"Every lover of his country should desire to vindicate its institutions, of which this is one."
—Charles J. Ingersoll, 1856, referring to abolition as a challenge to the American institution of slavery. [19]

"You are requested to attend and unite in putting down and silencing by peaceable means this tool of evil and fanaticism."
—An anonymous ad posted in a newspaper in 1837, asking the public to disrupt a meeting of abolitionists. [20]

The rhetoric hasn't changed much. The last quote is, to me, the most shining example, as a pro-slavery zealot manages to sell his position as one of peace and harmony while demonizing abolitionists as evil fanatics. Similarly, meat-eaters often refer to animal liberationists as "fanatical," "extreme," or "radical."

Fear of disrupting the status quo—exposing oneself to negative repercussions not currently experienced—prevents would-be activists from taking direct action. It resigns them instead to making personal lifestyle choices that make them feel better about themselves, like going vegan, or engaging in welfarism (improving the living conditions of nonhuman slaves)—without making any effort to end the Animal Holocaust once and for all. This issue is best highlighted by the anti-suffrage packet; you may have noticed that neither of the sentiments I've extracted from it demonize women's suffrage itself. Instead, these sentiments caution women not to rock the boat, playing to their sense of prudence in order to suppress their desire for justice.

Ingersoll questions the patriotism of anyone who challenges existing American institutions, whereas I and many other activists believe it is far more patriotic to seek to *improve* upon an institution—or abolish it if it cannot be improved upon, as in the cases of both human and nonhuman slavery—than it is to let a detrimental institution remain unchanged and watch idly as our country suffers the consequences. To challenge a failing American institution is an act of the utmost integrity. It shows that you truly care about the wellbeing of your community, and that you trust in your community's ability to do the right thing.

Single-Issue Campaigns that Target People of Color

Westerners often eagerly engage in animal advocacy campaigns against Eastern countries, demonizing foreigners for violating the rights of particular nonhuman animals. American campaigns against Japanese whaling (forming the basis of the popular reality TV show *Whale Wars*), against the consumption of cats and dogs in various Asian countries, and PETA's 2014 campaign against Chinese manufacturing of "dog leather" spring to mind. *Save the whales, screw the cows.*

Why is it that fewer Americans rage against the daily enslavement, exploitation, and slaughter of cows, pigs, chickens, and other animals on their own soil than against offenses committed unto dolphins, whales, cats, and dogs overseas?

The answer lies in *intersectionality:* where the roads of racism, sexism, speciesism, and many other harmful -isms meet. It is racist to claim that one race (such as Japanese) is "worse" than another (such as Italian), and speciesist to claim that killing one species (such as dogs) is a more egregious offense than killing another (such as chickens).

We will talk more about where sexism and speciesism meet in a moment; first, let's explore some other ways in which race issues and animal issues interrelate—beyond the simple fact that every member of every race is also an animal.

Challenges in the Hispanic Community

Many middle-aged Hispanic immigrants who arrived in America in the sixties and seventies tend to feel somewhat removed from any "anti-farming" cause, as they can recall growing up in their countries in the forties and fifties—when, and where, animal slaughter was deemed a necessary part of survival. The challenge with which we are presented by this community—and many other communities besides, such as small-scale farmers in the Midwestern United States— is twofold: to illustrate that many of the farms on which animals are currently raised in the US—if you can even call them farms anymore—are not the farms on which *they* were raised (in home countries and/or previous decades), and to demonstrate how and why animal slaughter is unnecessary for human survival *independent of the farming methods employed prior to slaughter* (in other words, to truly drive home the Moral Imperative and illustrate how a regular practice they witnessed in childhood was actually anything but "regular"—it was murder).

In the Old Country, Back in the Day, etc., it was often necessary to kill an animal you had grown up with and come to truly love, because the alternative was starvation. Thus, farm children are encouraged from an early age to regard animals as commodities rather than friends and members of our community. When children fail at this, they are—if they are lucky—allotted a brief grieving period before being reminded that the animals are here to feed us, not play with us, and beseeched not to make the same "mistake" of befriending a farm animal again ("That's why we don't name the chickens.").

There's also the matter of gift giving. Gift giving serves the dual purpose of letting recipients know that you care about them and demonstrating your socioeconomic status to the surrounding community. Animals' bodies are often used in this way, particularly in parts of the world where meat is more expensive than in America: to honor one human or group of humans while visibly elevating the socioeconomic status of another human or group of humans—without any regard whatsoever for the individual whose life is stolen in the process.

In many countries and cultures today, this mentality persists; as meat is neither as abundant nor as affordable in much of the world as it is here, it is often regarded as a luxury item. Many cultures dictate that it is common courtesy to seek and prepare luxury items such as meat for honored guests.

My father once told me that he "first" shot a cow in the head when he was about thirteen years old. I have often wondered how this, as well as the implied subsequent instances of his having to commit acts of murder, has shaped his worldview and behavior as a grown man. I wonder who my father might have been if he had not been compelled for so many years to engage in murder; still, as we'll explore later in this book, not every farm boy grows up to be a farm man.

More than once, I've stood accused of not being "Hispanic enough"—another nod toward racism so pervasive that members of the stereotyped community begin to believe in the misconceptions perpetuated about them. One of the reasons behind this accusation, I suspect, is that veganism has been stereotyped as a "white thing." The truth is, I love my culture. I love our music. I love our balmy weather, our paradisiacal beaches, and our wild jungles. I love the spice element of our cuisine—our peppers, our herbs; most of all, *I love our love.*

Hispanics and Latinos are notorious for our passion in both familial and romantic love, as well as for the strength and longevity of our friendships. If ever there were a community ready to embrace the truly loving existence that animal liberation would bring about, it would be mine. The obstacles I've mentioned here are just that—obstacles, not barriers.

We just have to leap a little higher.

Challenges in the Asian Community

Wayne Hsiung addresses the socioeconomic significance of meat among Asian immigrants of the 1970s in a November 2014 post for *The Liberationist:*

> By the time he was in his 20s, my father was a popular and successful figure back home, as the #2 ranked student in his department at the prestigious National Taiwan University. But in the US, he was… nothing. Mocked for his broken English and deferential Confucian manner, stuck in the Midwest where there was nary a Chinese face to see, and warned by his boss that there was no place in America for a "Chinaman" ("You'll need to go home eventually," his boss said. "It will be better there."), there were a million reasons for him to leave.
>
> Weighing against it all was this: in the US, his family would have meat at every meal. After a lifetime of deprivation, that was perhaps reason enough to stay. Meat was not just a perk. It was not just food. It was a sign that we had made it.[21]

It is no secret that the Asian community is often criticized within the Animal Liberation Movement, as well as among meat-eaters. A video that went viral in October 2014 featured an intoxicated bus tour guide in San Francisco ranting against Chinatown:

Fuck your little seafood fucking markets with your turtles and your frogs inside, okay?...Okay, when you come to America, you gotta assimilate a little bit; and here in America, we don't eat turtles and frogs, okay? But they're gonna bring that here!

Matt Stone and Trey Parker's long-running, society-critiquing animated series, *South Park*, hit the nail right on the head with Season Thirteen's eleventh episode, "Whale Whores." In this episode, Americans express outrage over Japanese whaling practices, and the reality TV show *Whale Wars* experiences its apex of popularity. In the end, the South Park gang discovers that the Japanese engage in these practices because they hold whales and dolphins responsible for the atomic bombs dropped on Hiroshima and Nagasaki during World War II. A photograph suggests that the pilots controlling these bombs were a dolphin and a whale.

The solution? The South Park gang alters the photo so that the culprits now appear to be a cow and a chicken. Thus, in Japan, death industries proceed to focus on cows and chickens rather than whales and dolphins—which, to Americans, feels normal and "right." Queen's University scholars Will Kymlicka and Sue Donaldson refer to this notion—that what We do is right and ethical, and what They do is immoral and heinous—as "performing whiteness." I have often referred to the same phenomenon under the larger umbrella-term of *otherization*.

It is important to remember where your audience is coming from if you hope to reach it. It is quite a leap for some people with backgrounds like that which I've just described—whether they are racial minorities, or white people living in rural America where farming is a way of life—to accept that the animals they've been forced to regard as food can in fact be their friends, and that killing them is wholly unnecessary for survival. It may be a greater leap still for those who are used to thinking about meat as a hard-earned luxury to voluntarily forgo it after years of working to accumulate sufficient wealth with which to access it.

In Chapter Six, we will talk more about farm life and hear from Harold Brown, a former farm boy who found his way to the Animal Liberation Movement in adulthood and spoke of his transition into an animal-friendly way of life in the renowned documentary, *Peaceable Kingdom: The Journey Home* (2009).

The Color of a Movement

In March 2014, Direct Action Everywhere (DxE) organizers Wayne Hsiung and Priya Sawhney hosted an open forum at DxE's Oakland, CA headquarters entitled, "The Color of a Movement: Animal Rights and Racism."[22]

The following insights are an amalgamation of information presented on the slides for this talk and my own perspective and research. Video footage of the meeting, as well as the slides themselves, are accessible via DxE's website.

In an effort to defend dropping the atomic bomb on Japan and incarcerating Japanese-Americans into prison camps, President Harry Truman said the following in a letter to Samuel Cavert, General Secretary of the Federal Council of the Churches of Christ in America, in 1945:

> The only language they seem to understand is the one we have been using to bombard them. When you have to deal with a beast, you have to treat him as a beast.

This attitude exemplifies both speciesism and racism, as it perpetuates the notion that minorities are not just inferior to the majority (which would be bad enough), but that they are *as inferior as animals*; ergo, animals are also inferior to the majority. This way of thinking presupposes that while minorities are themselves animals, members of the majority are not, when in fact *all* humans—regardless of color, socioeconomic background, sexual orientation, or religion—are animals. To be human is to be an animal.

The year 1945 sounds like it was a long time ago, but it really wasn't. Truth be told, this rhetoric is still employed today to denigrate minorities. Video footage of a Tea Party rally in the 2000s shows a reporter asking a Tea Party member why he hates Mexicans. The reply? "Mexicans are filthy, stinking animals."

Not only did he and other Tea Party demonstrators offend Mexicans that day, in speaking forcefully against immigration and in favor of deportation, but they also insulted animals, demonstrating the belief that it is okay to abuse a group of people if that group resembles animals to you—because, of course, it's okay to abuse animals, isn't it?

The 2008 Stanford University study "Not Yet Human," conducted by Professor Jennifer L. Eberhardt and others, examined why racial prejudice still persists in this country. The study found that:

> U.S. citizens implicitly associate Blacks and apes…This Black/ape association…increases endorsement of violence against Black suspects.[23]

This proved to be true even among people who declared themselves at the start of the study to be "non-racist." The challenges presented by the results of this study are twofold: how can we prevent white people from viewing African Americans as nonhuman, and how can we prevent these same people from believing that violence against nonhumans is acceptable?

"The Color of a Movement" slides informed me that fewer than 3% of animal liberationists in America are people of color. While I was not surprised to see this, given my personal experiences as an activist—having attended various meetings, demonstrations, and so forth at which I was the only minority, or one of fewer than a handful of minorities—it is surprising in light of the similarities between the plight of the nonhuman animal and the plight of the human racial minority. Both are otherized: criticized and punished for being different while their abundant similarities to the "superior" group are ignored. Both have been oppressed, denied basic rights to family and freedom, and forced to work (and even die) for the benefit of the "superior" group.

Why, then, are there so few minorities in America engaged in the Animal Liberation Movement? The reasons are complex and unclear. From a personal perspective, I can deduce that the majority of Hispanics and other minorities, who perhaps have close friends or relatives who are farmers, would be reluctant to join the movement due to cultural pressure. I faced enormous social pressure from my family upon becoming vegetarian, and even more upon becoming vegan; still, they loved me enough to eventually get over it, and I was confident enough in my convictions not to allow anyone to sway me otherwise.

How might we better connect with persons of color, and spread the message of animal liberation to those who were raised on farms (both in the US and abroad)?

One strategy endorsed by DxE is to "achieve buy-in from minority communities"—in other words, to form connections with local businesses, governing bodies, and other such organizations with minority members and influence. Professor Nicholas Christakis's research at Harvard University illustrates the importance of this strategy. His research indicates that, regardless of how much information you foist upon a community, you cannot hope to truly change that community unless and until you've formed strong, lasting connections with other leaders in that community.

One way in which the Animal Liberation Movement can, and should, achieve this is to show up for demonstrations and meetings regarding *human* rights violations, such as solidarity protests with Baltimore against police brutality. Animal liberation *is* human liberation; you can't have one without the other, and by demonstrating our commitment to the rights of humans we not only add credibility to this statement but also increase the likelihood that we will encounter and form bonds with leaders in communities of color—individuals who are already committed to social justice (otherwise, they wouldn't be out protesting anything) and therefore may be persuaded to adopt a vegan ethos.

In some cases, persuasion won't even be necessary; many social justice advocates of color are already vegan, yet do not actively engage in vegan communities. Showing up in solidarity with the concerns of human groups gives us an opportunity to extend an invitation—not to mention walk the inclusive, intersectional vegan walk about which we're constantly talking.

It is not a matter of lack of interest. "Minorities" (members of the global majority) don't generally care less about nonhuman animals than white Americans do; rather, the Animal Liberation Movement has unfortunately done a better job, at this point, of integrating white-owned businesses and political groups than it has of reaching out to minority groups.

Theory of Racism (and Speciesism and Sexism...): Identify the Other→ Suppress Empathy → Trigger Animosity

The above outlines three basic steps toward instilling racism in the mind of an individual as well as disseminating racist sentiments throughout a society. The first step speaks directly to otherization: how we come to define Us and Them. What is required of an individual to be considered one of Us, and what distinguishes them immediately as "not like us" and therefore one of Them? Racism achieves this by pointing out the color of one's skin; the way one speaks, dresses, and eats; one's taste in music and art; and so forth. Speciesism achieves this by focusing on the ways in which nonhuman animals differ from humans—they have feathers, they have scales, they don't speak using words, they don't have opposable thumbs (except for apes), etc.

Once we've identified a being or group of beings as the Other, we set about creating the dynamic of Us vs. Them. Our needs outweigh Their needs. Our priorities are more admirable, more sophisticated, and more respectable than Their priorities. Our culture is superior, and therefore should ultimately supplant, Their culture. What We do is right and what They do is wrong. This is how we learn to *suppress empathy*—Phase Two of the "harmful –ism" model above. We suppress empathy by convincing ourselves that *Their* plight is justified by *Our* success, that *Their* pain is secondary to *Our* comfort.

Finally, animosity is triggered among Us against Them. This serves as a safety net for racism and speciesism alike, as many people who would be reluctant to engage in these behaviors or adopt these beliefs due to an inability to suppress empathy would readily change their tune once convinced that there is a reason not just to lack empathy for, but also to *actively dislike,* the Other.

The Relationship between Speciesism and Sexism

Speciesism, as previously discussed, overtly violates one of the primary tenets of feminism: the autonomy of individuals over their own bodies. Sexism, like racism and speciesism, stems from otherization: identifying females as different from, and therefore inferior to, males. While other species provide flavor profiles or clothing aesthetics enjoyed by some humans, women provide sexual and aesthetic pleasures desired by straight men while competing with men of any orientation for jobs, resources, and recognition. Women also differ from men in visually obvious ways, just as cows differ obviously from humans.

Once the Other has been identified, empathy is suppressed: men decide that their success is more intrinsically valuable and necessary than that of women, members of one race decide the same about all other races, and humans decide that their existence is of a higher importance than that of all other species.

Finally, animosity must be triggered. More and more frequently in America, men compete with women directly in the workplace—for everything from initial job placement to promotion, from raises to perks, and on to awards, invitations to luxurious business trips, and other distinctions. This direct competition, which one might hope would garner *increased* respect for women as they prove themselves over and over again to be equal to men in both intelligence and capability, often has the opposite effect: it makes men angrier at women, less trusting of them, more judgmental—and far less empathetic. This coupling of decreased empathy and increased animosity prompts them to look the other way—or even *celebrate*—as women continue to make less money than they do for completing the same tasks, or when their company refuses to promote any women for the third consecutive year.

Sexism is also apparent with respect to how vegan men are stereotyped in our society—a major obstacle in changing the habits of some men who profess to sympathize with the cause privately, then proceed to mock the cause while in the presence of their peers or coworkers (I have encountered many such men). There persists a strong misperception that "real men" eat meat—that there is something weak, something "effeminate" about showing compassion for nonhuman animals. I think part of this has to do with the misconception that meat is nutritionally necessary for the development of strong muscles; suffice it to say, for the time being, that many of the most powerful animals on Earth—the ox, the elephant, the bison—are strictly plant eaters. Vegan bodybuilders exist. Vegan marathon runners exist. Vegan mountaineers exist. You get the idea.

Beyond this dietary misnomer, a larger part of the problem is the firing of the false synapse, "compassionate—weak—feminine." There is nothing weak about being compassionate, and the fact that something is weak does not make it feminine. To say that vegan men are That Vulgar P-Word demonstrates not only speciesism (*nonhumans are not worth caring about, so anyone who cares about them is weak*), but also sexism (*women are weak, so anyone who demonstrates weakness must be more feminine than masculine*).

Thus, liberationists are confronted with the task of disrupting two ongoing illusions: that to align with nonhumans is weak, and that to be weak is to be feminine. These illusions share a common father, aptly named *Patriarchy*.

In her essay, "Sexist Words, Speciesist Roots," Joan Dunayer—animal advocate and author of *Animal Equality* (2001) and *Speciesism* (2004)—asserts the importance of "a feminist perspective on the status of animals." She begins by succinctly outlining the historical relationship between speciesism and sexism:

> Historically, the ideological justification for women's alleged inferiority has been made by appropriating them to animals; from Aristotle on, women's bodies have been seen to intrude upon their rationality. Since rationality has been construed by most Western theorists as the defining requirement for membership in the moral community, women—along with non-white men and animals—were long excluded. Until the twentieth century this "animality" precluded women's being granted the rights of public citizenship.[24]

Responses to the equation of animals and women abound in feminist communities. Toward the end of the eighteenth century, feminists sought to declaim that women are not emotionally or instinctively driven, like animals, but are instead rational and logical, like men—a challenge to sexism that regrettably reinforces speciesism.

Some feminists later rejected this notion and instead embrace their connection to animals and nature while rejecting society's positioning of these entities as inferior to the Rational World of Man. Marilyn French's *Beyond Power* (1985) attributed the domination of women to "the Western masculine denial of the human-animal connection."

> Patriarchy is an ideology founded on the assumption that man is distinct from the animals and superior to [them.] The reason for this superiority is man's contact with a higher power/knowledge called god, reason, or control. The reason for man's existence is to shed all animal residue and realize his 'divine' nature, the part that seems unlike any part owned by animals—mind, spirit, or control.[25]

The third argument—in my view, the weakest—is that female oppression has nothing whatsoever to do with animal oppression. Various feminist publications in the 1990s and the twenty-first century have rejected the notion that the Female Problem and the Animal Problem are linked. Perhaps these feminist writers fear that attaching themselves too strongly to what appears to be a "separate" or "outside" cause will hinder the progress of their own social movement. In any case, as Dunayer passionately declaims, "there is no neutral place from which to observe evil. To observe in silence is to be complicit."

The needs of animals and the needs of women are not mutually exclusive; these needs can be met side-by-side, and ignoring or declining to speak about animal issues in fear that they will interrupt dialogue about women's issues are fundamentally speciesist acts. These actions imply not only that the needs cannot both be met, which is patently untrue, but also that the needs of one group—women—outweigh the needs of another group—nonhuman animals.

Any initiative that helps women—anti-rape initiatives, breast cancer awareness initiatives, and so on—inevitably benefit animals: specifically the subset known as *human women*. Conversely, initiatives to free enslaved dairy cows benefit women: specifically *bovine mothers* and *bovine rape victims*. Initiatives to end chicken consumption and the egg trade also benefit women: women whose sons will be murdered, whose mouths will be cut off, and who stand to die even before their scheduled date of slaughter of anything from suffocation to inhalation of toxic agents if we continue to ignore their cries.

An Intersectional Web of Oppression

I abandoned social media for a few years until recently, dismissing it as a set of venues for vanity, procrastination, and stalking. I was pleased to discover upon re-entering the world of Facebook in early 2015 that much has changed since I first registered for the site around 2004, when I'd just completed high school. While there are still those who choose to use Facebook and other social media outlets to share selfies of which they are particularly proud, post offensive messages about their exes, and so forth, it has also become a hub of social justice activity. I have had many a critical conversation and have met multiple inspiring activists through Facebook, and groups such as World Intersectional Liberation strengthen social justice communities across state and national borders. (I confess, I still don't *love* social media; I just hate it a little bit less now.)

I'd like to share with you a brilliant chart I recently discovered on Facebook. David Kirk and other members of the World Intersectional Liberation Facebook group created it, and it pretty much says it all. This chart clearly outlines the way in which all forms of oppression are structured; it is my belief that, in order to truly eradicate any of these, we must all work toward the common goal of eradicating *each and every one of them*:[26]

THE INTERSECTIONAL WEB OF OPPRESSION

Fundamental Process	Instance	Instance	Instance	Instance	Instance	Instance
Each and every manifestation of oppression	RACISM	SEXISM	CLASSISM	HETEROSEXISM	ABLEISM	SPECIESISM
involves members of one group abusing their power	Person from one race	Men	Upper class/Middle class	Heterosexuals	Person with ability X	Human animals
to dominate members of another group (and vice-versa)	Person from another race	Women	Middle class/Working class	LGBTQ+	Person without ability X	Nonhuman animals
which is "justified" by arbitrary "differences"	exploitable, weak, beasts, worthless, savages, lacking language, unevolved, less moral, uncivilized, less educated, unnatural, less intelligent, less human					
that encourages unequal, even cruel, treatment	denial of moral personhood, suffering is trivialized or denied, exclusion, exploitation, ridicule, dismissal of rights, confinement, ownership, slavery, verbal abuse, physical violence, rape, murder					

The arbitrary acceptance of any one instance implicitly approves of the fundamental process.
This sets a precedent that allows the justification of EVERY instance.

<u>Oppose the fundamental process - Reject ALL oppression - Demand social justice for ALL beings.</u>

Being an Effective Ally

Now that we've explored the ways in which various forms of oppression are connected, what do we do with this information? How can we effectively support advocates for various social justice causes outside of those with which we are most familiar?

There are a few tips I've picked up—through experience (on both the oppressed and the privileged side of a given fence), conversations, and readings—that you may find valuable when engaging in dialogues about intersectionality. The first and perhaps most important of these is to focus on the commonalities among *systems* of oppression rather than among *victims* of oppression. For instance, it is far more effective, generally, to speak of the similarities between speciesism and racism than it is to speak of the similarities between nonhumans and people of color. At first, these might seem like one and the same, but the truth is, the former is more likely to inspire empathy than the latter. The latter may even have the opposite effect; rather than inspiring empathy for nonhumans, comparing nonhumans to people of color when talking about racism with a person of color might offend that person. When we are offended, we are not inclined to be empathetic toward others. Instead, we are often tempted to redirect the conversation toward our own struggles and downplay the struggles of others.

Yes, we humans are also animals; therefore, ideally, we should not object to being compared to nonhumans. The fact remains, however, that some people will immediately become offended, and assessing whether or not someone has a "right" to be offended is ultimately a waste of time when you are trying to spread a message of compassion. It is also worth noting that, historically, nonhuman-related rhetoric (such as "beasts," "animals," and "brutes") has been employed aggressively to degrade persons of color. Some examples of this were provided earlier in this chapter. So it may be traumatic for a person to hear such a comparison made today, even if it is made in an entirely different spirit and with an entirely different intent.

Another important factor in discussing intersectionality is to commit to *cooperative learning: sharing your experiences and perspective with others while actively listening to, and learning from, theirs—and not passing judgment.* Two important elements of cooperative learning are *active listening* and *maintaining a safe space.*

Active listening is a difficult skill for us to master—increasingly difficult in today's technological age, when information is distilled into tweets and lists and updated every thirty seconds. In contrast to passive listening (in which you are still, quiet, and allow someone to talk "at you" while your mind does whatever it wants to), *active* listening involves clearing your mind of all other content and focusing exclusively on what you are being told, mentally bookmarking bits of information about which you may have questions. The most obvious and yet increasingly overlooked aspect of active listening is simply *looking at the speaker;* I frequently find that when talking to someone, they have their eyes set on their iPhone, checking emails or reading the news. I find this offensive, and tell them so. They usually apologize at the time, but still, the next time I see that person, it typically happens again—at least once.

You may think that listening involves exclusively, or at least mostly, your ears, but you can learn an awful lot about how a person feels about a subject by studying that person's face and body while they speak. Active listening also involves your mind, in that you are analyzing what is being said and trying to recall things you don't understand or don't agree with so that you can later ask for clarification. Active listening is, *at minimum*, a mental, auditory, *and* visual exercise. (Not that anyone who struggles with any of these can't be an active listener; those with poor eyesight, for instance, develop other ways of *seeing*.)

Maintaining a safe space, to me, means hosting a space—either physical or virtual—of mutual respect and acknowledgement, where people feel safe speaking openly about their views. This, too, is a bigger challenge than it may appear at first. Typically, when people discuss safe spaces, they do so from the point of view of marginalized and/or victimized persons; this makes perfect sense, as these people are perhaps most in need of our compassion, having suffered as they have at the hands of an oppressive system (or multiple systems). When it comes to cooperative learning, it is also important that we provide a safe space for those on the other side of the fence—those with privilege(s) we ourselves may lack—who actually want to learn about social justice issues and contribute to a solution rather than perpetuate the problem.

To be clear, I am not speaking in defense of persons who are actively, willingly racist, sexist, heterosexist, ableist, or any other "ist." I am speaking strictly of those who acknowledge that they are the products of privilege and want to help level the playing field—people with a genuine interest in understanding oppression that they have not experienced firsthand.

What follows are a series of observations I made recently in a blog post on *The Liberationist*, regarding cooperative learning:

There are words and phrases in our culture that are overtly racist, such as the N-word that was used against African Americans hatefully for so long and is still used today by some racists. At the same time, there are multiple manifestations of racism that are far subtler. An example from my own experience would be the phrase "We are all one race—the human race." I've said this many times in the past, in an effort to foster a sense of global cooperation and emphasize our common needs, desires, etc. It wasn't until recently that someone, not even addressing me in particular, publicly explained why that phrasing is racist: it seeks to ignore obvious differences in people's struggles, experiences, and access to privilege by pretending that race doesn't exist. It is a scapegoat commonly used amongst those who would rather not talk about race at all than engage in constructive dialogue about it.[27]

I was embarrassed to learn that people perceived this statement that way, and thinking back on past instances of having used it, I wondered how many people walked away from those conversations thinking that—gasp!—*I* was racist! I am grateful to have received that explanation. I learned something, and while I still believe that we all have a lot in common and should treat one another as one big happy Earth-inhabiting family, I now seek less offensive ways of expressing that belief—ways that neither deny nor suppress the experiences of others.

The reason I was able to learn this is that, when I asked what was offensive about the statement, I received a detailed yet *polite* response—a response that made me feel comfortable sticking around, asking more and learning more. I was not vilified as an ignorant racist; if I had been, I probably would have fled in my embarrassment, and never learned precisely *why* anyone was calling me racist. I would have been confused, hurt, and reluctant to engage with that same group of people again.

Unfortunately, my positive learning experience is seldom mirrored in various social justice communities. To an extent, people tend to be more polite and respectful in person, though not always; it is within Internet communities that I have witnessed especially poor treatment of individuals who, admittedly, *did* say something offensive. They were chased away with insults and accusations; then, once others in a given discussion realized that the alleged racist/sexist/speciesist/heterosexist/etc. had left, inevitably one or more persons would say something to the effect of, "See, they left; that person clearly did not want to learn. That person doesn't really care about social justice. What a jerk!"

Valuable insights on this issue have been provided in two important articles. The first, "Calling In: A Less Disposable Way of Holding Each Other Accountable" by Ngọc Loan Trần, is about *calling in*—the notion of inviting people into a community from which they have strayed, i.e., back into a racial justice group after having said something racist, rather than "calling out"—publically shaming someone and thus pushing that person further away from the community.[28] The second, "A Note on Call-Out Culture" by Asam Ahmad, specifically addresses politicized "call-out culture," in which people "publicly name instances or patterns of oppressive behaviour and language use by others."[29] While general "calling out" can be about anything at all, the call-out culture addressed in this article relates specifically to social justice communities and admits to the tendency of some social justice activists to see calling out as "an end in itself." In other words, we sometimes use someone else's poor choice of words or lack of understanding to highlight our own proper word choice and perfect understanding—rather than actually trying to inform or enlighten the other person.

The intention of such behavior is not cooperative learning but, rather, to emphasize one's own purity. It is an exercise in "one-upsmanship." Another example, beyond merely criticizing one's word choice or statement of opinion, is when we use our academic credentials and/or employment to shut someone else down—to convince them that they are simply incapable of having a relevant opinion about a given topic. Yes, you may have a degree in economics; that does not mean your opinion on every single matter having to do with the field of economics is correct, or even that all of these opinions are naturally "more correct" than those of people who do not have an economics degree. This simply means that, with respect to the specific subjects (countries, time periods, etc.) of which your curriculum was comprised, you have more knowledge than most people. There are, undoubtedly, still gaps in your knowledge, and no matter how much knowledge you have, you are still limited by your own perspective and experience.

There is no magic formula for how to have a social justice conversation, and I highly doubt there ever will be. There are, however, a few simple steps we can all take to make these conversations more effective, no matter how upset we become or how obviously "wrong" that other person is:

- When having a conversation with someone with whom you disagree, and that other person leaves, **ask yourself, "Is there anything I could have said differently?** Could I have expressed my point of view in a way that is more respectful of their perspective?" The answer might be *No.* Maybe they really did just leave because they don't want to learn, but we shouldn't *assume* that to be the case.

- When you sense yourself or the other person growing agitated, and the conversation is currently public, **consider moving to a private space.** People often become more agitated in public than in private because embarrassment plays a role; perhaps this person would feel more comfortable hearing you out, and be more willing to accept that they did something wrong, if they didn't feel compelled to do so in front of a dozen—or a thousand—others.

- **Avoid one-upsmanship at all costs.** There's no need for you to prove to anyone that you are more educated than they are, or that your brand of activism is more effective than theirs. Stick to the subject at hand and avoid generalizations or resume-recitals that shift the focus from, "Which opinion is more valid?," to "Who is a better/smarter/more progressive person?"

I strongly believe that *the best teachers are those who are also students.* We can all learn from each other, even those of us with the "right" opinion in any given situation. We can learn how to better express that opinion and encourage people to rethink their values, rather than intimidating or embarrassing people such that they shut down or run away. It is through cooperative learning that we can each strengthen the various communities of which we are a part.

Once you've highlighted the similarities in systems of oppression and have committed to cooperative learning, it's time to *ask what is needed of you.* Often, when we are experienced in engaging in one form of social justice work, we assume that we know what another movement needs in order to succeed. In our eagerness to be helpful, we might step on someone's toes—or an entire race's toes, or an entire gender's toes, or an entire sexual orientation's toes. The best way that you can illustrate to a marginalized group (of which you are not a part) that you want to help is to *ask that group how you can most effectively do so.*

Sometimes, the answer might be, simply, "Do nothing." The group might just need you to sit this one out, giving it space to voice its own views and tell its own stories. At other times, a marginalized group might need your support in getting non-marginalized people to attend an event; for instance, a women-centric group might need the support of willing men to encourage as many men as possible to attend a speech about women's rights. That does not mean that the women need a man to speak *for* them—only that they need help securing an audience of *men* as well as women (and other non-women, such as people who identify as agender or gender-fluid).

Within the broad category of "women," there may also be times when transgendered women need the support of cis women in acquiring an audience of cis women. This does not mean that cis women are invited to speak at, plan, or otherwise facilitate the event, but only that they are invited to promote it.

Sometimes what is needed is something tangible, like money, space, or supplies. Sometimes it's encouragement; we all know what a bummer social justice work can be, and sometimes all we really need is for someone to say, type, or write, "Good job!" or "I'm with you!" or "Keep it up!" Sometimes what is needed might be an action: a letter to your congressperson, or participation in a rally. It might be a skill, such as video editing, writing, or web design. Whatever it is, make yourself available however you are able, without appropriating the roles that marginalized persons are already successfully filling as leaders of their own movement.

Being an effective ally isn't about taking over, or even pushing things forward; it's about being a prop on which others can lean for support. It requires us to take feedback constructively. When attempting to build bridges between social justice movements, don't take it personally when you are asked to step back or step down. Check your ego at the door, and commit to increasing the marginalized group's visibility and reach—not your own.

Finally, in keeping with my very first suggestion—comparing systems and not individuals—in order to be effectively intersectional, we must avoid falling into the trap of *ranking systems according to "badness."* Many social justice advocates refer to this sort of behavior as engaging in "Oppression Olympics." Steer clear of discussions about whether racism is "worse than" speciesism, or whether heterosexism is "worse than" racism. *All* systems of oppression are bad, precisely because they *oppress someone.* Attempting to establish a hierarchy among forms of oppression inevitably supports a false hierarchy amongst individuals, opening the door for such ludicrous statements as, "Women are more important than black people" or "Nonhuman animals are more important than homosexuals." The whole point of social justice—not just any one cause or movement, but Social Justice with capital letters—is that *everyone is important.* All systems of oppression are rooted in the notion that one group is more important than another; the oppressed must not adopt the ideology of the oppressor.

We will speak more of false hierarchies later, as they relate specifically to the Animal Liberation Movement—specifically, speciesist hierarchies that compel humans to care for and love one species while exploiting and murdering another.

Chapter Three

Lifting the Veil

If you put tripe in a bowl and tell them it's from a humanely raised cow, they're going to eat it.

—Nate Appleman, Culinary Manager, Chipotle Mexican Grill

Humanewashing: Why "Grass-fed," "Cage-free," and All of These Other Buzzwords Miss the Point Entirely

Perhaps the most potent threat to the Animal Liberation Movement to date is the perpetuation of The Humane Myth: the notion that there is a kind, respectful way to kill someone who does not want to die. We have witnessed in the past decade the emergence of *humanewashing:* the employment of compassionate rhetoric and imagery by abusive institutions to manipulate public sympathy for animals for the sake of increased profit margins. Humanewashing is not just factual, but also *moral* fraud: it completely ignores the victim's perspective by masking the inherent violence of slaughter. A corpse sold by *any* company is the body of someone who neither wanted nor deserved to die.

Humanewashing has successfully perpetuated The Humane Myth and converted many potential animal liberationists into animal welfarists: people who accept the violation of the rights of nonhumans, provided that nonhumans are awarded a certain amount of space, privy to a particular diet, and so forth. To put it another way, a welfarist campaigns for chickens to have more room to roam freely before the date on which they are slaughtered; a liberationist calls for an end to slaughter, *independent of how much space a chicken was awarded beforehand.*

To be fair, many welfarists claim to be working toward animal liberation while prioritizing the comforts of animals currently enslaved who, in their opinion, will not live to see a vegan world. While I empathize with the desire to make all nonhuman animals as comfortable as possible *right now*, within the confines of our current systemic oppression of them, this pessimism is perhaps one of the greatest dangers to our movement. We must constantly push toward liberation so that as many nonhuman animals as possible *do* live to see a vegan world. We need to stop thinking of liberation as some far-away, maybe-eventually half-goal and commit ourselves fully to making it happen *as soon as possible*. Welfarist initiatives, while well-meaning, make it all too easy for the powers that be to perpetuate oppression by satisfying the public with crumbs to distract it from demanding the loaf.

Phrases such as "cage-free," "free-range," and "grass-fed" aim to reassure the public that institutions treat animals with love and respect before they murder them. Consumers often take comfort in these buzzwords, and neglect the Animal Liberation Movement in favor of "humane" meat and dairy—or to put it bluntly, the illusion of "humane" slaughter and rape.

Ultimately, there is no right way to kill someone who does not want to die; for those of you who do not (yet?) subscribe to this school of thought, let's look at some of the more obvious, practical concerns regarding this rhetoric: it is highly misleading.

When most people hear words like "cage-free" or "free-range," they picture a quaint little farm where animals are allowed to do as they please until their date of slaughter arrives. This is seldom, if ever, the case. In Dan Shapley's article, "Nine Food Label Lies," he explains that, in order to have permission to use the term "free-range," all that an institution need accomplish is to grant chickens exactly *five minutes* of "access" to the outdoors every day.[1] No stipulations are made whatsoever with respect to what constitutes "access," meaning that a filthy shed brimming with five or six hundred chickens can be called "free-range" as long as there is a trap door in one corner of the shed through which the chickens can leave—if they ever *reach* and *find* the darn thing, that is…

On many allegedly "humane" farms, pigs that can grow to up to 300 pounds are kept in pens shorter than the length of a human arm. Dairy cows, regardless of what they are fed or how much time they are allowed outdoors daily, are nevertheless consistently raped in order to ensure constant pregnancy—and their resultant children are heartlessly stolen from them upon birth.

Chickens marketed as "cage-free" often spend their lives—instead of in tiny cages stacked on top of each other—packed into an overcrowded, poorly ventilated shed. Cages of wire have been replaced with cages of flesh. These birds are packed in so tightly that they are not even afforded enough room to flap their wings, while the air they breathe is highly toxic. They are also not exempt from the barbaric practice of debeaking, whereby their beaks are seared off with a hot blade—without the use of painkillers.

While the dairy and meat industries have both claimed in the past that debeaking is necessary "for the animal's own safety," the simple fact is that chickens in nature peck each other to assert authority and establish hierarchies within their communities (hence the phrase *pecking order*). It is only under these crowded, filthy, and psychologically distressing conditions that chickens peck themselves and each other in an uncontrollable and potentially dangerous fashion. Rather than improving their conditions—or better yet, liberating the birds entirely—the industries opt to cut off the offending beaks. This is not a necessary practice; it is a deliberate, violent choice.

What "cage-free" actually looks (and smells) like

Kelly Atlas, a former DxE Bay Area organizer who was popularized by Glenn Beck as the "Crazy Chicken Lady" in September 2014, participated in a rescue in March 2014. At the time, the details of this rescue were unclear to me; many months later, I would learn that she and the other DxE Bay Area organizers had in fact been engaged in a groundbreaking open investigation and rescue at a "certified humane" farm—the highest legal standard in the US for any farm—for the past year. The farm was owned by Petaluma Farms, a company already in hot water for lying to consumers; and the eggs produced therein were sold by humane-washing giant Whole Foods.

The following week, in late March, I accompanied Kelly to Animal Place to visit the previously rescued chickens and assist with "health-checking" a new batch of chickens coming in that day. On this trip, Kelly told me of the conditions she had witnessed firsthand the week before—conditions that would be exposed in January 2015 by the release of a Direct Action Everywhere video and subsequent article in the *New York Times*. She explained:

> The smell of ammonia was so thick, I could hardly stand to be in there for five minutes. I had to come out for air regularly. After my first few minutes there, I stepped out for some fresh air and blew my nose. What came out was pitch-black! Now imagine what the lungs of those poor chickens must look like!

The next day—Saturday, March 29, 2014—Direct Action Everywhere hosted an international demonstration as part of our "It's Not Food, It's Violence" campaign. DxE East Bay demonstrated at a Chipotle location in San Francisco, telling stories of individuals who were either rescued or escaped exploitation and abuse. Near the end of our demonstration, a few members performed "speak-outs," in which an activist just grabs the megaphone and speaks from the heart about the issues.

I was most moved by organizer and press liaison Brian Burns's speak-out. He had accompanied Kelly on the chicken rescue, and had helped rescue the same chickens I later visited with her while awaiting the new arrivals we would be health-checking. I *knew* the chickens of which he spoke. I had seen them, held them, pet them. I had borne witness to their injuries. Kelly had told me about the crowding, about the stench of ammonia.

I knew he was telling the truth:

> Chipotle is trying to convince you that they treat animals with respect, and that the animals in their care are unconditionally loved. They promote their food as Food with Integrity. I went to a so-called "cage-free" facility last week on a chicken rescue. I saw firsthand what "cage-free" really looks like. The foul stench of ammonia did not say "respect." The colonies of lice eggs on the chickens' feathers did not say "love."

There was one detail I would have liked to add: the sores and blisters on their feet did not say "integrity." One of the chickens I'd helped health-check had swollen, crippled feet; she couldn't walk. Jackie, a head honcho over at Animal Place, called a vet and, thankfully, had medication on hand that she could supply to the poor hen. Many of the hens I saw had also been debeaked; I watched as one desperately tried to pick up a morsel of food from the ground, only to have it consistently fall out of her permanently mutilated mouth.

In January 2015, as part of the unveiling of our *Until Every Animal is Free* campaign, which shifted the focus from Chipotle to Whole Foods, Direct Action Everywhere released a video about the open investigation and rescue its Bay Area organizers had conducted at the Petaluma-owned, Whole Foods-profiting farm. The video shows how filthy, dark, and cramped the conditions are. The chickens, too weak to properly groom themselves, are covered in their own feces. Many are missing feathers and almost all have been debeaked. Some of these poor creatures were so violently ill that they didn't even look like chickens anymore.

A veterinarian at Berkeley Dog and Cat Hospital in Berkeley, CA examines one of the rescued chickens on camera:

> This chicken's beak has been cut, right here…The problem with diarrhea like this is you get maggots in two or three days…I mean, for her to get this thin, she has not been right for at least the past couple of weeks…Her prognosis overall is really, really poor…She is suffering at this point.[2]

"Cage-free," "grass-fed," and all of these other humane-washing buzzwords miss the point entirely. They play on public sympathy for animals, convincing well-meaning people to pay an extra couple of dollars for "humane" meat, dairy, and eggs rather than confronting the fact that they are purchasing the corpses of individuals who did not want to die, and the products of the enslavement and repeated rape of nonhuman females.

These marketing ploys not only reinforce The Humane Myth, but also the Myth of Human Supremacy, as they convince the public that they are making the best of a bad situation—that "humane" meat and dairy is the way to go because *no* meat and dairy is simply unacceptable. Humans "need" (want) these products, and the cost to nonhumans is irrelevant because ultimately, We are more important that They are.

The Humane Myth and the Myth of Human Supremacy form the Twin Demons of Animal Abuse

Companies outright LIE about this all the time: Our history is ripe with examples of companies adopting this rhetoric only to be found guilty later on of having outright lied to the public regarding their practices. In spite of the loose standards in place for using these effectively meaningless terms, some companies still can't bring themselves to comply—but hike up their prices all the same.

In 2012, three years prior to the release of DxE's investigation video, the Animal Legal Defense Fund sued Petaluma Farms for using cage-free-indicative labels on their eggs and charging cage-free prices while continuing to keep their chickens in cages. According to the lawsuit:

> ...the estimated 13,000 hens at Petaluma Egg Farms 'spend their entire lives inside modern, barren industrial sheds with no grassy fields and no outdoor access,' says the group, and are not raised in wide open spaces in Sonoma Valley, where they are free to 'roam, scratch, and play.' Nor do they have access to the outdoors and enjoy large communal areas with natural ventilation and sunlight.[3]

In April 2014, approximately thirty animal liberationists from various groups demonstrated against Petaluma Farms. At the center of an international meat recall, the former Rancho Feeding Corp. slaughterhouse (now Marin Sun Farms) had reopened under new management.

Activists gathered at the site to raise their voices against The Humane Myth being perpetuated by said new management; Marin Sun Farms CEO David Evans claims, "The humane treatment of animals is in line with the principles of this company." Maybe so (assuming anyone who believes in the principle of humane treatment of animals has ever decided to purchase a slaughterhouse, which I doubt), but it certainly isn't in line with the company's *practices*, which are far more important to the animals whose lives are at stake than to whatever the company claims its *principles* are.

One of the demonstration's organizers, Lisa Soldavini, told reporters: "We thought that the slaughterhouse was going to get shut down and we were going to get rid of one more slaughterhouse....David Evans touts the fact that he is a humane farmer, but we believe there is no humane slaughter."[4]

I love synchronicity. This lawsuit already helps to beautifully illustrate why "cage-free," "grass-fed," and all these warm and fuzzy buzzwords don't mean a thing. This company lied to its consumers for who knows how long, tricking them into paying top dollar for eggs so as to alleviate their own guilt. Countless citizens naively thought that they were minimizing animal cruelty and supporting "humane farming" by buying Petaluma eggs rather than other eggs, and they were all wrong—fundamentally wrong, as Lisa's comment illustrates. In a more literal sense, they were incorrect. Petaluma Farms knows how to talk the talk, but as DxE's video reveals, neither the 2012 lawsuit nor the 2014 demonstration was enough to convince the company to walk the walk.

Lisa's comment pushes the envelope even further, and illuminates the truest, strongest, "real-est" reason that humane-washing buzzwords miss the point entirely: At the end of the day, slaughter is slaughter—and it is inherently cruel. Keeping hens enslaved to produce eggs, manipulating their bodies' chemistry with hormones, and leaving them susceptible to a host of diseases and maladies... All of this is inherently cruel, even though the hens themselves are not being slaughtered (yet). Some people have a hard time grasping the cruelty of an egg because the egg itself is not alive. It is the conditions in which egg-laying hens must live and the pain they endure as their egg-producing parts become infected from overuse that is cruel—and these realities are inescapable, whether we are talking about "cage-free" eggs or not.

Even if you think it's "okay" to eat eggs because they're unfertilized, the chickens "don't need them," or any of a number of explanations I've heard in the past, what do you think happens to the hens when they can no longer produce eggs, or can't do it quickly enough to turn a profit higher than the cost of feeding and housing them? To the slaughterhouse they go—or to the alleyway or field or even garbage bin, where they are abandoned and left to die of starvation and/or exposure. Unwanted farmed animals are abandoned in this way as a matter of course, leaving aside those who are murdered immediately upon birth because they cannot produce anything considered "of value," such as male chicks.

Justin Van Kleeck, cofounder of Triangle Chance for All (an organization that rescues farmed animals from county shelters in the Triangle region of North Carolina), asserts that as long as animals exist as "domesticated" beings, they cannot in fact be truly free, owing to genetic manipulation:

> Laying hens produce eggs to such a degree that their reproductive systems and entire bodies are self-destructive. Few hens live past age five, even if they are not slaughtered, because we have bred them to break down...Liberation, to me, means restoring their autonomy as much as getting them out of awful conditions, and such autonomy is not possible as long as they bear our exploitation in their genes.

Ergo, a pressing challenge for our movement is not only to provide space in which animals can live freely, but also to halt genetic manipulation. While those already affected unfortunately will remain affected, the best we can do is to stop mutilating others—not just by cutting off their beaks, which hurts a parent but not his or her child, but by mutilating their genetic makeup, which harms both parent and child. (This issue will be explored further in Chapter Seven: Liberation as Autonomy.)

Chipotle: Food with Integrity? Not quite.

In 2013, Mexican fast-food giant Chipotle launched a clever marketing campaign entitled "Food with Integrity." Among other things, Chipotle promised to treat its animals "with respect." Mind you, Chipotle serves meat and dairy; therefore, there is just as much blood on its hands as, say, the hands of Burger King or McDonald's. It may have added a vegan burrito to its menu in 2014, but it is by no means a vegan restaurant. So, what does this rhetoric really *mean*?

Chipotle spokesperson Chris Arnold has said, "I think the way we portray our suppliers is very consistent with how they operate in reality," and that Chipotle uses "a number of naturally raised meat suppliers." Chipotle in fact gets its pork from Niman Ranch Pork Company (or did, until it stopped selling carnitas at hundreds of locations at the start of 2015, refusing to name which pork supplier it had decided to cut ties with). Pigs at Niman Ranch aren't required to have outdoor access; they can be housed in "hoop buildings" with sunlight, instead. "Growing and finishing hogs"—the kind that you eat—are only required to have eight to eighteen square feet of space each, depending on weight, if they are housed in a structure that permits outdoor access. In cases where pigs are housed in hoop buildings, they only get five to fourteen square feet.[5]

Some of Chipotle's beef comes from Meyer Natural Foods, which finishes feeding cows in feedlots—so the beef isn't 100% grass-fed.[5] Meyer's website does not list a standard space requirement but rather appeals to its farmers to adhere to the vague "adequate space for comfort" standard—in short, no standard whatsoever. "Adequate" is not a unit of measurement.

David Sirota criticized the animated Chipotle commercial "The Scarecrow" in his September 2013 *Salon* article, "Chipotle's Self-Serving Deception: A 'vegetarian' bait and switch."

As a piece of buzz-worthy art, Chipotle's new three-minute ad (and attendant smartphone game) is no doubt a masterpiece. It is everything that all the worshipful articles about it say it is—beautiful, inspiring and politically significant for how it openly derides factory farming. What most of those articles don't say, however, is that it is either a deliberate endorsement of a plant-based diet or it is a deceptive attempt to appropriate the morality of vegetarianism and ascribe it to meat-based business.[6]

Among Sirota's many poignant observations concerning this humanewashing opus are:

- The scarecrow is clearly appalled by the Crow Industries' meat-based operation early in the short, and is later seen harvesting his crops—but not at an abattoir (slaughterhouse) engaging in what Chipotle wants us to believe is "humane slaughter."

- The scarecrow then heads into town in a truck that appears to be filled exclusively with vegetables—with no reference whatsoever to the scarecrow having produced, or intending to sell, meat.

- The ad ends with the scarecrow presenting "what could easily pass for a vegetarian dish."

The resulting message can be summarized thus: the scarecrow, horrified by meat production and what it entails—including slaughter—resolves instead to make his living selling produce. Clearly, Chipotle wants us to identify it as the scarecrow: so mortified by factory farming, so patently against cruelty, so devoted to loving animals unconditionally. None of these are the case. Chipotle has yet to lay down its throat-slitting swords and go veg; yet, as David Sirota and activists, consumers, and journalists across the country are increasingly noting, this hasn't stopped Chipotle from appropriating animal liberationist values to market its animal-exploiting products.

Chipotle execs have claimed that their marketing strategy is not about "product integration," but rather "values integration." What values are they trying to impart on us? None; what they mean to say is "values *manipulation.*" They seek to appropriate a value that is trending here in America—"We don't want to be mean to animals anymore"—and manipulate Americans into thinking that Chipotle is the solution. *Chipotle cares about the animals, too! Chipotle shares your values! Eat at Chipotle, where we pet and play with our animals before we rape and kill them.*

With each naïve consumer Chipotle draws to its establishment, one more would-be animal liberationist accepts the status quo. That's what is so very dangerous about this type of marketing. The people who eat at Chipotle as a direct result of these ploys (not all of its customers, but certainly most) are people who might otherwise be motivated to *actually* save lives. These are people who genuinely *want* to do the right thing, but when faced with doing the right thing "the hard way" (going vegan, engaging in nonviolent direct action) and the illusion of the right thing being achievable "the easy way" (eating at meat/cheese/dairy-serving restaurants that call themselves "humane"), they take the easy way out.

Whole Foods: The Humanewashing Champion

When most people think of animal-abusive corporations, they probably don't include *Whole Foods* on the list. Whole Foods is known first and foremost for, well, providing whole foods—natural, pure grains, nuts, and produce that customers feel proud of consuming because of their numerous health benefits. It's no secret that the company also sells meat and dairy, but it has done a spectacular job of preventing itself from being cognitively *associated* with these industries.

How did they do it? The same way Chipotle did: via humanewashing.

Three examples of Whole Foods's contribution to perpetuating The Humane Myth are:

- *Cruelty by Numbers:* In 2009, Whole Foods instituted a system for which I have coined the term "Cruelty by Numbers." This system categorizes corpses on a scale of 1 to 5, 1 being defined as "No cages, no crates, no crowding," and 5 being considered the most humane: "Animal centered, entire lives on the same farm." There is even a level below 1, "Not Rated," meaning that such animals' lives did not meet Whole Foods requirements. (Presumably, these animals are not sold at Whole Foods, rendering the category utterly superfluous. A subliminal reminder of the company's goodness: "We're so kind, we won't even *serve* creatures raised this way—just, you know, everyone else.")

  Not surprisingly, customers must pay more for 5s than 4s, 4s than 3s, and so forth, as purchasing corpses labeled 5 allows customers to have their cake and eat it too—to pat themselves on the back for making a humane choice while not having to deny themselves of anything they enjoy (heaven forbid!). Even those labeled 1 are advertised as having had decent lives; even the 1s aren't kept in cages! So the implications of this entire system are not only that there are degrees of cruelty where slaughter is concerned, but also that *even the most poorly treated animals served by Whole Foods didn't really have it that bad.*

As DxE's open investigation revealed, where Whole Foods is concerned, there most definitely is crowding—and ammonia, and animals covered in feces and lice, and a host of other inhumane conditions. So the numbers system, aside from being wildly insulting toward the animals whose lives have been stolen from them, isn't even remotely accurate with respect to how these animals *actually* live.

- *A hearty helping of ANIMAL COMPASSION with every order:* This and similar slogans adorn the top of meat and dairy shelves at numerous Whole Foods locations, in a pathetic attempt to convince customers that they are making a compassionate choice when buying corpses from Whole Foods rather than any other provider. In reality, the only difference between buying a corpse at Whole Foods and buying one at, say, your local butcher is that, in the former case, Whole Foods gets the money; in the latter, your butcher does. At bottom, a corpse is a corpse is a corpse— no matter whom you pay for it.

  The color chosen for this message's backdrop—a warm, cheerful yellow—is no doubt carefully selected to support the lie. Don't think *blood* or *death*, folks; think *sunshine!*

- *Know what kind of life your dinner lived:* A Whole Foods ad prints this offensive message over the image of a beautiful woman holding a live chicken. This phrase simultaneously acknowledges the individuality of the animal—by admitting that the animal once lived, and therefore once had feelings, experiences, and emotions—and objectifies the animal by referring to him or her as "dinner." Humanewashing incarnate.

We All "Drank the Kool-Aid" with Respect to Animal Testing

In his June 2013 talk at the National Institutes of Health campus in Bethesda, MD, Dr. Elias Zerhouni, who served as America's National Institutes of Health director from the years 2002–2008, said the following on the subject of animal testing:

> We all drank the Kool-Aid on that one, myself included. With the ability to knock in or knock out any gene in a mouse—which can't sue us— researchers have over-relied on animal data. The problem is that it hasn't worked, and it's time we stopped dancing around the problem. ... We need to refocus and adapt new methodologies for use in humans to understand disease biology in humans.[7]

Noteworthy publications such as the *British Medical Journal* and the *Journal of the American Medical Association* have published numerous studies concluding that, owing to our fundamentally different biological makeups, animal testing cannot reliably predict how humans will react to a particular product, nor can it adequately determine the effectiveness of treatments and cures designed for humans. In fact, a vast majority of animal experiments fail to lead to medical advances. Many yield misleading results that are useless at best, dangerous at worst.

None of this matters. Why? Because *even if* we "needed" to test on animals in order to ensure product safety or cure diseases, the bodies of others do not belong to us. Animals are not property. They are not instruments. As Alice Walker said, they exist for their own reasons. Therefore, we should not use products we cannot be confident about without animal testing, and not pursue lines of research that involve animal testing, independent of whatever results such research may yield. (And no, you're not going to find a cure for cancer by genetically manipulating a rat. If that were the case, we'd have one by now.)

This is perhaps the second most commonly brought-up topic among my non-liberationist friends (the first being, of course, the nutrition angle—*Where, oh where shall I ever get enough PROTEIN!*). It is one of their "aces in the hole"—or so they think. Animal testing and nutrition are the two arguments to which I've most commonly been exposed by individuals in my life; as a result, I've taken it upon myself to learn the ins and outs of both. Ultimately, activism isn't about just saying whatever we as activists want to say, or feel is most important for others to hear; it's about saying *everything that needs to be said in order to save as many lives as possible.*

To abstain from engaging in conversations like these, or knowing the facts with which to dispel myths like "we need meat for protein" and "we need animals to cure cancer" simply because those matters aren't important to *us* as individuals is, I think, a grievous error in judgment. If we want to change minds, we have to be prepared for these types of discussions—whether we like them or not.

Of Mice and Humans

In a series of articles published in *The Huffington Post* in the summer of 2013, Dr. Aysha Akhtar, author of the book ***Animals and Public Health: Why Treating Animals Better is Critical to Human Welfare***, revealed several key factors that prevent animal testing from yielding accurate, reliable, and/or useful results:

- *Nonhuman animal experiments simply don't make good "models" of human physiology and human diseases.* To drive this point home, Dr. Akhtar quoted Dr. Nicholson of Merck pharmaceuticals, one of many pharmaceutical and biotech companies that are now employing new means of testing (such as "organs-on-a-chip," developed at Harvard and discussed later in this section):

The limitations of animals as stand-ins for human patients are a major reason (for drugs to fail). Animal disease doesn't faithfully replicate asthma, for instance. The condition is uniquely human ... and animal models can't capture the constriction of airways and all of the other characteristics of the disease. We have found great mechanisms that can control asthma in an animal, and most of them have failed in humans.[8]

Dr. Akhtar also cited a study published in the *Proceedings of the National Academy of Sciences* in February 2013, which revealed that, as the title of the study purports, "Genomic Responses in Mouse Models Poorly Mimic Human Inflammatory Diseases." In other words, mice do a poor job of replicating the inflammation that occurs in humans and leads to various diseases, disorders, and conditions, such as Alzheimer's, celiac disease, and multiple sclerosis.[9] Beyond being unable to replicate asthma—one ailment—inability to replicate inflammation in general results in an inability to adequately replicate a wide variety of ailments—many of which are fatal if not properly treated.

Mice are the most commonly used animals in scientific research, yet they have proven to be incapable of mimicking one of the most common, most prominent conditions experienced among humans—a condition that can lead to crippling and even terminal illnesses. So, *why do we keep using them?*

In 2006, The Diabetes Research Institute announced that the human pancreatic islet cell (the focal point of diabetes development) differs dramatically from that of rodents. One researcher was quoted as saying:

We can no longer rely on studies on mice and rats. It is now imperative that we focus on human islets. At the end of the day, it is the only way to understand how they function.[10]

Unfortunately, this institution tested on mice and rats for over thirty years before making this discovery. That's thirty years' worth of lives wasted—countless lives daily, times 365, times thirty... So much pain, suffering, and ultimately, death—and no advancement in understanding diabetes made therefrom whatsoever. Those animals are gone now, and we cannot bring them back, but we *can* prevent others from experiencing the same fate.

- ***Stressed nonhuman animals yield poor data.***
  Dr. Akhtar states:

  Animals in laboratories are involuntarily placed in artificial environments—usually in windowless rooms. Routinely, these animals are caught from their cages, placed in restraining chairs, have blood taken from them, and subjected to experiments that cause significant pain. Dogs, cats, monkeys, rats, mice and other animals are often denied food, water and even pain medications. They are burned, irradiated, crushed, shocked, poisoned and infected. It's important to understand how animals live in modern laboratories because what we do to them—how we house them, how we handle them, how we experiment on them—all can cause misleading research results that eventually harm us... there is a phenomenon in laboratories known as "contagious anxiety." Blood pressure and heart rates shoot up in rats watching other rats being decapitated. Cortisone levels rise in monkeys watching other monkeys being restrained for blood collection. Just the routine laboratory procedures, such as catching an animal and removing him from his cage, in addition to the experiments themselves, cause significant and prolonged elevations in animals' stress markers, which can affect research results.[11]

The Moral Imperative here should immediately horrify you upon reading these words. These animals are being *tortured*. They are not simply being observed; they are living lives of pure misery, and often the effects of testing end those lives. For those of you who may not be sympathetic to the plight of these animals, these words should nonetheless drive the point home that any study based on the reactions of non-humans in these conditions simply cannot tell us anything of value with respect to how humans, in decidedly different conditions, would react to the same stimuli, or the same combination of chemicals.

The *New Scientist* article "Too Stressed to Work" reveals how stressed rats develop lasting inflammatory conditions—though not similar to those developed in humans—which cause intestinal leaks.[12] On a moral level, this should upset you; you should not want to contribute to the leaking of another living being's intestines. On a selfish level, this should also upset you; you should not want your medications to be developed based on how a rat with leaky intestines reacted to it. After all, you're not a rat with leaky intestines, are you?

PETA's website offers a detailed list of alternatives to animal testing, which includes but is not limited to the *use of available human tissue that would otherwise go to waste*.[13] Not only is this a more compassionate solution, but it also yields more accurate results. What could be better to help us understand the effects of products, illnesses, or medications on humans than testing them on cells that are decidedly human?

Human tissue can also be synthetically developed. Pioneering contract research laboratory CeeTox uses human cell-based *in vitro* (test tube) toxicity screening to test drugs, chemicals, cosmetics, and consumer products. These humane tests replace cruel tests that involve pumping substances into animals' stomachs and lungs and dripping chemicals into animals' eyes or onto their raw, shaved skin.

Researchers with the National Cancer Institute, the US military, private companies, and universities across the country have shown that MatTek's in vitro 3-D human skin tissue equivalent is an excellent substitute for animals when it comes to conducting burn research and cosmetics testing, as well as with respect to conducting research on radiation exposure and chemical weapons attacks.

Harvard is just one of many top-tier universities in the US that has eschewed the practice of animal testing. The scientists and engineers at Harvard's Wyss Institute have since created **organs-on-a-chip.** These tiny devices contain human cells in a three-dimensional system that mimics human organs. The chips can be used—instead of animals—in disease research, drug testing, and toxicity testing. This is one of the preferred methods employed at Merck pharmaceuticals, by scientists such as Dr. Nicholson.[14]

Human skin equivalent tests such as EpiDerm and EpiSkin have been validated and accepted in Canada, the European Union, and other countries as total replacements for animal-based skin corrosion studies. Government regulators in Canada accept the use of a "skin patch test" in human volunteers as a valid replacement for animal-based skin irritation studies (similar to allergy testing, a "skin patch test" is when a small part of skin is exposed to a small dose of the substance in question). The 3T3 Neutral Red Uptake (NRU) Phototoxicity Test was developed and validated in Europe, and has since been accepted at the international level as a replacement for animal-based phototoxicity studies.[15]

Cruelty isn't Fun

When speaking about veganism to those who are less engaged in the broader movement but have made or are considering making a personal commitment to vegan living, the focus tends to be dietary, but the food industry is only one of many industries that engage in animal exploitation. Fur, leather, wool, and a host of other garments are not nonhuman-friendly. By far the most widely accepted and least discussed form of nonhuman animal abuse in America, in my experience, is the entertainment industry.

You know who couldn't care less about whether you eat meat or not? Circus animals. Rodeo animals. Animals who are raced, such as horses and dogs. Those who are trained to fight one another, such as dogs and chickens. Animals at zoos and amusement parks. These guys don't care what you're eating, and they have just as strong a desire to be liberated as those who end up on your dinner plate.

Events such as circuses containing animal acts and rodeos have been celebrated and highly attended in this country for... well, forever. To the best of my knowledge, neither the use of animals in circuses nor the existence of rodeos has ever been illegal in the United States. While agricultural legislation is an increasingly hot-button issue, and more Americans go vegetarian or vegan every day, the matter of whether or not it is ethical to use animals for sport remains decidedly off the table. There have so far only been minor, single-issue allusions to the problem, such as the ban on elephants in circuses (but not tigers or baboons or bears...), and New York City Mayor Bill de Blasio's commitment to ending the use of horse-drawn carriages in Manhattan.

Consider the message circuses and rodeos send to children. It breaks my heart to see countless young children being led into circus tents and rodeo arenas, having no idea that what they are about to witness is the result of captivity and enslavement. I can't imagine that any parent actually tells his or her child, "These animals were stolen from their natural habitats and removed from their families so that they could be taught these tricks, and people like us can buy tickets to see them perform, so that the people who stole them will make money." What I overhear parents telling their children at these events, over and over again, is:

- The animals are having FUN! They LIKE performing!

- The animals aren't being hurt. Their trainers love them and are kind to them.

Since most small children cannot think critically enough yet to ask, parents don't even bother to explain where the animals came from—that they were stolen, ripped from their prides, their herds, their parents and children. Their silence leaves the impression that the animals joined the circus willingly—that they *chose* show business, just as human actors and actresses do.

No parent enjoys lying to his or her children, but any parent will tell you that there are some occasions on which this becomes necessary. Is it really necessary to lie to children about circus animals? What purpose does that serve? It simply allows the child to enjoy the show—and, by extension, the parent as well. Would it really be so awful if a child turned to his or her parent and said, "I don't like this. These animals don't belong here. I want to go home"?

So parents will have spent some money they will never see again; that's all there is to be lost here. Again, as any parent will tell you (at least, as many parents have told *me*, being that I am not one myself), throwing money away is pretty much par for the course when raising kids. They whine and plead with you for months to buy them that-super-expensive-thing for their birthday, you do, they love it for a week, and then it lives in the closet or under the bed for all eternity.

Ever see the movie *Chicken Run?* It's a great claymation film released in 2000 about chickens escaping a farm. The 2008 film *Bolt*, while illustrating humans eating chicken and burgers and other forms of meat throughout, focuses on the plight of a small canine actor who doesn't know he's an actor, and learns from friends he meets along his journey (particularly a cat named Mittens) how to just *be a dog*. In both films, humans are seen maliciously misleading animals and depriving them of their natural lives, attempting to convince them instead that a human industry (be it agriculture or entertainment) is the one and only place for them; and in both films, the moral of the story is that *the humans are wrong.*

Movies like *Chicken Run* and *Bolt* encourage young children to have respect and compassion for animals; later, these same children are taught that in the "Real World," people eat animals all the time, and it's no big deal and nothing about which to get upset.

We all love watching heartwarming family films in which people motivated by greed or hatred lose and those who stay true to themselves and demonstrate kindness win. We actively seek these movies for our children; then, at some indeterminable point, varying from family to family, we slowly start to un-teach them. We train them to turn their empathy switches off and attempt to normalize for them the imprisonment, murder, and consumption of creatures we once inspired them to regard as friends.

Once upon a Forest (1993) is by far one of my favorite children's movies of all time. My mother rented it for me from the local public library when I was about six. It tells the story of the Furlings, a gaggle of woodland critters—a hedgehog, a raccoon, a mouse, and so forth—and their wise teacher, Cornelius the Badger. Humans—known to the critters as Shoemans due to their limited perspective from the ground of humans as large, rubber boots—are responsible for the release of poisoned gas into the forest. A driver throws a glass bottle out of his window, which breaks, causing the tires of his gas-filled truck to pop and ultimately overturning the truck. Michelle, Cornelius's granddaughter, inhales some of the leaking gas and becomes gravely ill. It falls to the Furlings to retrieve medicinal plants for her in a far-off region of the forest.

Children naturally empathize with Michelle and the Furlings when watching this movie, and adults allow them to feel that way; we even encourage it. We herald this movie as a lesson not to throw bottles out of windows—i.e., not to engage in land pollution. We sit alongside our children and actively pity Bolt for the trick Hollywood has played on him. We root for the liberation of the "claymated" chickens in Chicken Run.

Then we take them to the circus, or to SeaWorld, and afterwards, to KFC or Burger King for dinner...

Countries such as Bolivia, Cyprus, Bosnia, and Greece outlawed the use of all nonhuman animals in circuses prior to 2014; the US has yet to do so.[16]

What are we waiting for?

"What do you do with a horse?"

At one of our many circus demonstrations over the summer of 2013, someone approached Phoenix Animal Liberation Squad as we were wrapping things up and announced, somewhat timidly, that he raised horses. "How is that wrong?" he asked us. "I mean, what do you *do* with a horse?"

Unlike many others who approach us at demonstrations, this man was not trying to antagonize us; he seemed to genuinely want to know. He didn't *want* to be an animal abuser, but he currently had horses in his charge. What might we expect him to do with them? Open the barnyard door and let them run away? Take them to some other place where wild horses abound and set them free, *Free Willy*-style?

This is by far one of the most difficult questions I face, and though I have faced it many times in various forms, I still stumble a bit in trying to answer it. Like many of the world's problems, the fact that you can see the problem doesn't mean that the solution is equally clear. So, I like to start with what is *not* the solution. Opening the barn door and letting them run away is not the solution. Where would the horses go? They would run into the street and be hit by oncoming traffic. They would get lost in some region with minimal food and starve. They would be attacked by some other wild animal, shot by a human who felt threatened, or meet any of a number of other catastrophic ends.

What may surprise some of you is that I am equally certain that relocation to The Wild is not the solution. Why? These horses have been domesticated. They have been taught that food is brought to them—not that they need to find grazing lands, much less to *compete* for said lands. They've been taught that they will be groomed regularly, and so may not remember how a horse keeps clean in nature. Perhaps they're not the best swimmers.

They also smell, look, and may even sound different from wild horses. They would be met with rejection. They would be frowned upon as inferior. No wild mare would choose a domesticated stallion over a wild one.

Finally, it is not as if all horses are one family, all whales another; a domesticated horse is no more part of the family into which he or she may be imported than you are part of a family with everyone else in the room you currently occupy. That may be the case for you presently, but, if it is, it is purely coincidence. Occupying the same room does not a human family make. Similarly, occupying the same pasture does not a horse family make. Setting them free, rather than resulting in the sense of community and belonging we like to imagine for them, can often sentence a domesticated animal to a life of isolation and even victimization.

Now that we know what is *not* the solution, what is? The best I can offer is to treat these animals like the victims they are—victims of captivity and exploitation. What do we do with victims? We find them *sanctuary*. We provide them with *refuge*. There are numerous animal sanctuaries in the US, only some of which are listed in Chapter Ten of this book. We can, and should, also *stop breeding them*, and allow them to reproduce naturally and at will—just like we humans do. *That's* what you do with a horse.

Sure, it doesn't solve the family problem, but, honestly, I don't think anything will at this point. How do you track down a nonhuman animal's family? Unfortunately, we have permanently separated these animals from their families already, and there's nothing to be done about that; the best we can do is to *stop removing them*. For those who have already been removed, and whose natural defenses have already been weakened by years of domestication, the best solution I can offer is placement at an animal sanctuary, where animals can still be cared for in the way that we've compelled them to *need* to be, while living the lifestyle for which they are naturally best suited.

Getting back to our troubled modern horseman, how does this solution differ from his own? A lot depends on his personal situation—his finances, living arrangements, and so forth; in the absence of this knowledge, I can only presume that an animal sanctuary that has been designed for precisely this purpose can provide a more pleasurable existence for his horses than he ever could. Does he have the acres of land these other places have? Is he really letting his horses live however they want to, or is he using them for labor or recreation? I don't know the answers to these questions, but I do know that the average farm sanctuary is much larger and more liberating to farmed animals such as horses than any stable that can be afforded by the average American private horse owner.

That last bit is also of great significance: I referred to the American *horse owner* just now. At a sanctuary, no one really "owns" the animals; it is understood that animals are not here to be owned, but to exist *alongside* us. They are masters of their own destinies; the staff simply provides the amenities on which the animals have grown dependent *thanks to us*. Our fault, our responsibility.

A far cry from life in The Wild, I know. An imperfect solution, but nobody's perfect.

Oakland and the Bullhook Ban

On Tuesday, December 9th, 2014, Oakland City Council held a meeting at which, among many other issues, it would decide whether or not to enact a citywide ban against the use of bull-hooks in circuses to train elephants. Bullhooks—long poles with a sharp, hooked end—are used not only to inflict pain upon elephants, but also to instill fear. Circus-raised elephants are taught as babies that the bullhook means pain. Never forgetting this early trauma, elephants are controlled during training sessions via use of the bullhook and on stage via fear of it. Handlers often keep bullhooks up their sleeves during performances, hidden from the public but in view of the elephant—a constant reminder of the consequences of disobedience.

The start of the meeting was something of an Oakland Government Oscar Night. This meeting turned out to be both former Mayor Jean Quan's and Council President Patricia Kernighan's last, while retiring Director of Emergency Services and Homeland Security at Oakland Fire Department Renee Domingo was honored for her twenty-five years of service to the city. Neighborhood volunteer leaders of District 2, including Oakland Chinatown Chamber of Commerce Foundation President and unofficial "Mayor of Chinatown" Carl Chan, were also honored.

Finally, it was time to address the issues. The bullhook ban had been billed as the first non-consent calendar item of the meeting. The items were quickly reordered, however, after it was determined that an overwhelming 110 US citizens had signed up to speak their piece about the ban.

The discussion was delayed until roughly 10 p.m. Right from the start, it was evident that this was not to be a traditional discussion. Typically, citizens are given one minute to speak each. The discussion of bullhooks instead opened with a ten-minute presentation by those in favor of the ban—a motion that had been approved previously by Councilman Noel Gallo, one of the two who brought the issue to the fore in the first place (the other being Councilman Dan Kalb), but of which no one thought to request the approval of President Kernighan.

In her momentary absence from the chamber, a video began, showing Ringling Brothers employees using bullhooks to abuse elephants in an effort to "train" them in 2009.

Needless to say, Madame President was not pleased. In the interest of fairness, she apologized to the opposition and allowed it a ten-minute presentation, during which various Ringling Brothers employees insisted that the "guide" (bullhook) was just that—a harmless instrument used to guide the elephant's movements, and not an instrument of abuse. They completely ignored the video we had all just watched and stuck to their carefully rehearsed talking points.

Predictably, several concerned citizens spoke about the threat this ban posed to their jobs—seemingly unaware that it was neither City Council nor the animal activists of Oakland but rather Feld Entertainment, Ringling Brothers' parent company, who threatened their jobs (and, consequently, their access to healthcare). While some of these people beseeched activists to "Have compassion for humans, too," they would have been better off pleading with Feld for compassion—or raging against Feld for toying with their livelihoods for the sake of winning a political debate. Unfortunately, many low-income-earning individuals shy away from criticizing their employers under any circumstances, and it may have appeared safer to them to criticize activists than to demand that Feld stop using them as pawns in its chess match against city government.

Another deplorable chess move on Feld's part was to threaten not only to stop bringing the circus to town (which would be a cause for celebration among local liberationists), but also other shows under its corporate umbrella, such as Disney on Ice—shows that have nothing at all to do with nonhuman animals.

Councilwoman Rebecca Kaplan—who had charmingly announced at the start of the meeting that she was wearing a sports cap in celebration of the Warriors' recent victory over the Lakers—proposed a compromise: following Los Angeles's lead, she proposed that the ban be passed but that it not go into effect until September 2017, giving those concerned about job security ample time to be retrained in elephant training methods that did not involve bullhooks (or, possibly, to find other employment). This would also give the council time to further discuss matters with the county. The compromise swiftly replaced the original motion to institute a ban effective immediately.

Elephant trainers on both sides of the debate spoke, some insisting on calling the bullhook a "guide" and claiming that they used it regularly and humanely, while others revealed that they had been training elephants for over a decade *without* the use of bullhooks.

After nearly two hours of debate, Councilwoman Kaplan's amendment to the ban was passed. Aside from this single-issue victory, however hard-won, I have to say that by far the most inspiring part of the meeting was hearing Mayor Quan's words prior to casting her vote in favor of the ban:

> Honestly, I am certain that the day will soon come when we will see a ban on elephants being used in circuses altogether, but we made some moves tonight, and with this ban we will keep moving forward.

Here we arrive at the heart of the matter—total animal liberation. While banning circuses was not the issue of the evening, it was evident that many of the Oakland residents present would support such a ban, but there needs to be a starting point, a nexus. Oakland has now joined Los Angeles and other cities in adopting a bullhook ban; it is my sincere hope that soon, Oakland will join Mexico City, Bolivia, Peru, Greece, and the many others who have banned the use of wild animals in circuses altogether.

Mayor Quan's words give me restored faith in the value of single-issue campaigns in the movement. In the past, I have struggled to find peace with these campaigns, such as Mayor de Blasio's push to ban the practice of horse-drawn carriages in Central Park. While I am happy for the horses who will be retired (hopefully, to an animal sanctuary), I worry constantly that issues such as these distract the public from the broader issues—such as the fact that animal abuse is being profited from all over Columbus Circle, including the Time Warner building: home of humanewashing giant Whole Foods.

However, just as the *Cambridge Declaration on Consciousness* laid important groundwork for increasing humanity's deference for the cognitive abilities and capacities of nonhumans, so too might issues such as horse-drawn carriages and the use of bullhooks pave the way for humanity's reexamination of how we coexist with—as it stands, habitually oppress—them.

The only trouble is, the animals cannot wait. It's up to us humans to engage in direct action *now* in order to speed up the process, rather than rest on our laurels at the slightest indication of victory and say, "There, at least we've done *something.*" This is not to say that our actions should not be planned, the Bigger Picture always considered, but planning and acting are not mutually exclusive. We can act out publically to draw attention to the issue while being strategic about achieving our end goal: animal liberation.

It is also worth mentioning that the terms "single issue" and "welfarist" are not interchangeable. I do oppose welfarist campaigns, such as those that aim to improve the lives of animals in captivity by granting them bigger cages rather than campaigning against the very fact that they are caged. Such campaigns, in my opinion, fail to adequately challenge the speciesist mindset and reinforce the false notion that there is a "right way" to exploit someone. By contrast, campaigns such as the ban on elephants in circuses—which resulted directly from the bullhook ban—employ preexisting empathy for a particular species in order to encourage empathy for other species experiencing similar forms of oppression. They utilize how we as a society regard *one* species of nonhuman animal to challenge how we regard *all* nonhumans.

Mayor Quan's assertion, coupled with the relative swiftness with which the Oakland Bullhook Ban was followed by the end of "circus elephants" in America, give me hope that these initiatives, rather than helping the powers that be remain stagnant while quelling criticism, are in fact compelling the powers that be to sit up and take notice.

There will, of course, be campaigns for tigers and baboons and all other nonhumans exploited by circuses; I look forward to participating in them.

Effective 2018, Ringling Brothers Says Goodbye to Elephants

On Thursday, March 5, 2015, Feld Entertainment announced that it will be phasing out the use of elephants in its circuses and will end the practice altogether by 2018. The thirteen elephants currently used by the company will be sent to the Center for Elephant Conservation in Polk City, Florida.[17]

Kenneth Feld, President of Feld Entertainment, told the *New York Times* that "The biggest issue is, there has been a lot of legislation in different cities and different municipalities...There's been, on the part of our consumers, a mood shift where they may not want to see elephants transported from city to city."[18]

In other words, Feld has decided to remove elephants from its circus acts as a direct result of protests from individuals across the country—protests that have resulted in long, expensive litigations. Ultimately, keeping elephants in its act is simply not lucrative enough for Feld to commensurate with the expense of arguing for the "right" to use these animals in more progressive cities and counties.

One could argue, rightly, that this is a victory for activists; we asked for something—the end of the use of elephants in circuses—and, at long last, we got it...Sort of. We've been promised, at least, that it will happen in 2018. We know already that this is not a victory for the tigers; is it, as it may appear at first glance, a victory for the elephants?

Let's take a look at this Center for Elephant Conservation in Polk City, Florida, and ask ourselves whether any elephant can be expected to be happy living there.

A Red Flag is raised within my first five minutes on their website. In the "About Us" section of the Center's website, it declares itself "…dedicated to the conservation, breeding, and understanding of these amazing animals."[19] Ahem, *breeding?* Alarmed, I sought clarification. Naively, I hoped perhaps the term *breeding* was being misused here, to indicate that the animals did occasionally mate with one another voluntarily and that the babies were protected alongside the parents; in other words, that this was a haven not just for individual elephants, but also for *elephant families.* I didn't want to jump to conclusions, so I did a bit of digging.

I soon encountered a statement by Samuel Dewitt Haddock Jr., who was hired in August 1997 to work as an elephant handler at "Ringling's breeding farm, called the Center for Elephant Conservation (CEC) in Polk City, Florida."[20] While working there, one of his primary duties was to train baby elephants. In his statement, Haddock reported that baby elephants were "typically pulled from their mothers around 18-24 months of age. Once they're pulled from their mothers, they've tasted their last bit of freedom and the relationship with their mother ends."

His report goes on to expose other horrific practices at the Center, including tying up babies for days on end, taking them for only two brief walks per day while they spend an average of twenty-three hours per day restrained; keeping bullhooks in front of their trunks during walks and applying pressure if the babies pick up the pace; tying ropes to babies' legs, necks, and trunks, while up to four humans pull in various directions, forcing babies into particular poses; and the constant playing of super-loud rock music to acclimatize babies to the noise they will encounter under the big top.

So, here's the question: Now that Ringling Brothers has decided to stop using elephants in its circuses, is this still how elephants will be treated at the Center? Given that they no longer "need" to be trained for performance in circuses, can we safely assume that they will be allowed to stay with their mothers and roam freely, without the use of ropes and bullhooks by humans to control their every movement? Will they still even "need to" be bred?

Presumably, breeding occurred so as to maintain an adequate supply (Ugh, I loathe speaking about sentient beings as "supplies..." I may need to lie down after this.) of elephants for the many performances Feld hosts annually. Since they will no longer be used for this purpose, what further excuse can there be for breeding them?

It's too early, in my opinion, to say with certainty that this is a victory for the elephants currently "owned" by Ringling Brothers. We won't know until they are at the CEC, and we can see the life with which they are provided. In a more general sense, this is still a victory for the Animal Liberation Movement as a whole, as it is proof positive, alongside the *Blackfish* backlash and ensuing anti-SeaWorld demonstrations that caused the company's stock to plummet 33% in August 2014[21], that nonviolent direct action *works*. Whether it's a crowd of people making noise and holding signs on the freeway, or a thought-provoking documentary including footage of real animals, exposing the public to corporate lies *does* have a measurable impact.

It's like Jesse Pinkman warned Walt on *Breaking Bad*, after abandoning his recent arson attempt: "Burning your house down is nothing...Next time, I'm gonna get you where you *really* live." We have to hit 'em where it hurts—their wallet.

Is the removal of elephants from circuses by 2018 precisely the effect for which we'd hoped? No. Is it preferable to the status quo, from the victims' perspective? Definitely—provided this CEC place adopts the role of *sanctuary* and abandons its current role as a *training and breeding facility*. Does banning elephants from the circus now increase the likelihood that tigers will be banned from it later? Probably—but *only if we keep fighting for them*. If we rest on our laurels now, Feld might abuse tigers and other sentient beings for the next hundred years.

We can pat ourselves on the back for a moment, hold up our glasses, and toast this exciting new development; then, it's time to roll up our sleeves and get back to work.

Understanding Exploitation as a Cultural Staple—and Rejecting It Anyway

Rodeo demonstrations are the toughest, in my opinion, with respect to performing nonviolent direct action. While people look upon circuses as a frivolous pastime, rodeo fans are *hardcore*. There are both patriotic and sexist perceptions of the rodeo; it is affiliated with cowboys, the Old West—with being a *MAY*-un, gosh darnit!

PALS demonstrated against a rodeo in 2013, a demonstration I did not personally attend; when I heard about how it went, I felt relieved to have missed it. I confess, I may have been tempted to behave violently myself had I attended, as I was informed that a bunch of rowdy rodeo spectators dumped buckets of cold water on my dear friend and fellow activist, Eddie James. (The rodeo demonstration I did attend that year, at the Arizona State Fair, was a quiet affair by comparison, likely owing to the fact that we were forced to demonstrate outside of the event—not directly on-site.)

Rodeos provide us with a solid example of how our culture has normalized animal abuse (aside from, you know, everyone you know who is eating someone's body *right now*). Whereas abuse is denied or politely ignored at the circus, people actually *cheer for* abuse at a rodeo. They whoop and holler like it's the coolest thing they've ever seen in their lives. Whereas most Americans probably wouldn't be too put out if the use of nonhuman animals in circuses were one day outlawed nationwide, I envision a violent uproar would ensue amongst rugged *MAY*-uns and their female counterparts should anyone try to ban rodeos in America.

Still, it has to be done, and there's an important lesson to be learned in doing so. The fact that something has become a cultural staple—that it's been going on for decades, hundreds or even thousands of years, engaged in by our forefathers or even our ancestors—doesn't mean it is the best option available to us. I'm reminded of the scores of individuals I've encountered at demonstrations and on the Internet who talk about how cavemen ate meat. Not only do these individuals obviously not know that humans are herbivores by design, but they're also suggesting that the way cavemen lived should serve as an *example* to us!

When talking about politics, philosophy, technology, or pretty much any other aspect of our culture, no one ever says, "We should keep doing it this way, because that's how cavemen did it," or "We should stop this and start that instead, because that's how cavemen did it." The pursuits of both technology and academia are perhaps the most obvious examples of how our increasingly intelligent and progressive society *eschews* the ways of the caveman in favor of that which is most beneficial to itself, to surrounding communities, and to our planet. Why then, do people still feel justified in eating meat on the sole basis that a bagillion years ago, in the face of starvation and with few or no alternatives available to them, individuals who are biologically *just barely* related to us humans resorted to this practice?

Rodeos also exemplify the intersection of sexism and speciesism explored in Chapter Two. They promote the stereotype of rugged manliness as being dependent on exploitation and violence. They reinforce the false associations "cruelty—strong—masculine," which imply the aforementioned false associations "compassion—weak—feminine."

Which behavior requires more strength: following the crowd in doing what you instinctively know is wrong, or giving peer pressure The Finger and going your own, compassionate route?

Married to Our Own Convenience

The success of humanewashing in impeding the progress of the Animal Liberation Movement highlights a fundamental flaw in our culture that needs to be rectified: We have become married to our own convenience. It has never been as easy to go vegan as it is right now, yet scores of individuals have gone vegan long before the twenty-first century. As emphasized in the Prologue, the term *vegan* was coined in 1944—and vegans existed long before that. They didn't have the luxury of Daiya or Chao cheeses, of Yves or Tofurkey faux deli meats. They didn't have organs-on-a-chip. There weren't a bagillion doctors and nutritionists out there writing books and publishing studies proving that we humans require neither meat nor dairy to survive.

Today, in countries around the world, vegan convenience foods and products are still lacking, yet people have made, and continue to make, the commitment to animal liberation in these places. Historically, people have made the switch not just before the emergence of fake cheese and meats, but even before the medical community had confirmed beyond a shadow of a doubt that meat and dairy are harmful to humans—thus putting their own health at risk, as far as anyone knew at the time. In the face of mounting pressure to eat meat and dairy for nutritional reasons, they still dared to defy conventional wisdom, and embrace plant-based eating. (Most, though not all, plant-based dieters inevitably become full-fledged vegans by also eschewing animal-abusive garments and forms of entertainment.)

The convenience of the status quo is by far one of the largest barriers to convincing people to accept speciesism. Humanewashing satiates our lust for convenience by assuring us that integrity does not require sacrifice—we can have whatever we want, and, as long as a particular word or phrase is on the package, we're all still wonderful people. Arguments abound as to why it is "impossible" to live truly vegan. We've all heard about the insects we step on and swallow, about the air and land pollution committed by our cars and even the public transportation we hold so dear, about the nonhuman animals we displace by building our homes, and so forth. There is this pervasive notion that because we can't eliminate *all* of our negative impacts on nonhuman animals, we should all just stop trying.

If, when walking down the street, I risk bumping into someone and hurting that person, does that mean I should immediately shoot everyone on sight? Is accidentally stepping on a bug on occasion the moral equivalent of voluntarily consuming corpses daily?

Someone very close to me, who consumes animal byproducts on nearly a daily basis, recently confessed, "You are on the right side of history," in relation to my position against the exploitation of nonhuman animals. In spite of this, he continues to consume animal byproducts. This is a clear indication to me that ending our dominion of nonhumans is not just about telling people what's right, which many already know, but also convincing them to make the necessary sacrifices in order to *live* what is right—to bridge the gap between what we *know* and what we *do.*

I could sit here and tell you of the many products and services that exist to make veganism convenient, but I won't. Why? Because this isn't about our own convenience. It isn't about us at all. It's about them. Yes, I do honestly believe that liberating nonhuman animals will yield positive results for humanity, but even if it didn't, I would still support the movement. Their bodies are simply not ours to use.

Chapter Four

Putting Animal Liberation on the Public Agenda

An ounce of action is worth a ton of theory.

—Ralph Waldo Emerson

Organizations and individuals go about putting animal liberation on the public agenda in a variety of ways. There are far too many valuable institutions working away at this for me to list here, so for the sake of brevity, I've chosen to highlight four: Animal Liberation Victoria, Direct Action Everywhere, the Nonhuman Rights Project, and the Animal Legal Defense Fund.

Animal Liberation Victoria is a direct-action-oriented, abolitionist organization making great strides for the movement. It was Patty Mark, founder of both Animal Liberation Victoria (ALV) and the Open Rescue Movement, who paved the way for Compassionate Action for Animals (CAA), an organization based in Minneapolis, to conduct the first-ever open rescue on US soil in 2000, at a farm owned by Michael Foods (a major Midwest supplier). Roughly fifteen years later, Direct Action Everywhere would follow suit, conducting an open rescue at Petaluma Farms and launching an international Open Rescue Network.

The Nonhuman Rights Project (NhRP) provides us with a good example of what I typically consider a "bad thing"—single-issue campaigning. What NhRP does well that other single-issue groups often do not is challenge the very notion of *what it means to be a person.* The legal definition of "personhood" is being turned on its head by this group's court battles on behalf of chimpanzees. This gives me hope that the day will soon come when chickens, pigs, and other exploited animals can sue their captors; and, perhaps more importantly, humans will identify all nonhuman animals, not just chimps, as having "personhood"—as sentient beings deserving of autonomy over their bodies and lives.

The Animal Legal Defense Fund (ALDF) is another legal force to be reckoned with in the Animal Liberation Movement. This group strives to bring industrial cases to court, yet struggles because not only is animal agriculture exempt from many animal abuse laws, but these companies also have big bucks with which to pay for their defenses (or settle out of court). I think it crucial for those among us who are able to support ALDF to do so, so that it may one day have the resources with which to go after Big Agra.

These are not, by any means, the only paths toward putting liberation on the public agenda. Besides participating in demonstrations and farm investigations (ALV and DxE), and duking it out in court (NhRP and ALDF), dedicated activists push the movement forward regularly by writing articles, songs, and stories; creating visual art installations; circulating petitions; and even just talking to the people in their lives (in person or via social media) about the issues. There is a plethora of ways in which people with various skill sets can contribute to the movement; herein lay just a few.

Animal Liberation Victoria

Animal Liberation Victoria is an organization devoted to challenging the property status of animals—with the goal of ultimately abolishing it, which is why members refer to themselves as *abolitionists*. This organization, which is based in Melbourne, Australia, employs nonviolent direct action to draw attention to animal abuse and exploitation. Founded by Patty Mark in 1978, ALV has been a driving force for the Animal Liberation Movement on an international scale, inspiring younger organizations such as Direct Action Everywhere with its ethics, goals, action models, and pioneering of the Open Rescue Movement.

Animal Liberation Victoria's Statement of Purposes[1]

TO ABOLISH THE PROPERTY STATUS OF ANIMALS

Animal Liberation Victoria endorses an animal rights position that maintains that all sentient beings, regardless of species, have the right to be treated as independent entities, and not as the property of others.

TO ABOLISH, AND NOT MERELY REGULATE, INSTITUTIONLISED ANIMAL EXPLOITATION

Animal Liberation Victoria supports only those campaigns and positions that explicitly promote the abolitionist agenda, placing primary emphasis on animal agriculture. We recognize we will not abolish animal exploitation and the property status of animals overnight, but will encourage at all times the adoption of a vegan way of life as the most appropriate course to achieve these aims.

TO ABOLISH HUMAN'S SPECIESIST ATTITUDES AND PRACTICES

Just as we reject racism, sexism, ageism and homophobia, we reject speciesism. The species of sentient beings is no more a reason to deny any individual the basic right not to be the property of others, than is race, sex, age or sexual orientation a reason to deny membership in the moral community to other humans.

TO ENCOURAGE AND NURTURE ANIMAL RIGHTS EDUCATION

Animal Liberation Victoria commits itself to public education concerning the rights of animals and the importance of defending any other animal whose language communication is different to our own, and who are thus unable to 'speak' for themselves.

TO ENDORSE THE PRINCIPLE OF NON-VIOLENCE

All campaigns and positions of Animal Liberation Victoria use non-violence as their guiding principle and rule of operation. Our work fosters giving aid and rescue to any animal who is suffering in pain and left unattended.

Campaigns and Actions

Animal Liberation Victoria was initially founded specifically to benefit battery hens.[2] *Battery hens* are hens who are kept in wire cages stacked on top of each other, where they are not afforded room to stand up or flap their wings; and can be used for egg production or simply housed this way until their date of slaughter, at which point their bodies become "chicken."

While the lack of space afforded to battery hens has been widely discussed already, some of the lesser-known disturbing facts revealed on ALV's campaign website are that the parents of egg-laying hens are kept in breeding sheds, forced to mate constantly on an excrement-covered floor while inhaling ammonia-filled air; and that egg-laying hens are slaughtered not when egg-laying ceases (as I previously thought and many fellow activists believe), but *as soon as egg-laying productivity decreases.* In other words, an egg-laying hen can be killed for producing not zero eggs, but simply for producing fewer eggs today than she did yesterday.

(It should be noted here also that being bred and manipulated to produce large quantities of eggs often results in swollen, infected vents—hen vaginas—which are not only painful for the hen, but ultimately yield fewer eggs. So we humans create the "problem" of decreased egg production and then kill the offending bird—as if she had any choice in the matter. As though she'd been a naughty employee, when in fact she has been a tormented slave her entire life.)

On April 4, 2012, ALV's Open Rescue team rescued 14 of 15,000–20,000 hens held in battery cages at Somerville Egg Farm in Moorooduc, Australia. ALV had reported the egg farm to police over a decade prior, but nothing had been done, so upon being contacted by a concerned citizen in 2012, ALV decided to take matters into its own hands.[3]

The following morning, at 4:30 a.m., four ALV activists— Patty Mark, Jo Osborne, Lisa Manning, and Felicity Andersen— chained themselves with the remaining caged hens. In a video of the action, two of the activists are seen holding victims. One activist gently lifts a victim's wing to expose a canvas of missing feathers and blotchy skin. The video then informs viewers: "Today's hens lay 320 eggs per year, not the 20 that nature intended, causing calcium depletion and severe feather loss."[4]

The tubular "chains" the women wore to connect with the hens and with each other bore the word "FREEDOM" in bold black letters. Some also held signs in their free hands, one of which read: "Where's the Justice?"

Police arrived on the scene and proceeded to drag the activists onto the floor, blocking the public road leading to the "crime scene" from media and supporters alike—shielding the company responsible from being held accountable by either group. After what must have been a grueling four-hour wait, the activists were thankfully released on bail. The fourteen rescued victims were taken to a vet, where they were treated for worms.

Images of these victims are painful to see. In many cases, their entire backsides were devoid of feathers, while their featherless wings had been reduced to long, sharp sticks. A close-up of one victim's vent showed signs of severe infection—extreme redness and swelling.

Outrageously, Luigi Napolitano, owner of Somerville Egg Farm, publically accused the activists of having "upset the hens."

ALV now also speaks out on behalf of *broiler hens*—hens raised for their flesh rather than their eggs. In fact, it was their 14-month investigation of Parkhurst Farms and rescue of over 200 hens therefrom that resulted in a lawsuit by a major Australian "chicken purveyor" in 2010 (more on that later). ALV is a longtime participant in a global campaign against famous chicken chain KFC, returning weekly to Melbourne's busiest KFC location to demonstrate against the company's sale of corpses. The group has conducted numerous investigations at KFC suppliers, and uncovered birds starving and dying of dehydration, birds with crippled limbs, and other such atrocities.

Other ALV campaigns include anti-whaling initiatives, anti-fur initiatives, advocating for the shut-down of puppy breeding factories, educating the public about the horrors of animal experimentation, and fighting for a ban on live export—the transportation of live animals across national borders.

While it is important for the public to see firsthand what happens behind closed doors, in an effort to instill empathy for creatures we are used to regarding as products, it is important to note that independent of the horrific conditions revealed by Animal Liberation Victoria, Compassionate Action for Animals, Direct Action Everywhere, and other organizations engaging in open rescue, ***all animals raised for food of any kind die premature deaths***. They are either slaughtered for their flesh or slaughtered because they no longer produce by-products at a financially lucrative rate. *None* of these animals—even those who some imagine live on picturesque hillsides—are allowed to live out their lives according to Nature's design. *Everyone* in the system is ultimately killed; images exposing the suffering that these victims endure while still alive merely highlight the storm before the storm.

Where There's Life, There's Hope

In an interview by Mark Hawthorne of the animal rights blog *Striking at the Roots*, Patty Mark shared the story of a chicken named Apricot, whom she and others had rescued from a KFC broiler shed. Sadly, Apricot suffered from a condition quite common among birds raised for food—one Patty refers to as "splayed legs," in which both legs are dysfunctional and just stick out in front of the bird while he or she helplessly sits atop them.

Patty delayed and delayed a visit to the vet after rescuing Apricot, as past experience had taught her that vets typically put down these otherwise reasonably healthy birds. After just under two weeks of hand-feeding, hand-watering and grooming the helpless, audibly grateful Apricot, Patty woke up to a surprise:

> On about day 12 after the rescue when I got up one morning she wasn't sitting in her basket. I freaked and thought, 'Where's Apricot?' I looked about and noticed her amongst the others, and she was standing! Only for a few seconds, but she stood up and held her weight. I got teary eyed. Anyway, as the days have passed, she is walking about with a hobble, but walking around, and right now she's outside enjoying a mild autumn day with the others in the sunshine.[5]

Where there's life, there's hope. The painful, miserable existence of caged or crowded animals who are continuously exploited and inevitably killed can hardly be called a "life." All animals—be they human or nonhuman—will fight to live when they feel there is something worth fighting for, and that's what rescuers such as the brave souls at ALV give to the victims they save. They provide them with a life worth living, a life in which they feel safe and happy—so much so that a condition from which they may have died on a flesh farm or in an egg shed can begin to heal after just two short weeks of experiencing love and joy.

Of course, the credit can't all go to any human, however well-meaning that person is. The resilience of the animal spirit deserves the bulk of the credit. The fact that creatures such as Apricot are able to bounce back from the horrors inflicted upon them, to trust humans again and to fight to regain their strength after years of confinement and weakness, is nothing short of a miracle.

Exposing the RSPCA: Corruption and Fraud

Since its inception in 1978, Animal Liberation Victoria has been conducting rescues at battery cage farms all over Australia and the world, videotaping and photographing the conditions and victims they find at each. These places of violence include barn sheds that had been approved by Australia's Royal Society for the Prevention of Cruelty to Animals (RSPCA). Animal Liberation Victoria continuously challenges the RSPCA to live up to its name by exposing, rather than cooperating with, major players on Australia's meat, dairy, and egg scenes.

Patty Mark and ALV activist Erik Gorton revealed several offensive and troubling truths about the RSPCA in an article entitled, "What's Wrong with the RSPCA?" Such truths included:

- The RSPCA accepts sponsorship from Australia's largest battery egg producer, Pace Farms.

- The RSPCA accepts money from the sale of pig corpses by Otway Pork.

- The RSPCA consistently serves meat at public events and social gatherings.[6]

How any organization can claim to exist for the sake of defending animals while both serving and profiting from animal corpses with a straight face is beyond me. The hypocrisy is astounding; thankfully, ALV and others are fighting back.

As of 2013, the group had conducted a total of sixteen investigations at RSPCA-approved facilities, rescuing eighteen pigs from therein. The rescued pigs suffered from pneumonia, testicular hernias, broken legs, cerebral palsy, open necrotic wounds, septic arthritis, and scoliosis. The conditions exposed by ALV's many videos include filth, overcrowding, illness, decomposing corpses, and even acts of cannibalism amongst the pigs—acts rarely, if ever, witnessed in nature.[7]

In August 2013, James LaVeck and Jenny Stein, cofounders of Tribe of Heart (a film company that produced such animal-centric hits as *Peaceable Kingdom: The Journey Home* and *The Witness*), issued an open letter to animal advocates about ALV's fight against the RSPCA. LaVeck and Hart confirm that the RSPCA is being paid by animal exploiters to accredit farms and sheds as "humane," and share one of the many videos in which ALV exposes what really happens behind RSPCA-approved doors. The letter calls on readers to sign a petition demanding that the RSPCA halt all cooperation with animal abusers, as well as to share ALV's video widely.[8]

Here we see just one of many examples of how ALV excels at putting animal liberation on the public agenda. By leading by example, challenging institutions that many of us would take for granted as being "animal-friendly," ALV has inspired others to fight for justice—not just against the RSPCA in Australia, but against animal abuse everywhere.

In an interview with Claudette Vaughan of Abolitionist-Online, Patty Mark offered the following poignant commentary on the importance of open rescue:

> When there is a "disaster" like a flood, hurricane
> or earthquake, there is a groundswell of support

and assistance to help those in need. What is happening to animals inside factory farms and abattoirs is every single bit a "disaster"—maybe not a natural one, but a human one. It is up to animal activists, those humans who deeply understand how wrong and cruel animal farming is, to activate the rescue chain. Our movement must make nonhuman animal rescue just as valid and expected as human rescue...Besides saving a few of the 55+ billion animals we 6.5 billion humans. kill each year to eat, open rescue is also a tactic to throw open the doors on how low humanity has sunk in its dealings with other beings.[9]

Aside from viral videos, petitions, public demonstrations, and inspiring activists around the world to engage in open rescues, there's a particularly compelling and unique aspect of Animal Liberation Victoria of which all liberationist organizations should take note: the existence of its junior league, Animal Liberation Youth.

Animal Liberation Youth

One of the many ways in which Animal Liberation Victoria distinguishes itself while pushing the movement forward is by empowering young people—not just college-age liberals such as abound in many US-based activist networks, but teens and yes, even *children*. Animal Liberation Youth (ALY) was founded in 2007 with the expressed purpose of empowering activists who have not yet reached adulthood. While I have seen children and teens attend particular actions or activism-centered meetings in the past, I'd yet to encounter any activist organization designed specifically for this demographic prior to discovering Animal Liberation Youth (aside from PETA's PETA2, but whether or not one can concretely label PETA an "activist organization" given that it is neither strictly volunteer-based—people who work for PETA get paid—nor strictly activism-based is debatable).

In 2009, Animal Liberation Youth demonstrated at a KFC on Swanson Street in Melbourne. Young activists wore white bio suits with a black letter on the back of each of their tops. Turned with their backs facing the camera, eight activists read: "KFC KILLS."

One young activist identified himself as Jack, an ALY co-ordinator. Holding a chicken named Blueberry in his arms, he tells viewers of the demonstration in a YouTube video:

> This is Blueberry, a crippled chicken we res-
> cued at a KFC supplier farm. This is the chicken
> you're eating at KFC. This is how old they are
> when they're slaughtered. Please boycott KCF
> and save these animals.[10]

When I saw this, I nearly cried—and I don't cry very easily. When I do, it's typically because I'm upset; it took me many years to understand what it's like to cry from happiness. I've only done it maybe twice, I think. This would have been the third time, but, thankfully, I somehow managed to contain myself. I've never heard a child speak so beautifully or so boldly about animals before. Children are known for asking poignant questions, and I do feel both proud of and impressed by children from non-vegan households who ask their parents directly, "Did this cow used to be alive?" However, it's one thing to ask questions and then struggle to believe whatever answer you've been given, and quite another to not only form your own convictions, but to also stand up publically for them—and for the rights of those who cannot speak for themselves. Even as adults, this is difficult to do; now remember all of the hazing you faced as a child over the slightest thing.

Remember kids making fun of you or each other because someone talked funny, had an ugly [insert facial feature], was too smart, too stupid, too disruptive, or too well behaved? Children are the harshest critics; with them, you're either a goody two shoes or an obnoxious attention-seeker. You're either too fat or too skinny. You're either a nerd or a simpleton, and so on.

If a child can stand before his or her peers, relatives, and strangers with equal confidence, and speak from the heart about a pressing social justice matter... Then there's simply no excuse for us adults not to do so.

The truth is, *I HATE speaking out.* My heart races and my palms sweat every time I do it. I recently made contact with a fellow activist in Cleveland who endures the same sensations; she too suffers from anxiety. I'm not so anxious standing alongside my fellow activists at a demonstration, as I'm lucky enough to live in a place where animal issues are popular and so many activists turn out to the demonstrations I attend, but I get terribly nervous when I'm supposed to actually *say* something. I was also frankly embarrassed just to be standing there when I was in Phoenix at times, as PALS was much smaller than the group I'm in now, which made it easier for people to single us out and criticize us as individuals. I have the utmost respect for people who are bold enough to engage in actions with small numbers, and especially for those who just barge into places and perform speak-outs all by themselves. I highly doubt I will ever do the latter. I need people by my side, from whom to draw strength.

The reason people like me and my new Cleveland friend speak out, in spite of hating the feeling of actually doing so, is because it isn't about us; it's about the animals. Jack must undoubtedly share this conviction, as I'm sure he encountered animosity at school from classmates and perhaps even teachers and parents about his beliefs. I highly doubt he has had the luxury of attending all-vegan schools throughout his lifetime, assuming such schools even exist.

Other campaigns and initiatives by Animal Liberation Youth include promoting veganism at the annual Sustainable

Living Festival in Melbourne, demonstrating against the use of animals in cancer research, and engaging in open rescue.[11]

Is it Working?

YES! Not only has ALV inspired countless activists around the world to take nonviolent direct action and engage in open rescue, but it has also caused such a fuss regarding the Animal Problem that in 2010, Parkhurst Farms sued Patty Mark and her crew, with the help of Australia's largest producer of chicken meat, Baiada Poultry.

Why is this a good thing? Because not only do lawsuits like these serve to incite public dialogue, but they also provide the defendants with an opportunity to explain publically why they engaged in their actions. Lawsuits provide a platform through which people can explain *why* they trespassed, for instance—to save the lives of animals who are suffering and will die without proper care—rather than just defaming these people as "vile trespassers" and outlaws.

Patty Mark and a team of activists visited a Parkhurt-owned farm near Werribee, on which there were eight windowless chicken sheds, each of which sold a horrifying 200,000 hens per year to grocery stores, restaurants, and fast food joints all over Australia. In total, 1.6 million hens would be housed by this one farm per year, then sent to slaughter.[12] The rescue team photographed and videotaped the entire experience, highlighting the horrendous living conditions of these poor animals while reinforcing the fact that they simply did not belong there—their mere presence, never mind the conditions, was itself criminal in nature, as they were being regarded as property rather than sentient beings.

The story was featured on ABC's (Australian Broadcasting Corporation) *Lateline*, exposing the plight of the animals to viewers far and wide. Regrettably, much of the dialogue was centered on matters such as "free-range" and "organic" as they apply to raising animals, rather than the fact that animals are being raised "for food" in the first place; still, the footage spoke for itself. Patty also reinforced the plight of the chickens, independent of any discussion of labels or marketing, by stating early on, "We only hit a quarter of the shed and *fifty-one* dead rotting bodies. They were moldy, they were decomposing ... and there were birds just sitting on them eating them, picking at them."

Perhaps controversially, Patty also brought attention to the risk that consuming such creatures poses to humans:

> We have made complaints to all the legal authorities, we're totally ignored. And it's a real... We are here for the birds, cause... [chokes up] It was so hard to leave that shed tonight but we are also here for the people who are eating those sick crippled little babies.[13]

Some activists would instinctively object to such a statement, as it turns the camera away from the plight of the poor birds to the plight of the humans who eat them, and our compulsion is to constantly focus on the victims. However, I personally think this was a wise choice on Patty's part—to remind the many viewers who unfortunately may not care about nonhumans that these conditions pose a threat to them and their families as well. Later in this chapter, we will talk more about striking a balance between compromising and strategizing—a crucial tightrope that every activist must walk.

Direct Action Everywhere

Shortly after my move to Oakland, in April 2014, I spoke to DxE cofounder and Bay Area organizer Wayne Hsiung about how DxE came into being, what he hopes it will achieve, and how he and cofounder Ronnie Rose grew DxE in just under two years from a small, California-based operation to the international coalition it is today. His responses were richly intelligent, deeply personal, and truly inspiring. Here are a few of them:

SR: What inspired you to start DxE? Why not just join any of the many pre-existing animal liberation organizations out there? What did you hope to bring to the table that others perhaps do not?

WH: There are a million animal groups out there, but what makes us different is primarily that *we are squarely focused on movement-building*. Most animal rights groups attempt to shift particular actors (whether corporate or state) or the public. While we don't neglect those objectives, we also are keenly aware of the importance of building a stronger and more robust movement to effect real change. I was influenced in this by my studies of intervention into human rights causes. It turns out that most attempts to fix problems have little to no effect. The reason, as Nobel Prize winner Douglass North found, is that institutions—particularly "soft" institutions, such as culture and trust—are the ultimate cause of (and solution for) most social ills.

The primary way to change those institutions, in turn, is to create political or moral campaigns. It was shocking to me to read this literature, but the main basis for this thesis is a University of Chicago economist (and another Nobel Prize winner) named Robert Fogel, who showed that human slavery was won via a moral, rather than an economic, cascade. It was the mass of dissenters speaking out against slavery—and not changing economics, or the availability of alternatives—that ultimately drove antebellum chattel slavery to its deathbed.

A couple of other factors were also very important to me. The first is that *I wanted to be a part of an animal rights platform that expertly used modern technology and the latest research.* One example: Behavioral economics and psychology has shown that impersonal approaches to outreach—leaflets, billboards, advertisements—pale in comparison to the effect of one's peers. For instance, top-down anti-smoking campaigns have been working for decades to limited ultimate effect, but if a single friend of yours stops smoking, it causally increases the odds that you will stop smoking by over 20%!

The third and most important factor, however, was that *I saw the Animal Liberation Movement losing its soul to cynicism and corporate manipulation, and wanted to be part of building a better and stronger network for animals.* We have enough obstacles as is, and don't need to create more obstacles with a self-defeating attitude, yet even the largest and most popular animal liberation and advocacy groups practically *encourage* people to be evasive and depressed. This is contrary to the best evidence on effective advocacy, and I wanted to be part of spreading a stronger and more beautiful message.

SR: Aside from the message, would you say there is a common denominator to all DxE actions, or are they each a bit different? Have you developed a "style" of sorts, or is it always a bit touch-and-go?

WH: You've noted one common denominator: the strong message. The other big common denominators are that we focus on creating activists (rather than just vegans) and that we focus on social media (rather than just the handful of people at a protest). Stylistically, we are known for being young, confident, and energetic; but the truth is that there are different styles all over the world. Our allies in Moscow, at the Alliance for Animals, use extremely aggressive tactics, including chaining themselves to the Russian Parliament. In contrast, we have just as important contributors in places such as Augusta, Georgia, where one of our organizers (Breeda Mahoney) focuses almost entirely on leafleting and outreach. So our primary style is...that we have no style. Rather, we seek to empower activists anywhere and everywhere under the same strong message, regardless of what style they find most appropriate.

SR: How do you measure the success of your actions? How can you be sure any of this is "working"?

WH: We look at three different measures: impacts on the target, impacts on the public, and impacts on the movement. Unlike most campaigns, we reverse the typical priority; impacts on the *movement* are key. Again, if you look at the model of social change that works most effectively, pursuant to work by ground-breaking scholars such as Christakis, North, and Fogel, you have to create strong social movements to effect real and permanent change. Without that social base for your movement to take root—think of it as fertile ground for social change—any changes to a particular target or even the public at large will quickly dissipate. As so many politicians have noted, you have to first shore up your base—and, at this point, we as animal liberationists hardly even *have* a base!

That is not to say, however, that we don't look at other measures of success. We regularly assess our progress with respect to all three categories of impact. We have made incredible progress in all three in less than a year's time. With respect to the target, two of our most important objectives were to provoke a significant public response by the company we are currently targeting (Chipotle) and to slow down its truly astonishing growth. We've now achieved both objectives, as the company was forced to shut down its largest San Francisco store last month due to concerns over bad press and social media during the Macworld Expo, and its growth has slowed to almost zero—including a $1 billion loss in shareholder value on a single day!

With respect to the public, we set out to achieve press "pings" in five cities, trigger national press attention, and achieve at least 500 visitors to our campaign website on a daily basis. These were all no small feats for a grassroots platform with a budget of $0, yet, again, we've achieved all of these objectives, with a glowing piece in *Salon* about our campaign against "humane slaughter" being the most prominent success to date.

Finally (and as I said, most importantly), we look to our effect on the movement. Here is where we've had the most astonishing success. We set out a goal of gaining participation in twenty cities. We've now had seventy-one. We hoped for five countries.

We're now up to seventeen. We hoped to trigger a dialogue on our movement about humane slaughter and corporate manipulation of our movement. The best example of this is an amazing interaction I had with the famous author Jeffrey Masson. I met him prior to a book talk, and he started *raving* about this campaign against Chipotle and humane slaughter that he had read about. I blushed and informed him that the campaign at issue...was ours!

When the biggest and most influential voices ·in the movement are talking about your campaign, when the press and public have shown nothing but support, and when you're scaring the bejesus out of one of the largest multinational corporations in the world, you KNOW that you're achieving incredible progress.

Direct Action Everywhere's Organizing Principles[14]

WE BELIEVE IN, AND FIGHT FOR, TOTAL ANIMAL LIBERATION.

We are animals. We work for the immediate liberation of our brethren (human and otherwise). We speak and fight for nonhuman animals in the same way that we would speak or fight for our brothers, sisters, or children. We take the victim's perspective, aspire for total species equality, and contest the moral elevation of human traits ("humane" is not the same as "good;" "reason" is not the same as "value").

WE TAKE, AND ASK OTHERS TO TAKE, NONVIO- LENT DIRECT ACTION.

We directly confront the ideas and institutions that leave animals in cages and chains. We are open and proud in standing up for the oppressed. We believe in the spirit and power of creative protest, of dissent, and in a beautiful vision of a just and peaceful world. We strive to create heroes out of ordinary people—heroes who take the liberation of animals into their own hands.

WE TELL STORIES TO INSPIRE.

We tell stories from the animals' perspectives. Stories to radicalize. Stories to move people. Stories to change the world.

WE ARE A COMMUNITY.

We believe in the power of friendship and community, of social support and companionship, and of virtuous cycles and memes. We believe in the wisdom of crowds, and in the spontaneous creativity of the masses. We are going viral, and we won't stop until every animal is free.

WE DREAM BIG, AND HAVE THE COURAGE AND CONVICTION TO SEE OUR DREAMS COME TRUE.

We see beyond the next frontier. We believe in a world where the quiet oppression of complacency is replaced by the vigorous dissent of a movement for change.

Humanewashing: How DxE Fights Back

In 2013, Direct Action Everywhere launched a massive campaign against Chipotle, in response to the astounding success of its "Food with Integrity" marketing campaign. Chapter Three explored how humanewashed marketing tactics, such as those employed by Chipotle, pose an enormous threat to the Animal Liberation Movement. Here is how members of this organization, spanning coast-to-coast and with foreign syndicates as distant as Copenhagen, Denmark and Lisbon, Portugal, are fighting back:

- A nationwide "Die-In," in which activists in six cities converged in Chipotle restaurants and collapsed to the ground, to represent the animals who die for food.

- Disruption of a Chipotle-financed documentary at Stanford University—the film *American Meat*. The disruption received press attention in almost a dozen outlets.

- Multiple flash-mob-style disruptions inside stores: a banner unveiling *Someone, Not Something; Peace, Not Violence*.

- Disruption of a talk by Chipotle's Nate Appleman (famous for mocking animal advocates in the *New York Times*) at Chipotle's Cultivate Festival in 2013.

In addition, in January 2014, the group issued an open letter to the company entitled "Broken Promises, Stolen Lives," calling upon Chipotle to live up to its promise to treat animals humanely—by not killing them.

I know not everyone is a fan of the word "disruption." *Disruption* implies chaos, anarchy. Yes, these actions disrupt previously prepared presentations; they disrupt the ebb and flow of business as usual. These are the only means left to animal liberationists through which to spark dialogue, as those who stand in opposition to us seldom solicit our opinions outright; and, yes, despite all of its rhetoric, Chipotle stands in direct opposition to us.

It may appear, on the surface, that we *chose* to name them our enemy, but it's actually quite the opposite. They were, for starters, our natural enemy due to the very nature of their business: promoting slaughter of animals for human consumption when it has long ago been verified—and continues to be verified over and over again, through study after study, book after book—that humans do not require animal consumption for healthful living. They then decided to kick things up a notch by simultaneously *claiming to be our ally*, adding insult to injury—like someone who punches you in the face, unprovoked, and then declares, "Hi there; I'm a pacifist."

As author Daniel Quinn wrote in his stirring sociocultural fictions *Ishmael* and *The Story of B*, our culture has reared us to believe that the world was created for us alone, that it is our duty to rule it and our right to consume it—while enslaving or killing anyone who might threaten our ability to do so. "We can compete, but we cannot wage war," the mentors of Quinn's stories tell their protégés.[15] In other words, it's one thing for ancient humans to have killed a deer and then eaten it; it is quite another for all of humanity to decide, "All deer is for us! We must kill as many deer as possible, so that we can eat them; and we must kill anyone else who eats deer, so that there is more deer for us!"

It is also one thing to engage in *subsistence-based* agriculture and another to engage in what Quinn calls *totalitarian agriculture*. Most people trace the history of Humans as we know Them to the Agricultural Revolution in the Fertile Crescent some 10,000 years ago, but the truth is, smaller cultures scattered throughout the world were already engaging in various agricultural activities *before* the so-called "revolution." So what was different about *this type* of agriculture? How did it come to all but erase its competitors, such that 99.9% of the world we currently inhabit consists of cultures that rely on this, and only this, type?

The difference was that this type wasn't about subsisting—it was about expanding. That's not to say that it was anyone's specific *intention* that it would expand—only that the very nature of this type of agriculture *requires* expansion. The form of agriculture born in the Fertile Crescent produced far more food than any type that was practiced prior to its conception. It wasn't quite a *new* way of doing things so much as a *more efficient* way of doing things.

This method brought about humanity's relative freedom from strict reliance on solely what Nature provided. Now, people could control their food supply, which allowed them to "settle down." I put this, too, in quotes, because the notion that everyone who existed before the Agricultural Revolution was a nomad is a misnomer. Many tribes "settled down" to varying degrees prior to the Agricultural Revolution, storing gathered foods in specific areas and returning to those areas in times of scarcity.

In nature, it is easy to observe that no animal is truly nomadic. Animals that appear nomadic nevertheless will return to specific areas to mate, meaning that, in the interim, they are to some extent bound to these areas and refrain from straying too far from them.

In any case, I don't want to spend too much time on agriculture. The intention of this book is not to tell you whether agriculture is "good" or "bad." It's a facetious question, if you ask me. Agriculture is no more good or bad than a hammer is good or bad. A hammer is a tool that can help you build things. It is also a weapon that can help you destroy things.

My intention here is simply to highlight how agriculture, in its prevailing form, has contributed to the Myth of Human Supremacy. As we got better at farming, we increased our food supply so much that the result was more of us—which meant that we needed more space, so that we could build more homes and grow more crops. This need for space, coupled with concern over other members of the animal kingdom damaging our crops, positioned us as enemies to our animal brethren. Eventually, we figured out that we could even *use* our animal brethren to do some of the heavy lifting on our behalf; animal husbandry ensued, and we ended up not just killing and eating animals (and driving them off of their land) but also enslaving them.

We could no longer think of them as brethren, because that would be too painful; no one wants to steal land or food from, much less murder, his or her brother or sister. Instead we decided, as a culture, that we were superior to them and thus entitled to whatever we wanted—never mind the cost. It is this very mentality, and not merely the profit of any particular company, that animal liberationists aim to *disrupt*.

Our disruption is not to the "natural ebb and flow of things," but rather to the distastefully *unnatural* tide that has

swept up the bulk of humankind, giving it a false sense of importance from its view upon the crest.

Is it Working?

YES! There is strong evidence that Chipotle took notice
of DxE's campaign, and is concerned about the impact our actions may have on future sales. The company's regulatory filing
for the fiscal year ending December 2013 reported that:

> Our commitment to Food With Integrity may
> also leave us open to actions against us or crit-
> icism from special interest groups whose ideas
> regarding food issues differ from ours or who
> believe we should pursue different or additional
> goals with our Food With Integrity approach.
> Any adverse publicity that results from such
> criticism could damage our brand and adversely
> impact customer traffic at our restaurants...[16]

That Chipotle felt it necessary to address our criticisms
and admit its own vulnerability in a massive, critical financial
document just shy of a year after DxE's inception proves that we
have most definitely made it onto its radar. Chipotle also lost $1
billion in shareholder value from 2013-2014. *USA Today* reported in April 2014 that Chipotle lost $32.79 (6%) to $519.61 in
heavy trading volume.[17]

I was fortunate enough to witness firsthand another
manner in which we have impacted Chipotle on March 29,
2014, when DxE East Bay demonstrated at a Chipotle location
in San Francisco. This was part of an international day of action,
in which animal liberationists around the world participated.
After just a few months of such demonstrations, my fellow activists and I were pleased to discover that the San Francisco

branch we had chosen had actually shut down in anticipation of our protest.

Upon learning that the branch would remain closed to all customers until our demonstration was complete, we decided to keep things going for two hours straight. So for two hours on that one Saturday afternoon, that one Chipotle branch did not earn a single dollar. We took direct action and, in a rare and precious moment, witnessed a direct result.

In January 2015, Chipotle announced that it was temporarily removing carnitas from its menu at several locations nationwide because one of the company's major pork suppliers, which it refused to identify, was not meeting Chipotle's "responsibly raised" standard.[18] While this is certainly not what DxE demonstrations called for, as we demanded instead that the company remove all nonhuman animals from all of its menus, it certainly illustrates that we've gotten their attention.

In the face of falling profit margins and bad press, Chipotle felt compelled to at least *appear* more compassionate. So, carnitas went bye-bye, at least for a while, and the vegan sofritas is still going strong, nearly two years after its addition to the menu in February 2013.[19]

An Intelligent, Poorly Founded Concern

Many animal liberationists in Middle America and other places where vegan options are scarce are concerned that DxE and other nonviolent direct action groups are "doing it wrong"— that campaigns such as "It's Not Food, It's Violence" pose a threat to veganism by challenging companies that offer vegan options, thus making it harder for those who have made a commitment to animal liberation in these areas to uphold said commitment.

While I empathize with this concern, it rests on a false premise: that DxE is trying to "shut down" Chipotle, Whole Foods, and others with our campaigns. We are not. Ours are not boycott campaigns; if members of DxE want to eat Chipotle's vegan burrito, they are free to do so. Our campaigns are not about making any one company disappear; rather, they are about pressuring companies to be honest with the public and to stop engaging in violence against nonhuman animals. Chipotle can easily afford to go vegan and stay in business—even if, say, half or a third of its clientele jumped ship. It is that rich. (This also assumes that Chipotle would only *lose* customers by going vegan; who knows how many new customers it would attract by doing so?)

I have been lucky enough to live in "vegan paradises" for most of my life. I was born and raised in New York, living in Manhattan and working in Brooklyn from about 2004–2012, and now live in Oakland, CA; it was the one year I spent living in Phoenix that really opened my eyes to the reality that committing to animal liberation is so much harder in most of America than I had initially thought. *Most of America is NOT Brooklyn or Oakland.* Most vegans in Middle America can't just decide, "I'm never going to eat at a place that serves animal flesh ever again," unless they want to eat at home forever, which almost no one does (except maybe hermits). Since vegans are more heavily concentrated in places like New York and California, animal liberation organizations often neglect the needs of Middle Americans, and try to solve The Animal Problem from a deplorably limited perspective.

Now here are some reasons why, in spite of all this, I ultimately still believe in the value of our Chipotle campaign in particular:

- As previously mentioned, **we are not trying to close Chipotle**, so vegans with no other options in their area are free to still enjoy Chipotle's vegan burrito.

- **Our campaign ensures that the vegan burrito sticks around.** In 2010, Chipotle introduced vegan Gardein items at *some* of its locations. For this, animal advocacy groups and vegans across the country praised the company. It became a media darling; then, once the lights were shut off and the camera crews went home, Chipotle quietly dropped Gardein items from the few menus to which they had been added.

Since DxE began "It's Not Food, It's Violence" in 2013, not only is the vegan burrito available at pretty much every location, but it has also survived much longer than the Gardein items did. Having this option helps the company fight us—which provides rural Americans with a place to eat when they're on a tight budget and can't go home to cook or, heaven forbid, would like to eat amongst other people!

- **Chipotle's rhetoric is dangerous to the Animal Liberation Movement.** Allowing Chipotle to use this rhetoric unchecked would perpetuate any or all of the following negative beliefs: that Americans are stupid and can't see through the lies; that Americans are apathetic and don't care when they're being lied to; that there are no consequences for lying to the American people, economic or otherwise; and that moving toward a Vegan America is less important than accommodating the few vegans who exist right now.

It has been argued that the campaign targeting Chipotle may send the wrong message to other restaurants: that if they're not "perfect" (i.e., 100% vegan), they shouldn't even try—and by "try," I can only suppose critics mean "have vegan options," because Chipotle actually doesn't try to treat nonhuman animals better than other establishments do—at all.

What message would it send to other restaurants if we did *not* campaign against Chipotle? That all it takes is one vegan menu item to halt the Animal Liberation Movement in its tracks? One burrito to dam the tide of animal liberation in America?

We do not intend to tell Chipotle or any other restaurant to stop trying; rather, we challenge Chipotle and others to try *even harder*—to move beyond offering a single vegan menu item, and take animals off of the menu altogether. Yes, it's an ambitious goal. No, I have no idea how it's going to work out, but I'm not giving up. Our campaign against Chipotle is not about removing options. It's about accountability. It's about social progress. It's about demanding respect from an institution that clearly doesn't respect its clientele any more than it respects the animals it enslaves and murders.

Open Investigation and Rescue

For over a decade, "Certified Humane" has been the gold standard of animal welfare around the world, supported by over sixty prominent animal advocacy organizations, including the Humane Society of the United States. Whole Foods, with its Cruelty by Numbers game and paradoxical advertisements, has been hailed as an animal rights hero, but DxE's open investigation has revealed that this fame and fortune was built on a foundation of lies.

(From a welfarist perspective, that is; from a liberationist perspective, the violence of Whole Foods has always been evident, because the company serves meat and dairy.)

In Chapter Three, we talked about the horrific conditions DxE encountered at the "certified humane" Petaluma farm (a Whole Foods egg provider): darkness, filth, lack of space, lice infestations, and nutritional disorders, just to name a few. The story broke in the *New York Times* on January 8, 2015, and international protests ensued that weekend, but that was just the beginning. DxE has since launched an international network to facilitate *open rescue:* civil disobedience in which one rescues animals from farms openly, without concealing one's identity. Prior to DxE's excursion to a Petaluma/Whole Foods farm, open rescue had not been successfully enacted in the United States in over a decade.

Inspired by Animal Liberation Victoria and Patty Mark's Open Rescue Movement, DxE's Open Rescue Network combines the benefits of many different tactics. At much lower cost, one can rescue animals from abuse who otherwise would have been left behind in an undercover investigation. Openly showing one's face—individualizing the activist—garners much more public sympathy for those rescuing animals than masked, undercover actions. It presents us with a way of combating stifling "ag-gag" laws, which hinder and criminalize undercover investigations by outlawing videotaping, photographing, or otherwise recording the violence and cruelty that takes place behind closed barn doors.

The Nonhuman Rights Project

Veganism as a lifestyle, or at minimum a dietary, choice has experienced an increase in popularity in the United States in the past twenty years. Various sources have estimated, from 2009–2014, that somewhere between 7 million and 7.5 million Americans self-identify as vegans. Vegan options are increasingly prevalent at high-end supermarkets (and are even extending to some low-end supermarkets—particularly soy milk and vegan burgers), while companies such as Vegan Publishers in Boston, MA and Vegan Wedding Photographers in Brooklyn, NY have developed liberationist business models outside of the culinary and fashion arenas.

While the vegan diet may be said to be going "mainstream" (or at least "de-shamed"), the topic of animal liberation itself is not entirely fashionable just yet. Discussions of animal ethics appear to be polarized with respect to venue between quiet, intimate conversations with friends, and loud, confrontational street demonstrations. Here and there, an academic pokes his or her head up, gives a lecture at a university that ends up on You-Tube, and ethical e-wars ensue. What must follow is a concerted effort to put animal liberation on the *public agenda*, giving it the same reverence, press coverage, and legislative influence that past social justice movements have achieved. ALV, DxE, and other animal liberation coalitions achieve this through nonviolent direct action.

Another group that has taken great strides in this area, utilizing the letter of the law rather than public displays of discontent, is New York City's Nonhuman Rights Project, headed by renowned animal lawyer and project president Steven Wise. The group's mission is to "...change the common law status of at least some nonhuman animals from mere 'things,' which lack the capacity to possess any legal right, to 'persons,' who possess such fundamental rights as bodily integrity and bodily liberty, and those other legal rights to which evolving standards of morality, scientific discovery, and human experience entitle them."[20]

Naturally, I object to the use of the phrase "at least some"—but I get it. Everyone has to start somewhere, and this group may not have been able to achieve the traction necessary to launch into the public eye if it came out and said immediately, to the surprise of many, that *all* animals deserve legal personhood. (For instance, I can envision some malcontent shouting from the bleachers, "So, you want to give legal rights to cockroaches? HA!") This issue arises time and time again as I examine NhRP cases; nevertheless, let's look at some of their most notable cases before launching into any assessment of their effectiveness.

In early December of 2013, Mr. Wise filed writs of habeas corpus on behalf of four captive chimpanzees. The lawsuits were dismissed, but Mr. Wise said he planned to appeal. Roughly four months later, in April 2014, the *New York Times* reported that the NhRP would help a chimp named Tommy sue his captors for unsuitable living conditions, such as solitary confinement:

Inside the shed, the repairman inched open a small door as though to first test the mood within. A rancid milk-musk odor wafted forth and with it the sight of an adult chimpanzee, crouched inside a small steel-mesh cell. Some plastic toys and bits of soiled bedding were strewn behind him. The only visible light emanated from a small portable TV on a stand outside his bars, tuned to what appeared to be a nature show.

"It's too bad you can't see him when he's out in the jungle," the repairman said, pointing to a passageway nearby, which opened onto an enclosure that housed a playground jungle gym. "At least he gets fresh air out there."

. . .

On the way back out to the car, Wise paused.

"I'm not going to be able get that image out of my mind," he said, his voice quavering. "How would you describe that cage? He's in a dungeon, right? That's a dungeon."[21]

Tommy was once a circus chimpanzee, whose caregiver recently passed away, leaving him under the care of the man referred to as "the repairman." Wise met Tommy and the repairman at Circle L Trailer, the owner of which apparently also makes his living renting out reindeer during the holiday season for photos and such, including commercials for Macy's and Mercedes-Benz. (No data concerning the fate of these poor souls was provided by the article.)

Wise, Natalie Prosin (Executive Director of the NhRP) and Elizabeth Stein (New-York-based animal rights expert) filed their petition at the Fulton County Courthouse in Johnstown, NY. The petition described in detail Tommy's miserable living conditions, such as his isolation and lack of space, and culminated in a series of nine affidavits from primatologists around the world asserting the cognitive sophistication of chimpanzees and the suffering Tommy was being forced to endure. In essence: "Chimps have feelings, JUST LIKE US!"[22]

Unfortunately, on December 4, 2014, the Supreme Court declared that Tommy is not a "person" entitled to a common law writ of *habeas corpus* because he is "unable to bear duties or responsibilities." Roughly two weeks later, the NhRP filed a motion seeking leave to appeal to New York's highest court on the grounds that this decision contradicts previous decisions made by the Court of Appeals and that numerous cases bestow personhood on petitioners who are unable to bear duties or responsibilities. The motion was denied in January 2015. The NhRP is therefore currently seeking permission to appeal directly from New York's highest court.[23]

Fourth Time's the Charm: Habeas Corpus Hearing Granted for Two Chimpanzees

On April 20, 2015, the NhRP announced that its fourth demand for a hearing under habeas corpus on behalf of nonhumans since the organization's inception has met with success. For the first time, in May 2015, a hearing will be held on behalf of two chimpanzees—Hercules and Leo—who are being unlawfully detained at Stony Brook University on Long Island, New York.

While Justice Jaffe, who issued the decision to hold the hearing on April 20th, downplays the significance of the habeas corpus statute and New York State court spokesman David

Bookstaver maintains that "All this does is allow the parties to argue their case in court," this unprecedented event will inevitably call into question the legal definition of personhood and, independent of the results of the hearing itself, I anticipate a domino effect in the months and years to follow.[24]

NhRP is calling for the release of Hercules and Leo to a sanctuary in Florida, and the burden will rest on Stony Brook University to prove that there is just cause for further detaining these individuals.

Looking at the Nonhuman Rights Project's work alongside the *Cambridge Declaration of Consciousness* and former NIH director Zerhouni's bold statement against animal testing ("We all drank the Kool-Aid on that one, myself included"), it appears that the moment is ripe for the Animal Liberation Movement to flourish. Sure, there are still ample obstacles to overcome, but both the scientific and legislative communities—which are, admittedly, often more highly regarded and granted greater credibility by the masses than animal liberation organizations—are making great strides in putting animal liberation on the public agenda. These recent events, while not asserting any genuinely "new" information, nonetheless have potential to make a major impact on both the factory farming industry and the use of animals in scientific research and product testing in the years to come.

Now here's the rub. I love these guys for fighting the good fight—for caring about someone other than themselves, and especially for caring about someone who isn't human, but... Okay, well, there's racism, which says one race is better than another (or all others), and there's speciesism, which says one species is better than one (or all) other species. What concerns me about the NhRP cases is the potential for *development of a speciesist hierarchy*. These actions don't entirely dispel the Myth of Human Supremacy so much as they add a footnote to it, an addendum: "Humans are better than all other animals, but primates are pretty close."

I'm reminded of one of Orwell's Animal Farm laws: "All animals are equal, but some animals are more equal than others."

Chimpanzee cases are only the beginning for the Non-human Rights Project. Along with chimps, the NhRP plans to file similar lawsuits on behalf of other members of the great ape family (bonobos, orangutans, and gorillas) as well as dolphins, orcas, belugas, elephants, and African gray parrots—all beings with "higher-order cognitive abilities."

Let's pretend for a second that that even *matters*—that possessing what human scientists label "higher-order cognitive abilities" somehow makes one superior and more deserving of life and liberty than others. Were that truly the case, there are several animals left off of this list: *pigs*, for instance—among the smartest animals in the world. With respect to birds: Why only the African gray parrot? Many bird species possess exceptional cognitive abilities. Some even have the capacity for aesthetics, such as the bowerbird.

Why were these and other "higher-order cognitive abilities"-havers left off of the list? Because *this isn't really about cognitive ability. At all.* This is about who is "like us" and who is "not like us." This is otherization at its finest. It's easy to sympathize with chimps because they look and act a lot like humans. It's relatively easy to sympathize with parrots because they (well, most breeds, anyway) can be taught to speak in human tongues. It's harder for most people to sympathize with pigs, in spite of their cognitive abilities, because all most people seem to know (or want to know) about pigs is that they are delicious. They hear pig, they think *pork*; they do not think *friend*.

Pigs have an especially bad rap in our culture, as calling someone "a pig" is an insult on multiple levels. It can be meant to imply that a human is physically dirty, that a human is sexually perverted, that a human lacks grace or agility, and those on the other side of the law refer to cops as pigs as a display of pure hatred. Rather than "dirty cop" or "perverted cop," what is typically meant when a cop is called "a pig" is roughly, "I hate you, cop; so I will degrade you by calling you a lesser being. And as much as I hate you, I'm going to go ahead and assume that all pigs are worse than you, simply because you're human and they are pigs." Or to put it another way, "I hate you so much, I don't think of you as human; you are subhuman, and pigs, by virtue of not being human, are by default also *sub*human, so you're more like them than like me."

What implications might the standard of "higher-order cognitive abilities" have for us humans, if universally accepted? Should humans with lesser cognitive abilities be subjected to mistreatment, isolation, and exploitation? Should adults have to take an IQ test before society determines whether they get to live in peace or under a boot?

Ultimately, in spite of its limited scope, I still believe that what the NhRP is doing is valuable, as they are challenging what it means to be a person. While, at the moment, their focus is on chimpanzees, they do plan to expand, and I hope that they do soon; but more important than any tangible result they may achieve in the short term, what I find so compelling and exciting about their work is that they are laying theoretical groundwork for revolutionizing the way humans look at nonhumans. Perhaps focusing initially on chimpanzees is a strategic move on their part, as they know it is easier for the masses to care about chimps than pigs. Perhaps one day the NhRP will represent a pig, chicken, or cow in court, suing its captors for mutilation, confinement, or rape.

We can't let it end here; even if chimpanzees and dolphins see their day in the sun, we mustn't forget the "lab" mice, the "veal" calves, the consistently violated "dairy" cows. We can't allow the law to define a group of creatures as "special" and deserving of better treatment than others. Not only is this unfair to the others, but it also leans dangerously toward the welfarist mentality. The issue can't be how the captives are treated or how big their cages are; the issue at the forefront of our minds must always be *the fact that we have nonhuman captives at all.*

Animal Legal Defense Fund

I had long ago heard of the Animal Legal Defense Fund, and knew vaguely that they worked with animal abuse cases, but beyond that, I didn't know much. I presumed that they were a mostly "dog-and-cat" organization—that they may focus on, say, removing pets from homes in which they are abused or neglected, or breaking up underground animal-abusive industries such as dog fighting rings. Somehow I assumed they would steer clear of circus, meat and dairy industry, and other animal abuses that "omnivores" tend to overlook; perhaps because it was such a high-profile organization, perhaps because I didn't know where their funding came from—but most likely, as often happens to us liberationists, I was growing increasingly pessimistic in general.

After learning of their involvement in the Petaluma cage-free egg case, my curiosity was further piqued. Fortunately, in the summer of 2014 I encountered a lovely couple here in Oakland with some connections to the ALDF. When I mentioned I was writing a book on animal liberation, they offered to put me in touch with the organization.

I was directed to Matthew Leibman, a senior attorney in the Litigation Program at ALDF who works on all aspects of ALDF's civil cases, including investigating reports of animal cruelty, conducting legal research, developing new legal theories, and appearing in court. Later, through him, I was directed to another ALDF attorney, Jessica Blome. I thank them both for the insights that follow, which definitely raised my spirits and renewed the hope I was scarcely aware that I'd been losing.

The first thing I heard from Matthew that really lit up my life was that the ALDF, contrary to my previous pessimistic assumptions, does not deal strictly with "dog-and-cat" legislation. This group advocates on behalf of a wide variety of animal species: "…everything from rats to chimps to frogs to birds."

In May 2014, the ALDF filed a "friend of the court" brief on behalf of the city of West Hollywood—the first city in the nation to ban the sale of products made from animal fur within city limits. Thanks at least in part to this brief, a constitutional challenge to West Hollywood's legislation was dismissed. This case sets the critical precedent that municipalities ought to have the right to make ethical determinations for themselves and forbid products and practices that harm animals within their borders. While bans such as the bullhook ban in Oakland and Los Angeles outlaw certain practices within cities, in the case of West Hollywood, an entire family of products has been forbidden—an issue that affects many more residents and businesses than the alteration of a circus procedure.

In July 2014, the ALDF settled a lawsuit against Duane Freilino, organizer of the annual JMK Coyote Hunting Contest in Crane, Harney County, Oregon, and successfully put a stop to this contest. Jessica Blome was the lead attorney on this case. I asked her whether she considered this an isolated case or part of a larger program to end hunting contests in America:

> Since winning the Oregon case, we joined a working group comprised of several other animal rights and conservation organizations with the goal of stopping as many of these contests as possible. Right now, we are focused on predator killing contests. We do not consider this a larger "program," so to speak, but we are escalating our efforts in this area.

Owing to their success in this case, I wondered if the ALDF currently engages in cases about other recreational events that involve the oppression of nonhumans (such as circuses). Matthew confirmed that the ALDF, in fact, often deals with animals in entertainment, including circuses, zoos, rodeos, and other animal exhibiters. As is the case with every group dealing with animal abuse issues, I had to ask Matthew about ALDF's involvement—or lack thereof—in suing places like slaughterhouses for murder, or factory farms for abuse. What he and Jessica had told me so far had rendered me uncharacteristically optimistic; still, I couldn't shake the feeling that if ALDF had been going after Big Agra et al., I would have heard about it or read about it.

He replied:

> We definitely don't respect or accept cruelty at the industrial level any more than we accept it at the individual level. ALDF focuses not only on discrete or aberrant acts of cruelty by sadistic individuals, but also on systemic, institutionalized practices that exploit animals. Unfortunately, financially lucrative exploitation is often exempted from cruelty laws, but that doesn't deter us from litigating against larger industries such as industrial agriculture.

The financial power of the meat and dairy industries thus serves as one powerful obstacle in holding them accountable for their abuses. Some other points Matthew made on the subject include:

- Pigs and dogs share many of the same traits, capacities, desires, and emotions; but you can get away with doing things to a pig on a farm that you'd be imprisoned for doing to a dog.

- Rats and mice are exempted from the Animal Welfare Act, the main federal statute governing animal research—not because they don't feel pain, but because researchers oppose providing them legal protection.

Not only is there a dichotomy between what one can do to a dog and what one can do to a pig legally, but this dichotomy also exists within the realm of how farmed animals are treated. For instance, the Humane Slaughter Act, which is commonly violated by industrial farmers anyway, does not cover birds; therefore, even those willing to adhere to the law need not do so with respect to chickens, turkeys, or other farmed birds. Speciesist Hierarchy rears its ugly head once more. The issue is not simply that humans are more entitled than nonhumans, it is also that dogs are more entitled than pigs, pigs are more entitled than chickens, and so on.

Whether or not an item is legal seldom determines its popularity. Prohibition in the US in the 1920s and '30s failed to impact the popularity of alcohol, and was eventually repealed. Marijuana, in spite of the fact that it remains illegal in most of the US, is not only popularly used, but is also becoming "de-shamed," by which I mean that more and more people from various walks of life are now willing to admit to their peers—and even their colleagues!—that they smoke and/or eat marijuana. So no, I don't think making industrial meat or dairy farming in America illegal will end the sale and distribution of meat and dairy products in America. As long as there's a market, there will be a supplier.

Still, taking legal strides against animal products such as fur serves a purpose. Our legal system does not exist outside of morality. Even where legislation appears to contradict general American morality, *enforcement* of said legislation often directly mirrors our values as a culture. Therefore, I believe illegalizing meat and dairy—or even just industrially produced meat and dairy—would make a major contribution to turning the tide of morality in America toward greater empathy for farmed animals. Eating animals would, if not cease entirely, at the very least be considered gauche and scandalous—as it should be.

On March 11, 2015, the Animal Legal Defense Fund made the following announcement on its Facebook page:

> Free range. Cage free. Grass fed. We've all heard the terms meant to convince us that what the meat companies are selling is humane. But is it? The Animal Legal Defense Fund's Manager of Investigations, TJ Tumasse, has investigated all forms of animal agriculture. He takes on the question of humane meat at the upcoming 2015 Conscious Eating Conference. Register now.[25]

A link to the registration site for the conference was included. So it was that I not only learned about a promising social justice event happening in my area, but also learned that ALDF has an undercover investigations department devoted to exposing the truth behind animal agriculture—taking photos and shooting videos of the horrific conditions experienced by nonhuman animals used for food and sharing these images with the masses.

While the ALDF has perhaps yet to outright sue Big Agra for its crimes, the organization is nevertheless confronting the lies of industrial meat and dairy head-on. It simultaneously challenges the notion that nonhuman animals are void of personhood and the idea that there is a humane way to exploit and even kill someone—all of which are ideas that have been used to justify atrocities against nonhumans for centuries.

The illegalization of fur products in West Hollywood is a promising sign. Perhaps in the near future we will bear witness to the first case of a city or district banning meat and dairy within its borders. In the meantime, let us consider some other examples of single-issue campaigns and the extent to which they support or hinder the movement.

Low-Hanging Fruit: Political Appropriation of AR Sentiments

It's no secret that politicians—like magazine editors, TV producers, and others whose careers hinge almost entirely on The Now—love to claim the "it" issue of the day as their own. People caring about the environment? *I'll plant a tree on camera.* People worried about obesity? *I'll run a 5K and give a brief interview afterwards, sweaty and winded.* That sort of thing. We've all seen it, and it isn't new.

While in the past I have laughed at and mocked such desperate attempts to win public favor, I now find myself mired in a complex internal struggle as a result of them. Why? Because the issue of the day is our treatment of nonhuman animals. Politicians are now taking seemingly positive steps to end *certain forms* of cruelty to animals, and as an animal-lover, an end to *any* form of animal cruelty is naturally a cause for celebration to me. I struggle because while I appreciate these measures, I understand all too well that these politicos are simply grasping at low-hanging fruit. They latch on to less pervasive forms of animal abuse and launch legislative attacks against them to avoid having to confront the Big Picture—having to develop and implement any significant structural changes to how our society eats, dresses, builds, learns, or is entertained.

For instance, New York City Mayor Bill de Blasio promised during his campaign to ban horse-drawn carriages from use in the city, and in December 2014 the *New York Times* reported that he was making good on that promise.[26] As a long-time New Yorker, I was delighted to hear this. Many of my visits to Central Park—particularly the area around Columbus Circle—have been marred by images of depressed-looking horses lined up in rows, often standing in their own feces, wearing blinders that rendered them unable to see fully in any direction, surrounded by noise, fast-moving vehicles, and photo-flashing tourists.

As much as it relieved me to hear that soon, no horse will have to endure such suffering in New York City again, I cannot shake the mental image I have of Columbus Circle. This image includes not only rows of depressed horses (and people and fountains and traffic lights and statues...), but also features as a backdrop the Time Warner Center: home of both the meat- and dairy-serving restaurant Landmarc, and humanewashing giant Whole Foods. While the horses outside are being, to an extent, liberated, just behind them is a building in which other sentient beings are being dishonored, their corpses sold and served. Does de Blasio intend to do anything about that? I doubt it.

Also in the news in December 2014 was New Jersey Governor Chris Christie's veto of a bill to ban the use of gestation crates in his state. In this case, the politico in question actually voted *against* animals for the sake of his numbers (presumably, a ban on gestation crates would financially inconvenience some agribusinesses in the area, all of which have voting power and some of which may have contributed to his campaign). The reporting itself, independent of the governor's decision, perpetuates The Humane Myth in that by focusing on *gestation crates*—crates in which pregnant pigs are kept in isolation—it reinforces the presumption that *non-pregnant pigs must live in superior conditions*. The sad reality is that the vast majority of pigs raised for slaughter experience isolation, overcrowding to the point of immobility, or some combination of the two.

A *New York Times* article about Christie's veto confessed, "Passage of the bill would actually have little impact."[27] Unfortunately, the reasons cited are trite (one reason being that there simply aren't that many pigs in New Jersey in the first place). The bill would have little impact anywhere; ultimately, whether they are pregnant or not, farmed pigs are murdered. Male pigs, who have never had to face the gestation crate, are habitually subjected to castration as piglets, without the use of anesthesia or painkillers.

While I am grateful for any measure that is taken to protect animals, I often worry that this focus on low-hanging fruit will only delay that which is truly necessary: a complete overhaul of our speciesist industrial complexes. For that, we need to strike at the root of the problem—speciesism—and, as the Nonhuman Rights Project is currently doing, attempt to redefine *personhood*.

What Works vs. What Doesn't

As an animal liberationist, my number one priority at all actions and events in which I participate is to change the way people look at animal abuse and exploitation. I seek to educate, inform, and ultimately convince as many people as possible that animal cruelty is not a "necessary evil" to be tolerated, but an *unnecessary* evil to be eradicated. Animal liberationists across the globe have varying views on what the most effective ways to accomplish this are, as well as which ways simply don't work. Here's my personal perspective on some things that work and some that don't.

What works: **Showing images and videos of animals displaying their individuality and joie de vivre.**

While conventional wisdom proposes that exposing the violence that occurs against animals behind closed doors to the public is the most effective visual means of changing minds, I've since come to understand that the sad, depressing nature of these images is actually a huge turn-off to potential recruits. While the public has a right to know what happens, which is why conducting and filming investigations is so important, we cannot expect people to expose themselves to these images with any regularity. So many people who claim to sympathize with animals nevertheless avert their eyes to such graphic images, or will look only once for the sake of knowledge; meanwhile, as Kelly Atlas brilliantly pointed out in a post on *The Liberationist* (October 2014), images of violence fail to challenge the speciesist mentality:

> Unless someone can recognize the subjectivity and personhood of the animal whose body is being violated, that person will not be able to recognize the act of violence against the animal as violence any more than he or she regards the picking of a pear from its tree as violence.[28]

In other words, images of many nonhuman animals experiencing violence at once often fail to strike a chord with humans because, from their perspective, the animals appear to be more like units rather than individuals. The set-up in which many nonhuman animals are abused and slaughtered in industrialized operations is conducive to this perspective, as conveyor belts and other forms of standard factory equipment are used and therefore can be seen in these types of images—contributing to the milieu of *production* rather than *violence*.

That aside, there is also the concern that overusing graphic images will desensitize people and thus ultimately reinforce speciesism, by which I mean that even those who *are* able to recognize violence against nonhumans as violence will grow accustomed to it and not feel emotionally compelled to do anything about it.

Finally, we must ask ourselves upon showing violent images of nonhuman animals, *Would we show this image if the victim were human? Would we feel comfortable showing a human's throat being slit, or a human being locked in a stall or cage too small for their body?*

If the answer is *no*, then we shouldn't rely on such images of nonhumans either. To treat these images as different or somehow less scandalous than their human counterparts is speciesism incarnate.

An alternative Kelly heralds, and with which I wholeheartedly agree, is to display images in which humans can clearly see nonhuman animals experiencing love and joy, and showing personality. Animals with quirks. Mama and Papa animals caring for their young. Animals helping each other, exploring their surroundings. Such images may be more effective in challenging the speciesist status quo, and provoking compassion and empathy among humans, who will recognize themselves more readily in a happy, loving chicken than they ever will in a chicken who has been turned upside down and shoved into a funnel to await slaughter.

Yes, it is horrible that this happens to chickens, but as it does not happen to humans, such an image does not compel humans to *relate* to chickens any more readily. The chicken is still otherized, whereas an image of chickens, cows, or pigs engaging with family, friends, and their environment is far more relatable and emphasizes that these creatures are capable of complex emotions and strong interpersonal relationships—*just like us.*

I experienced this firsthand recently, watching for the first time a series on Netflix called *Wildest Islands.* I encountered so many strange creatures via that show—some of whom I'd never heard, others of whom I'd vaguely heard but about whom I knew precious little. These animals were not even remotely similar to humans with respect to appearance, but it was evident in how they treated their young, courted potential mates, and built their habitats how remarkably similar they are to us in spirit. Galapagos sea lion mothers, for instance, go out to hunt while one mother stays behind, with all of the pups. The interactions I observed screamed "Day Care Center." The children played, and sometimes fought, while the "babysitting" mother alternated between admonishing them and scanning the perimeter. It was cute, funny—and it was definitely relatable.

I strongly believe that watching that interaction, the co-operation of male and female frigate birds in building their nest together, and other such scenes would inspire empathy for these creatures more thoroughly than images of any of them being victimized or killed. These images emphasize universal truths that are far more poignant than "everyone is mortal."

What (sometimes) doesn't: **Dramatic displays in which humans pretend to be animals.**

I say this *sometimes* doesn't work because there is a wealth of examples in which this actually *does* work, but, with this type of demonstration, one must proceed with caution. First, let's take a look at a type of display that I feel doesn't work, then we'll move on to one in which I personally participated that I think *did* work.

I first encountered PALS at a First Friday event in the spring of 2013. First Friday is an art-walk-slash-mini-festival occurring in downtown Phoenix on the first Friday of each month. I heard a member, Eddie, speak on the megaphone, and his words aligned so closely with my personal beliefs that I had to find out who these people were and join their ranks. I took a small pamphlet from them, with limited information on it, and after much digging found the group on Meetup.com.

Upon finding the group online, I was bombarded with images of one of its members wearing next to nothing, wrapped in plastic and laying on a large tray. Upon joining the group, I learned that this was one of their preferred demonstrations at that moment—to parade this girl around town in her meat tray in an effort to illustrate the cruelty of meat.

When I first looked at the photos, I actually didn't think about meat at all. I thought about the girl. My first thought was, "This girl is HOT!" My second thought was, "Is she *naked?!*" (She wasn't—but close enough to warrant asking the question.) I later found that many other groups had utilized this strategy as well, from all over the US. I came across photos displaying multiple packages in which humans appearing nude or near-nude were wrapped with plastic.

Aside from my environmental concerns regarding the use of so much plastic (and possibly Styrofoam, which the trays appeared to be made of, but I could not confirm this), I worried that this type of demonstration was ineffective. I felt that most people seeing a woman on a tray would have similar reactions to mine—particularly on college campuses, where hormones abound and students see sex in *everything*; and at First Friday, where after the first hour or so pretty much everyone is drunk. Not the best way to acquire sympathy for animals; people look, possibly get aroused, make a joke, and keep walking. I was too shy to voice my concerns to the group, and decided instead that if it ever held such a demonstration while I was a member, I simply would not attend.

At what was perhaps my second or third PALS meeting, we discussed what to do at the next First Friday, which, if memory serves, was to take place in July. We wanted to call attention to the new vivisection lab that had just opened at ASU, on Fifth and Van Buren. We decided to do a dramatic display, and somehow it was decided (perhaps because I was the newest member and they wanted to "break me in," so to speak) that I would be at the center of this display. I was to be strapped to a board and affixed with various tubes running from my throat down into a jar full of blood-colored liquid.

So far, so good, I thought. Seeing a person strapped to a board and connected to tubes isn't sexy; it's sad. *That* was the emotion we wanted to convey, after all: that letting animals suffer like this, needlessly and with our tax dollars at stake, is *sad*. We also had information to distribute about alternatives to animal testing, which satisfied my nerdy, über-logical sweet tooth.

Then a discussion about my wardrobe began. One member started talking about flesh-colored mesh, underwear, and other looks-like-she's-naked types of clothing. I felt my heart race a bit as I struggled to force myself to object. I breathed a deep sigh of relief as a more senior member of the group took the words right out of my mouth: "I'm concerned about over-sexualizing the victim."

I ended up wearing a hospital gown for the demonstration, and it was a HUGE success. While the lab is still open, and people still work there, the community was struck by our presentation and many people approached us to ask questions and attain our literature. They got the message—and I'm pretty sure nobody got hard.

It's unfortunate that anyone should have to worry about these petty human tendencies when attempting to address the mass imprisonment and slaughter of nonhumans, but we do. Ideally, people would see a human in a tray and be reminded of the plight of nonhumans and nothing else, but we are not living in an ideal world. Sexism is real, and we must take care not to distract from the nonhumans' story by opening ourselves up to objectification. Think back to *Being and Effective Ally*; while it's a shame that so many humans still object to being compared directly to nonhumans, we must acknowledge that racism is real and not allow the story of the animals to be overshadowed by an unnecessary comparison that can be interpreted as racist, or call to mind racism-based trauma.

Aside from the attire, I think another reason the animal testing demonstration may have been more effective than human-in-a-plastic-case demonstrations is that this one expressed what animals endure in science labs *while they're still alive*. By contrast, once an animal's corpse has been chopped up and wrapped in plastic, the victim is already dead. So putting a live human in such conditions isn't quite the proper analogy. Wrapping humans with wire fences, by contrast, as Animal Place farm sanctuary did during its Brave the Cage demonstration at Lake Merritt, Oakland on March 28th, 2015, is a great way to illustrate just how confined farmed animals are *while they are still alive*. Many humans find it difficult to stand shoulder-to-shoulder with other humans in a wire "cage" for even five minutes; this experience truly drives home the suffering inherent in being in such close quarters for one's entire life.

While pretending to be nonhuman animals is a method that, used with caution, *can* work, I still personally feel that it's preferable to show *real* nonhuman animals whenever possible. It is commonly said in nonhuman animal liberationists circles that we give "a voice to the voiceless," but that isn't entirely true; nonhumans *do* have voices—they just don't speak in human tongues. Our task, then, is not to provide a voice to the "voiceless," but to *elevate their voices*—to enable nonhumans to be heard by an ever-widening audience. We should, as much as possible, default toward letting the animals "speak for themselves." This can be done via imagery, such as photos and videos showing them living joyfully and naturally with their families, as well as via audio, such as at DxE's Silenced Voices demonstration in 2014, during which sounds from a factory farm were played—including a pig being castrated and a cow's horns being sheared off with a hot iron. Silenced Voices is my favorite of all DxE demonstrations in which I have participated for this very reason. Consumers of animal byproducts were confronted with the screams of terror and pain resulting directly from their consumption "choices."

What works: **Taking questions seriously—demonstrating willingness to talk about alternatives.**

Most people I know personally who claim to "sympathize with" or "support" the Animal Liberation Movement while still engaging in behaviors that directly *jeopardize* the movement aren't cruel or insensitive people; they simply uphold the belief that things are the way they are because they *need to be.*

For instance, many people believe that it is necessary for us to test on animals in order to save humans from disease. I hope the material provided earlier in this chapter has clarified to any of these individuals who may be reading this book that this is simply not the case. Alternatives to animal testing abound, and are currently being practiced by some of the most noteworthy universities, hospitals, and medical research labs in the world.

Americans who simply can't bear the thought of giving up the *flavor* of meat and dairy are in luck; our cup overfloweth with alternative meats and cheeses. Brands such as Daiya, Follow Your Heart, Vegan Gourmet, Yves, Tofurkey, Field Roast, Heidi Ho, and Smart Deli—just to name a few—have created a wealth of products that taste and feel like meat and cheese. Salami, bacon, cheddar, Monterey Jack, pepper jack, turkey, chicken, mozzarella, Parmesan, beef, duck—we're not just talking one generic "cheese-flavor" or "meat-flavor" here. There are a wealth of flavors and textures from which to choose.

Not all of these things are delicious. For me, good faux bacon has been the hardest to track down. I don't really like *any* of the faux bacon sold in stores and *very few* restaurants do it well, in my opinion. A close second would be good vegan fish, though Nature Vegetarian on Franklin Street here in Oakland makes a mean faux cod clay pot. While many non-vegans use one or two negative dining experiences to justify not making the switch, the same "not all delicious" statute applies to animal-abusive cuisine; not all flesh burgers taste good, on top of which, if the burger were served in its natural state—uncooked and unseasoned—it would be universally considered revolting by humans, because *humans are not designed to eat flesh, and must manipulate the shit out of it in order to make it palatable.* So if you're not vegan, tried some vegan specialty food and didn't like it, I encourage you to try a different one (and don't forget about all those veggies, fruits, and grains you already know and love!).

It's gotten to the point where we now even have alternatives to our *alternatives*! Want to go vegan, but concerned about eating too much soy? Never fear; Daiya brand faux cheeses are tapioca-based, come in many flavors, and actually *melt*. Chao cheeses are coconut-based and all the rage this season in the vegan community. (The company that makes Chao cheese, Field Roast, also has a yummy line of faux deli meats and even mushroom slices, for a quick and easy mushroom sandwich!) Seitan is a great wheat-based meat alternative, with a thick, rough texture that can easily replicate beef as well as chicken; so hop off the tofu wagon and experiment with seitan instead if you're worried about soy.

This isn't about consumerism, though I know some liberationists will read it as such. The food alternatives are just a fun, cherry-on-top thing to mention; they are not crucial to the movement. No one is going to go vegan solely because of the existence of Chao cheese.

What *is* crucial is that people understand they do not need meat, animal testing, etc. to survive. The veil must be lifted, the lies exposed. If someone says to you, "How can we study lung diseases without using animals' lungs?" and you say "Uhhhhh, I don't know, but it doesn't matter because testing on mice is *mean!*" then you don't have a right to act surprised or affronted when that person doesn't join the movement. The question might not be important to you, or to the movement as a whole, but it's important to the individual, otherwise that individual wouldn't have bothered to ask. You can try to explain that their bodies are not ours to use, but to someone who isn't naturally inclined to respect even the autonomy of all humans much less the autonomy of all sentient beings, such a justification for ending animal testing will sound inadequate and can easily be dismissed.

What's important is not to be able to list all of the faux cheeses available, but to be able to reply, "Organs can be developed on a chip now, so we can make fake lungs that act exactly like human lungs." Even something less specific, such as "There have been great advancements in ways to study diseases that are far more effective than using nonhumans; you should look it up!" may suffice in illustrating to people who ask these questions that you've heard them and are taking them seriously.

Some activists seem almost *afraid* to answer these questions—possibly because they don't know the answers at times, but even when they do, the fear persists that this information somehow detracts from the Moral Imperative: the fundamental truth that all sentient beings have a right to autonomy over their bodies. I personally don't think this is made any less valid or viewed as any less important when I tell people about organs on a chip. I always use the Moral Imperative first, but when people want to get into the nitty-gritty, I go there with them. Why? Because I'm not just interested in talking about what's most important to *me*, I'm interested in *changing minds*.

Please bear in mind that in this instance, I've employed the example of an individual conversation—not a demonstration. What works best amongst individuals may not work so well with respect to movement-building; we'll get to that in just a moment.

What doesn't: **Tugging at people's heartstrings—and refusing to talk about anything else.**

I believe most people do, naturally, sympathize with the plight of animals. Therefore, telling people they should join the Animal Liberation Movement because animal cruelty is, well, *cruel*, is sometimes insufficient. While the Moral Imperative is the most important, most broad-reaching reason that everyone should become an animal liberationist, the sad truth is that this argument alone isn't always enough to sway people. It often yields responses such as:

> Duh—I know cruelty is cruel, which is why I only buy GRASS-FED beef and CAGE-FREE eggs.

Or, an evermore depressing yet surprisingly common response is:

It's the Circle of Life, man! Everything eats something, so I eat animals, and I don't ask where they came from or how they lived.

I can hear my fellow liberationists sighing. We all want so badly to believe that the Moral Imperative is enough, and with respect to *movement-building*, I believe it is. With respect to *individual conversations*, however, focusing for too long on this Moral Imperative while neglecting to talk about practical concerns such as medical advancement has resulted in my driving repeatedly into a brick wall. When you tell people with logical, intelligent counterarguments that those counterarguments simply "don't matter," you lose them. You are now labeled childish, naïve, overly emotional. Your credibility has crumbled.

Individual vs. Movement-Building Strategies

One of DxE's organizing principles is that we *tell stories*—actual stories about real animals with names and photographs. Animals who were destined for slaughter and/or a lifetime of abuse, but who were ultimately rescued by farm sanctuaries and similar organizations. On the TV show *Community*, which once upon a time I liked for five minutes, Jeff Winger once said: "...I can pick up this pencil, tell you its name is Steve, and go like this [snaps pencil in half], and part of you dies just a little bit on the inside."

An inanimate object with a name ceases to be a mere object and becomes personified in your imagination. The same is true with respect to elevating the status of nonhuman animals in human psyches. Errol is not just a chicken to anyone who knows his story—or indeed, even just his name is enough to evoke more sympathy for him than for the countless others just like him in battery cages or filthy sheds all over the world.

In spite of the success of this method with respect to movement-building, as it challenges the pervasive notion that only humans have meaningful life experiences, I do not think it is enough to change every individual mind. Like I said, most people *already* feel sorry for nonhuman animals; perhaps these stories will make them feel sorrier, more personally connected, and ultimately motivated to *do something about it*. Maybe, but there are practical, inescapable realities that this way of thinking fails to address.

For instance, consider the plight of human mothers. I have an immense amount of sympathy for mothers—particularly those who tell me they are interested in the Animal Liberation Movement and wish they could join, but feel that they cannot do so because of their children. Never mind the amount of time having a child takes up in one's day-to-day existence; the primary reason so many mothers I know continue to eat meat and dairy—and feed it to their children—is that they are operating under the misguided notion that *meat is necessary for humans to stay healthy*. Most human mothers would readily choose their own child over some calf they have never met; ergo, as long as mothers believe their children need meat, they will not stop providing it—*no matter how many stories you tell them or how many pictures you show them.*

This is why discussing alternatives with individuals matters. Sure, it makes it about the person, and ideally, we want people to focus on the animals. We want them to take the victim's perspective. We want them to realize that whether or not meat is "good" for them is irrelevant, because it is fundamentally immoral. However, humans, like all other species of life on this planet, are hardwired to engage in behaviors that promote their own survival—even at the expense of other species. The challenge we are faced with is not just to make people feel *sorry* for animals, but also to show people that animal consumption will not only fail to prolong their survival, but will actually *hinder it*, making them more susceptible to illnesses (such as heart disease) and life-threatening occurrences (such as strokes).

It would likely change a human mother's mind more thoroughly to know that giving infants meat and dairy increases their susceptibility to ear infections—which often cause fevers, which, if not reduced quickly enough, can ultimately result in such tragedies as permanent hearing loss and brain damage—than it would to show her a picture of a calf and say, "This calf is just as important as your baby. Whether the statement is true or false is beside the point. The point is that the statement is generally *not effective.*

Most people won't consider vegan living if they think they will have to eat tofu and rice for the rest of their lives and be malnourished and tired. They won't vote to outlaw animal testing so long as they believe it is the only way we can, say, cure cancer or AIDS one day. They just won't. Those are the facts; I didn't create them—I just acknowledge them, as a rational human being. The public needs to be made aware that living a nonhuman-animal-friendly lifestyle is not only *possible*, but also beneficial, while living an animal-abusive lifestyle is incredibly harmful to all sentient beings—including humans.

This isn't compromising; this is *strategizing.*

What I've just said may appear to challenge one of DxE's fundamental tactics, which is that in all demonstrations and movement-building events it is most important to focus on the Moral Imperative against animal exploitation rather than the alternatives to practices that engage in said exploitation. I do in fact agree with this tactic, *with respect to building a larger movement;* however, I cannot fully agree with it on an individual, conversational level, as ample experience speaking with individuals about animal liberation—rather than addressing corporations, the media, and so forth about the issue—has shown me otherwise, and I simply can't ignore my own experiences.

What follows are two poignant examples highlighting the need for flexibility in our approach. The first illustrates how emotional authenticity—upholding the Moral Imperative for animal liberation above all other concerns—can broaden the circle of debate, and is thus a compelling and effective *move-ment-building* strategy. The second is a parable that also upholds the Moral Imperative, but that may be a less effective movement-building strategy and is better suited for one-on-one discourse.

The Crazy Chicken Lady

On September 27, 2014, DxE hosted an International Day of Action. Activists all over the world visited numerous venues profiting from animal exploitation, including restaurants and high-end clothing stores, spreading our message of animal liberation. One disruption that took place in the Bay Area was led by Kelly Atlas. The video from this particular action went viral, and famous conservative Glenn Beck spent approximately twenty minutes on his television show discussing Kelly—referring to her as the "crazy chicken lady." The story was later picked up by both CBS San Francisco and CNN's *On Call*.

In the days that followed, DxE released a video in which Kelly responded directly to Glenn Beck's criticisms; shortly thereafter, Glenn himself released a video responding to Kelly's video. Meanwhile, at that very first event of major press exposure—Glenn's televised segment criticizing Kelly—Glenn could not help but be reminded of a chicken he befriended as a boy, by the name of Charlie.

> I had Charlie the chicken. And it was this nice little chicken and it was my chicken. Well, Grandpa ate my chicken, and I was very upset. He ate my chicken. He took my chicken, and one day, we were eating chicken… And my grandpa said, that's why we don't name our chickens. And he said the whole time, don't name the chickens. Don't name the chickens. He warned me and he's like, Glenn, we eat chickens. This is what we do.

We grow them so we can eat them. This is what we do. We gather their eggs.[29]

The message Glenn seems to have derived from this boyhood experience is: Turn your empathy switch off. Do not personalize nonhuman animals; they are merely tools for production, and not individuals with whom we can form friendships. I don't expect one of the loudest conservative mouthpieces in the country to ever admit it, but I know that deep down, Glenn still feels that pain, that loss. No amount of money, fame, or "success" will ever bring Charlie back.

It was undeniably effective for Kelly to not only *tell an animal's story*, but also to demonstrate *emotional authenticity*: refusing to hide how upset she was about the violence Snow, her adopted hen, had experienced prior to being rescued by Animal Place.

Before Kelly's video went viral, Glenn never talked about DxE. In all likelihood, he didn't know we existed; and if he'd heard of us, he certainly didn't consider us newsworthy. Glenn is not someone who typically engages in conversations about animal liberation or speciesism, but Kelly's emotional authenticity put these issues on the table. Kelly successfully broadened the circle of debate, and while yes, she was characterized negatively as the "crazy chicken lady" (a phrase which implies both speciesism and ableism), she nevertheless increased the movement's level of exposure.

Kelly didn't say a word about vegan alternatives. She didn't mention any of the numerous health benefits of abstaining from animal byproducts. She told a story, arguably tugging at heartstrings, and it *worked*. This is a prime example of why, while talking about alternatives might be more effective in reaching individuals in one's (relatively small) social circle and is therefore something every activist should be prepared to do, "tugging at heartstrings"—focusing on the Moral Imperative—is a more effective *movement-building* strategy.

The Parable of the Liver

While many people wouldn't be willing to engage in a nonhuman-animal-friendly lifestyle if it meant they had to eat tofu and rice forever, some members of DxE and other animal liberationists *would*. Why? As DxE Bay Area organizer Chris Van Breen put it to me one morning, at a metal table in Jack London Square, "Need isn't enough."

> Say you had liver disease, and there was no treatment available to you—you knew, absolutely knew, that without a new liver, you would soon die. Now say you knew someone, or encountered some stranger, who had a perfectly healthy liver that just happened to be compatible with yours. Would it be ethical of you to kill that person and take his or her liver, just because your own life depended on it?

I have said earlier, and it bears repeating, that all species— including human—are programmed to promote their own survival; still, I believe most, if not all people, would reply to the above query that no, they would *not* kill another human being for his or her liver—*even if one's own life depended on it*. This response may well stem from the fact that the individuals in the query are both human—in other words, the response is speciesist.

Here's the rub: in thinking about the "Circle of Life" argument, I feel that in spite of this mind-blowing parable, if I *had* to eat meat...I would. I wish I could say I wouldn't, but I'd be lying. If it were necessary for my survival, I would eat it—just as hyenas and lions eat their prey without experiencing any moral qualms whatsoever. I would probably hunt my prey though, as true carnivores do, so as not to contribute to the prolonged pre-slaughter enslavement of nonhumans.

The parable gnaws on me; I know I wouldn't kill another person for his or her liver. So why would I hunt an animal if I needed his or her flesh to survive? I guess the only way to know for sure whether my position is natural or immoral would be to ask a lion if he or she would kill another lion for his or her liver—which, of course, is impossible. Thankfully, since I know that I don't require meat to survive, I don't have to think about this problem too hard; I start to, let it roll around in my head a bit, then move on to something else when I find myself feeling nauseated. Feel free to do the same.

That morning, still being relatively new to the Bay Area, I was struck by the aptness of DxE's base of operations being located in Jack London Square. I'm not sure whether this location was chosen intentionally, due to the area's namesake, or if that's just a happy coincidence, but I am a great fan of the author/philosopher/sociologist. I was reminded in that moment of this quote of his: "A bone to the dog is not charity. Charity is the bone shared with the dog, when you are just as hungry as the dog." These ideas of sharing our world with nonhumans and equating our needs to theirs ("when you are just as hungry as the dog") ring true to me, and it is these values for which animal liberationists fight. We fight for a world in which we live *amongst* animals—not on top of them. A world in which we accept them as our brothers and sisters—not as our slaves. This is the Moral Imperative we hold so dear, and no discussion of nutrition, animal testing, or any other complex issue should detract from this vision of universal harmony.

In concluding my thoughts on compromising versus strategizing, one important element of the activist strategy that we must bear in mind is to *be flexible.* Tout the moral message first and foremost, as it trumps all other messages; at the same time, we have a responsibility to be educated about alternatives to animal abuse should we face objections from *individuals with whom we converse.* We must be willing to adapt our strategy to our audience, rather than expecting our audience to consistently respond positively to whichever strategy we personally find most compelling.

Back to our regularly schedule programming.

What works: **Making foundational philosophical distinctions, such as welfarist vs. liberationist.**

This distinction is of the utmost importance, as it highlights an objection not just to the poor "treatment" (day-to-day experiences) of nonhuman animals, which can be incrementally rectified, but more importantly, to the *subjugation* and *objectification* of nonhuman animals—which must be outright rejected and is not subject to incremental change. Understanding philosophical differences such as this is paramount to our success as a movement and developing strategies that push us ever forward toward the ultimate goal of animal liberation. Later, we will explore some of the ways in which the welfarist mentality actually directly challenges the liberation of wild (undomesticated) animals (Chapter Seven). Distinctions such as these, as opposed to the semantic hairsplitting that abounds in any social justice movement, are essential to understanding the scope of the Animal Liberation Movement, and serve to clarify rather than confuse the issue.

I must confess that even within this fundamental distinction, there is often confusion. For instance, is an organization that opposes slaughter, yet supports legislation for bigger cages, welfarist or liberationist? I would call them welfarist, but other liberationists have told me recently that they feel such organizations are still liberationist, because they oppose slaughter. In my opinion, however, while I certainly do celebrate welfarist victories (as all of us who love animals must celebrate *anything* that improves their lives), it is far more valuable to focus in all demonstrations, literature, and other outreach opportunities on liberating animals once and for all. This is the more "extreme" approach, and asks the most of the public and our society, which is presumably why it's less popular. For the same reasons, it requires the most effort, while focusing efforts on welfarist initiatives makes it easier for animal abusers to prolong their abuses by providing small comfort to the ethically minded: "*At least* the slaves are more comfortable now." I don't want to waste my time on *at least*. I want to focus on the Big Picture and get us where we need to be ethically *right now*.

I highlight the confusion already inherent in this *necessary* distinction as a prelude to the danger of *unnecessary* distinctions such as the one that follows.

What doesn't: **Reducing the term *veganism* to a plant-based diet, limiting its scope to that of consumer options.**

It may or may not surprise you to learn that some animal activists who engage in a vegan lifestyle and uphold vegan ethics nevertheless object to the term "vegan" itself. One explanation that has been offered is the concern that the word "vegan" makes veganism about the individual's consumer choices, and takes the focus off of the plight of nonhumans. Some modern activists believe that talking about "going vegan" yields discussions dominated by Daiya cheese and MooShoes—discussions that neglect the victim's perspective.

In his 1944 Vegan Society newsletter, Donald Watson defined veganism thus:

> The word "veganism" denotes a philosophy and way of living which seeks to exclude—as far as is possible and practical—all forms of exploitation of, and cruelty to, animals for food, clothing or any other purpose; and by extension, promotes the development and use of animal-free alternatives for the benefit of humans, animals and the environment.[30]

The issue here, then, is not that the word itself is consumerist or objectifying of nonhumans in any way, but that it is often misused or not employed in its fullest sense. The definition of veganism does not refer to animals as commodities, but, rather, does the exact opposite—reinforces the fact that animals are *not* commodities and therefore one must exclude, as much as possible, *all forms of animal exploitation* in one's lifestyle.

Dietary veganism alone definitely isn't enough; truth be told, a "dietary vegan" is not really a vegan at all. I refer to these individuals as *plant-based dieters*. A true vegan, naturally, adheres to a plant-based diet, but this is just one piece of the puzzle. A plant-based dieter who attends circuses, for instance, or who buys leather shoes, is not a vegan. Similarly, I do not consider people to be vegan if they are racist, sexist, or engage in any other negative –ism, regardless of how they regard nonhumans, as veganism upholds the need for respect and justice for *all sentient beings*—including humans.

The fact that individuals and/or corporate entities employ a term improperly doesn't mean we have to throw away the term. While I understand the dismay of those who attest that the term has been coopted by consumerism, I worry that many who are poised to join the movement will not do so because they feel excluded or even overtly antagonized by this rhetorical controversy. Veganism is hardly the first ethical term to be appropriated by marketing firms for financial gain (see: *green*), but the term itself cannot be blamed for this.

In *Circles of Compassion*, author and philosopher Will Tuttle makes plain the fullest, truest definition of veganism behind which one can stand:

> Even though we may be vegan in our outer lives and choices, veganism, we begin to realize, is far more than consumer choices, talking points, and animal rights campaigns. Veganism demands us to question absolutely everything in us that has

been modeled by our cultural programming, and to bring our thoughts and deeds into alignment with a radically more inclusive ethic that calls for respect and kindness for all beings, including our apparent opponents. We see that veganism, as boundless inclusiveness, is the essence of all social justice movements, and that it is the antidote to what ails our world.[31]

I went vegetarian three years before I went vegan, and even after I became vegan, it would be several more years before I'd become an activist. If I hadn't gone vegan, I may never have come to the conclusions I have now come to, and that I am sharing with you. It was through veganism that I found my voice and became an animal advocate; so, in my experience, the goals of veganism and animal activism are intrinsically linked—not opposed.

Forcefully rejecting the term vegan may have the end result of pushing people *out* of, when what we should be doing is *inviting people in* to, the movement. It positions vegans and liberationists on opposite sides of an imaginary spectrum. It implies a hierarchy that doesn't exist. A vegan and an animal liberationist want the same thing, so they should be working together—not squabbling over what to call themselves.

I can't help but be reminded of another *South Park* insight, from the two-part episode "Go, God, Go!" In this episode, Cartman freezes himself and is thawed in the year 2546—a time when all world religions have been abolished and Science alone is subject to worship. In this Brave New Atheistic World, citizens can't agree on what to call themselves. The result of their semantic hairsplitting is a three-pronged war between the Unified Atheist League, the United Atheist Alliance, and the Allied Atheist Allegiance—all of which uphold identical beliefs.

Similarly, vegans (as opposed to plant-based dieters) and animal liberationists believe in the same thing: respecting the autonomy of all sentient beings over their own bodies. So why should we care about what others choose to call themselves, or how others refer to us?

John Sanbonmatsu shared my views on the relative harmlessness of the term "vegan" while suggesting a clever alternative in our December 2014 interview:

> The word "vegan" is rather unavoidable, I think— at least in the context of eating. At the same time, "veganism" is often a weak substitute or placeholder for the broader theme of animal liberation or animal rights. "Veganism," as you know, is associated in many people's minds with one's food preferences, even one's "lifestyle." Being vegan is seen as akin to being gluten intolerant, diabetic, or merely a finicky eater (as in, "Oh, I forgot— you're vegan! Where should we go where you can find something to eat?").
>
> More radical or political "vegans," of course, view veganism more broadly than this, encompassing a variety of other animal rights concerns with that term...
>
> Some years ago, I coined the term "metahumanism" to describe an ideology and praxis of universal freedom for humans and nonhumans: a democratic, feminist, socialist praxis that would include animal liberation at its center. Apparently, though, it was a non-starter; so someone else should think of a way of representing our project to the broader public!

Ultimately, I don't care if a liberationist wants to call him or herself a vegan, or if someone calls me a vegan or a liberationist. I'm willing to meet people where they are; as long as they are fighting for animal liberation, I don't care which word they employ to label themselves. What matters most to me with respect to the term "vegan" is that people define it in the fullest sense, as John mentions "radical or political vegans" do: not as a dietary choice, but as a life-long commitment to abstaining from *all* forms of animal abuse.

Another critique I've encountered about the term vegan relates to its use as a model for social change. Many vegans, myself included, have experienced the Lonely, Isolated Vegan existence: that feeling, even after you've made all the right lifestyle choices and "gone vegan," that you are alone and not really making a difference—that the speciesist machine will just hum along without you. That said, I think it would be a mistake to fault the term itself with this. The definition of veganism is not to blame for the isolated existence of some vegans; isolation is common when you first adopt a way of life outside of the norm. Not only is it harder for those around you, who don't live your lifestyle, to understand you, but it also becomes painful at times for you to be around them, now aware of the violence inherent in acts they commit every day.

The challenge becomes finding a community. It is through community that you can then incite the social change you'd like to see in the world, rather than abstaining from injustice personally while it continues all around you. Activism is one surefire way to meet likeminded people and form new friendships while working toward the creation of a more compassionate society. It is through activism that many isolated vegans find that sense of community and strength they previously lacked, and feel empowered to halt the speciesist machine once and for all.

There is nothing inherent in the word vegan that prevents one from doing this. Like anything else worth doing, all it takes is time, effort, and commitment. Veganism is not antithetical to activism; rather, the two walk quite readily hand-in-hand.

What works: **Coming from a place of love: meeting people where they are.**

I'm a big believer in encouraging people who are making an effort to live more ethically, even when this effort results in different actions than my own. Some people are only just starting to embark on their animal liberation journey; that's why they do things like go vegetarian instead of vegan, or support "grass-fed," "cage-free," and all the other nonsense. No, I don't agree with what they're doing. I *do* appreciate their concern for nonhuman animals and encourage them to keep researching and keep asking questions. The more they learn, I am convinced, the less they will want to support animal cruelty in any of its many guises.

We must also acknowledge and accept that going vegan is not universally "easy." A lot depends on things like *access*; for instance, those living in food deserts, or in the far north where crops are scarce if not altogether nonexistent, face far greater challenges than those of us living near a plethora of grocery stores and farmers' markets. New technologies such as hydroponic indoor growing are promising, but until those are improved upon and made accessible to every community in need, some simply won't be able to "convert" overnight. We must accept this if we truly seek to be an inclusive movement and show respect for all life, including the lives of less privileged humans.

What doesn't: **Coming from a place of hatred: demonizing meat-eaters, slaughterhouse laborers, and other human victims of the Animal Holocaust.**

In Chapter Six, we will examine the Animal Liberation Movement from their perspective in greater detail; I'll just say here that I do sympathize with people who work at factory farms and other such facilities. No one *wants* to kill cows for a living; those who do, do so to support their families, under the misguided belief that there's no other way to do so. Many of them speak little English and/or lack a college education. Many are migrant workers who don't even live in the US full-time. They are not monsters; they are simply underprivileged and uninformed.

In Arizona, I took part in an ongoing campaign concerning JBS Slaughterhouse, located in Tolleson. Over 2,000 cows are slaughtered at this facility daily, and activists visit the facility approximately once a month to host a vigil for these victims. This serves as a reminder to the surrounding community that this facility is literally a house of death. Live creatures go in, and they don't come out.

One thing I don't love about these demonstrations (or some of them, anyway—the group doesn't always do this) is a particular chant that was created to be spoken at JBS. I don't know if it was written by just one person or if it was a collaborative effort. It goes something like this:

"One, two, three, four: open up the cage door; five, six, seven, eight: smash the locks and liberate..."

So far, so good. I agree with both of the above statements—not literally, but metaphorically. We should open the cage door behind which all of these animals are collectively imprisoned, and free them, thus freeing ourselves from our addiction to meat and dairy as well as our blind acceptance of violence against nonhuman animals.

The last line is: "....nine, ten, eleven, twelve: JBS, GO TO HELL!"

I have never recited this line. Why? Because I am no one to condemn *anybody* to Hell. If there is such a place, then there is also such a being as will determine who goes there and who does not. That being is not I. To me, animal liberation is all about showing love and respect to *all fellow creatures*. That includes the slaughterhouse laborer. How can we claim to embrace a kinder, less cruel, less vicious way of life while simultaneously condemning people to Hell?

Meat-eaters are victims, too. They may not be forced to commit violent acts on a daily basis, surrounded by the sights and smells of death, but they are victims nevertheless of both the Myth of Human Supremacy and the Humane Myth. They were, as everyone has been, lied to; they just don't know it yet. They have been culturally encouraged, as everyone has been, to poison themselves regularly with animal flesh; to allow Big Agra to threaten our water supply; to turn their empathy switches off; and so forth. Veganism is, as Will Tuttle said, about *boundless inclusiveness*—compassion and consideration for all sentient beings, including those who believe that there is at least one excuse for animal abuse. Liberationists can articulate the falseness of this belief without actively *hating* anyone—without the use of violent speech or aggressive body language.

Hey, vegans, remember that time *y'all ate meat, too?* Unless you were born and raised vegan, there's blood on your hands, too. Remember that when talking to current "omnivores." You were there once. Would you have responded well to a message delivered with hatred? Or might you have been more inspired to fight for nonhumans by *love?*

The Sound of Silence

In closing, I'd like to share with you an excerpt Elizabeth Costello's first lecture in Coetzee's novel, *The Lives of Animals*:

> Between 1942 and 1945 several million people were put to death in the concentration camps of the Third Reich: at Treblinka alone, more than a million and a half—perhaps as many as three million. These are numbers that numb the mind... In the abstract way, we may be able to count to a million; but we cannot count to a million deaths.

The people who lived in the countryside around Treblinka—Poles, for the most part—said that they did not know what was going on in the camp; said that, while in a general way they might have guessed what was going on, they did not know for sure; said that, while in a sense they might have known, in another sense they did not know, could not afford to know, for their own sake…

I was taken on a drive around Waltham this morning. It seems a pleasant enough town. I saw no horrors, no drug-testing laboratories, no factory farms, no abattoirs. Yet I am sure they are here. They must be. They simply do not advertise themselves. They are all around us as I speak; only we do not—in a certain sense—know about them.[32]

Silence is not an option. Nonhuman animals have already been silenced, their murders carried out miles away from residential areas, behind thick walls and heavy, sound-insulating metal doors. Every day, every minute that we avert our gaze from what we know *must be happening* in order for there to be so much meat and dairy on the shelves, lives are lost in astronomical quantities. Our nonhuman brothers and sisters need us to speak for them, to stand up for them, and to continue to fight for them—until every animal is free.

Chapter Five

Where to Draw the Line?

It's okay to eat fish, cuz they don't have any feelings.

—Kurt Cobain
"Something in the Way," on the 1991 album *Nevermind*

Us vs. Them: Pests

Lice Are People Too!

On March 28, 2014, Kelly invited me to accompany her to Animal Place, an animal sanctuary located in Vacaville, California—about a two-and-a-half-hour drive from DxE's Oakland headquarters. I had just moved to Oakland roughly three weeks prior, and had spent two evenings at DxE house, getting to know my new comrades in arms and getting high on our plans for the Future. My first direct action with DxE Oakland was scheduled for the following day.

While I was looking forward to this first action, I leapt at the opportunity to engage in some hands-on activism with actual animals in need. So much of animal activism involves talking about animals, speciesism, factory farming, and so forth in the abstract. We use photographs and tell stories in an effort to spark emotional and personal connections with our audience; still, the fact remains that most Americans have not spent a great deal of time with cows, pigs, and chickens—the animals who we've been taught since childhood are food, not friends. I certainly didn't spend a whole lot of time around farmed animals as a kid, except during some of the summers I spent in Puerto Rico, but even then I don't recall meeting reps of many different species.

As soon as I met Kelly, she informed me about her work with Animal Place, which consisted of rescuing abused and/or exploited animals, performing health checks on the animals, and helping them find permanent homes. All adopters of animals from Animal Place are required to sign a contract forbidding them from ever selling or murdering their new friend, while the intensive interview and screening process aim to ensure that applicants have the means with which to provide comfortable and loving homes for the victims.

It was a sunny, breezy day in northern California. Delicate slivers of sunlight peeked out from behind whimsical cumulus clouds and stretched downward to greet the undulant, verdant hills—the verdant-est I'd ever seen, probably. The clouds teased us with their subtle art form—here a glimpse, there a glimpse. The view outside of my window might have been Ireland.

Kelly got lost ten minutes in, and about half an hour in I desperately had to pee; still, we made pretty decent timing. On the way, she explained to me her thoughts about the word vegan, as discussed above, and I was grateful for her insights. We were expecting the new arrivals at 1 p.m.; they in fact did not reach Animal Place until well after 3 p.m. This left me with more than a couple of hours to observe last week's flock, a plethora of white hens kept in a large fenced-in area with a rectangular cabin of sorts in it. The cabin had two long walls, but no short walls or doors, so the chickens could wander in and out to their hearts' content.

Before this experience, if someone had asked me, "What does a happy chicken look like?" I would have laughed heartily. I know enough about animals in general and animals used for food in particular to know intellectually that yes, chickens *can* be happy. Still, I never imagined I'd be able to actually *see* what that meant. That one could easily tell the *difference* between a happy chicken and an unhappy chicken—that their emotions were so *palpable*, so *readable* to me—was a revelation. I was awestruck.

Here, before me, after me, to my left, to my right, and OOPS! almost under my foot, were the happiest chickens I had ever seen. They scratched and dug at the dirt. They took dust baths—sometimes on their own, sometimes in groups of two or three or even five—rolling around in the dust and kicking dirt, grass, and hay onto themselves. They made the most adorable gargling noises. One bold little hen even dared to lay an egg right in Kelly's lap, using her bent knees and tucked-in feet as a nest.

I was surprised not only by the obviousness of the chickens' happiness, but also by its relatively swift emergence. They had, after all, only been rescued a week ago. Surely they must still be traumatized? Thankfully, chickens are apparently much more resilient than humans, and while Kelly informed me that many of the chickens had in fact been traumatized upon rescue, they seemed to be doing much better now.

(I did learn some months later, while assisting in a "de-clumping"—separating chickens when they clustered together at night—that just one of what I'm sure are many emotional tolls of having been oppressed as they were is that recently rescued hens, not accustomed to having so much space and undoubtedly startled by their new surroundings, often pile on top of each other post-rescue and can suffocate during the night. After another AP rescue, four hens died from suffocation.)

Aside from emotional trauma, a lifetime of exploitation leaves marks. Many of the hens had been debeaked. I watched helplessly as one hen tried several times to dig a worm from the ground and eat it, only to push it farther and farther away from her with her longer lower-beak, unable to snag the little fellow without the help of her upper-beak, which had been stolen from her. I felt both for her—frustrated, hungry, and confused—and for the worm, whose life was now hanging on by a thread. She had clipped him in the gut, so he could not squirm away; he flailed about, suffering and, if at all possible for a worm, undoubtedly frightened.

The Circle of Life, disrupted.

Before anyone asks, "But if she *had* eaten the worm, wouldn't that be murder?" I'd like to remind you all that she was *sucking him out of the ground*; she did not have to boil him or skin him or season him in order to consume him. That's not what *real* carnivores do; those are things only *humans*, who are incapable of consuming raw flesh due to their herbivorous design, do in order to make something inedible taste and feel edible.

Around 3:15, the recue team pulled into the yard and instructed us to follow them up the hill, where 300 brown hens would be health-checked and kept in a separate—MASSIVE—barn while they were treated. Upon approaching the transport truck, I was shocked at how *quiet* it was. I had expected a cacophony of clucks, cheeps, and gurgles to emerge from a truck weighted down with 300 hens; but they were silent.

As we unloaded the crates, it did not take long for me to realize why these ladies were so quiet while their white counterparts downhill were—literally and figuratively—kicking up so much dust. These girls had just been recued this morning; before that, their lives were pure misery, and they had no way of knowing while riding in the back of the truck that their struggle would soon be over. Hens cuddled close together, voluntarily smushing themselves into corners in spite of the ample room the crates afforded them. They resisted as we removed them, but once we held them, for the most part, they were still. This was convenient and even enjoyable for us, as it not only made health-checking easier, but also allowed us to cuddle and stroke the birds.

(I did find it depressing to see how lackadaisical some of them were about being handled by humans. They had lost the will to fight. They no longer cared what was going to happen to them. Grim resolve had replaced their fear.)

Health-checking consisted of checking the chickens' crops for stiffness, an indication that they may be either overfed or underfed; checking their mouths for sores; checking their feet for swelling, discoloration, or other signs of infection; and checking their feathers for lice. Large colonies of lice eggs were chopped from their feathers, while each chicken was dusted post-health-check with lice-killing powder. Then, the healthy or reasonably healthy chickens were set free from the barn to eat and drink outside, while those with severe health problems were kept in separate barn stalls while Jackie consulted a vet over the phone and administered medication.

I particularly enjoyed the end of the health-check routine with respect to reasonably healthy girls; I loved opening the barn door for them, spreading my arms out at an angle so that they could roll gently out of my arms and into the sunshine, and singing merrily, "Enjoy your freedom!" I felt sorry for those who couldn't join in the fun right away, but grateful to know that they would soon enough.

Everyone complained about the lice, and sympathized with the girls for having them, myself included; except that I couldn't shake the eerie feeling that we were rescuing one animal at the expense of another. We were, after all, killing the lice. Is it really right for us to choose the hens over the lice? Is that not the moral equivalent of having a dog you love, and protesting against dog fighting, while eating fried chicken or a burger for dinner?

I'm unsure of the ethical line to be drawn here with respect to chickens, as we made this executive decision for them. The chickens weren't killing the lice; *we* were killing the lice. I don't know if we had the right to make that choice, but I'm sure the chickens were grateful.

The second question I can answer with certainty: No. No, it is not the moral equivalent of respecting dogs and exploiting cows. Why? Because *cows aren't hurting anyone*. Cows are decidedly not pests. They do not hinder our own existence in any way.

When relating humans to cows, humans are the threat; when relating chickens to lice, lice are the threat.

I lived in Harlem for most of my adult life, having attended Columbia University from 2004–2008 and then remaining in the Harlem/Washington Heights area until a romantic relationship brought me to Arizona in 2013 and California the following year. One of the rooms I rented in Washington Heights shortly after graduation became infested with bedbugs. They feasted on me at night, and while at first I dismissed the bites I noted the next morning as being mosquito or spider bites, I was rudely awakened at 2 a.m. one morning to find bites covering every inch of my flesh. I felt feverish, and ran to the bathroom for a long, cold shower. The next day, I informed my landlord, who instructed me to place a phone call, which would result in a visit from an extermination team.

I didn't think twice about it. I called. I had them come. I let them kill every one. I didn't even feel a little bit bad about it. Not at all.

Why? Because when it's US vs. THEM, we have every right to choose US. Every living thing on the planet operates in this fashion, rejecting that which is harmful to it while actively seeking that which is beneficial. I could not live amongst the bedbugs; it was impossible. Nor could I relocate them or put them up for adoption. This wasn't me *creating* an Us vs. Them dynamic; I was compelled to acknowledge, and hastily adapt to the fact, that there already *was* an unavoidable Us vs. Them dynamic.

I imagine it's the same with hens and lice. I comforted myself over the death of the lice by imagining that being covered in lice felt to the hen the way being covered in bedbugs had felt to me. The only difference is that while I made the choice for myself—*I choose my own ability to survive over the lives of these bedbugs*—the hens were incapable of making such a decision. We made it for them. Did we have the right? Maybe; maybe not.

Do I still believe that the work we did at Animal Place that day resulted in more good than harm? Absolutely.

We can't expect ourselves to be morally perfect, because the world we live in is not morally perfect and we haven't anywhere else to live. All we can do is our best.

What Constitutes a Pest?

I personally define "pest" as *any creature that poses a direct threat to our own survival.* This definition may appear broad at first glance, but the key word here is *direct.* Lions, although carnivorous and therefore *capable* of posing a threat to us humans, are not pests because they do not do so as a matter of course. If you are in a lion's way and he or she is hungry, he or she will likely eat you, but humans are rarely the first choice for any carnivore. We are also a formidable threat, as animals have learned over the centuries that humans have things like guns and trucks, nets and poisons, with which to defeat them. (Okay, poisoning is a harder thing to prove or consciously remember, but when most nonhuman animals see a gun, I'm sure they know what that means: *time to go!*)

So, no, a lion is not a pest, nor is a hyena or any other natural carnivore. Bedbugs, lice, and mosquitos, by contrast, are pests. These creatures literally live off of human suffering; they are real-life vampires. They are bloodsuckers. They will not stop sucking your blood for any reason; they will continue to do so no matter how much you suffer or how much else is available to them for consumption. They *love* to drink your blood—and you have every right, in an effort to preserve your own survival, to use any means necessary to prevent them from doing so.

What about mice? To me, these are not pests, as they do not actually inhibit our survival; they are simply nuisances. There are tons of humane ways to get rid of unwanted mice in your home, without calling an exterminator or using poisons. A quick Internet search for the phrase, "humane mouse traps," will tell you all you need to know about this. Unlike the bedbug situation, were I ever to find myself with a mouse problem in my home, I would *not* call an exterminator. The mice invading my home would be no (or little) different from the mice currently being used in scientific laboratories. How could anyone reasonably object to testing on mice while consenting to domestic mouse extermination?

Nirvana was Being Sarcastic: The Truth about Fish

Over one trillion (1,000,000,000,000) fish are murdered worldwide every year.[1] If I had a dollar for every time I heard someone say he or she was "vegetarian, but I eat fish"—or employ the nonsense term *pescatarian* at me—I could have retired at age twenty-two. It never ceases to amaze me how so many people can come to the conclusion that exploiting and murdering land animals is wrong, yet continue to make an exception for ocean life. The only excuse I can come up with for this is that these people are concerned about their health. They've heard that eating "too much meat is bad for you," and once upon a time someone decided that fish, lobster, and other ocean-derived flesh is "not meat."

Still, even this reasoning falls short to me, because fish have been proven, over and over again, to actually *not be super-healthy for humans at all.* Yes, they are lean, but their bodies also contain mercury, sharp bones on which it is easy to choke, and so forth. Shellfish allergy is among the most common "food-related" allergies in America and the number one food allergy amongst American adults (2% of the adult population).[2]

Here, I will share some valuable information with you about the intelligence, emotionality, and socialization of various forms of ocean life, in an effort to convince these pesky pescatarians to either stop eating sea creatures altogether or to stop referring to themselves as "vegetarians who eat fish" and admit that they are just as "carnivorous" (*by choice*, as no human is naturally carnivorous) as people who eat chickens or cows.

Do Fish Feel Pain?

The study "Can Fish Really Feel Pain?" was published in late 2012, conducted by scientists from Europe, Australia, Canada, and the US. This study was prompted by an animal protection act passed in Germany the previous month, outlawing the killing or infliction of severe pain on vertebrates "without due cause."

It is not illegal to eat animals in Germany; therefore, this protection act is effectively worthless, anyway. Killing an animal to eat is not "due cause"—unless you are truly starving, and even then many animal liberationists would argue that it is not acceptable. Passing a law that implies there is ever "due cause" to kill someone doesn't bring us any closer to true animal liberation than a law stipulating how large a nonhuman captive's cage ought to be or how much time he or she should be allowed to spend outside per day prior to being murdered.

The study found that, as the title suggests, fish do not feel pain as humans do; they lack the "neuro-physiological capacity for a conscious awareness of pain." Fish do not possess a neocortex, and larger fish such as sharks do not possess C-nociceptors, nerve fibers found in mammals that "…have been shown to be involved in the sensation of intense experiences of pain." Now, here's where it gets interesting: "…all bony fish—which includes all common types of fish, such as carp and trout—*very rarely have them.*"[3]

I'd like to make two important observations regarding the previous paragraph. The first is with respect to the fibers found in *mammals* that are associated with pain. Fish aren't mammals; therefore, is it really such a surprise that they would have none— or fewer—of these receptors? Is this not an indication that they can't feel pain but rather an indication that they do not feel it *as mammals do?* The argument is structured to heavily imply that fish feel no pain at all. The lack of fibers similar to those found in mammals is not, in itself, a strong enough argument to convince me personally that fish do not feel pain.

Now let's talk about *very rarely*. The article does not define this any more clearly. The matter is given minimal attention, and then abandoned. What does *very rarely* mean? Only some fish have them? Many fish have them, but only one or two, whereas mammals have many more? Let's pretend for a moment that *very rarely* is to be interpreted in its most extreme sense—say, one in a million fish possess these receptors. So what? We have no way of knowing whether a fish we are eating possessed these receptors or not. So, even assuming these receptors *are* necessary for the sensation of pain, and even supposing only *one in a million* fish possess them, we still shouldn't be eating fish, because we cannot possibly know by sight alone which fish have these vital pain receptors and which do not.

If a million people are in a room together, and all but one of them is guilty of a crime punishable by death (another travesty of our society, but that's a story for another book), but we don't know which of the million people is innocent, do we kill all million people? Is the innocent person's life not valuable, and is he or she not entitled to it? Is one innocent man's death "not a big deal"?

What about that of one innocent fish? Or a million innocent fish?

Let us not get too wrapped up in this model, and remind ourselves for a moment that a fish with pain receptors is no more "innocent" than a fish without them is "guilty." The matter of pain receptors is ultimately irrelevant, as ample other evidence suggests that whether fish have these anatomical similarities to us or not, they are still capable of feeling…something very negative.

In her book, ***Do Fish Feel Pain?***, author and biologist Victoria Braithwaite says that "there is as much evidence that fish feel pain and suffer as there is for birds and mammals."[4] When

Braithwaite and her team exposed fish to irritating chemicals, the fish exhibited behaviors that are indicative, if not of pain in the human sense, at the very least suffering—they lost their appetites, their gills beat faster, and they rubbed the affected area against the side of the tank.

Aside from this behavioral evidence, Braithwaite discusses the biological fact that, while fish do not have a neocortex, they *do* have nervous systems. These complex nervous systems include neurotransmitters such as pain-relieving endorphins. Why would any animal naturally produce painkillers if he or she were incapable of experiencing pain?

Peter Singer addresses both behavioral evidence of pain and the production of painkillers in fish in his article, "Fish: The Forgotten Victims on Our Plate," published in *The Guardian* in 2010:

> When fish experience something that would cause other animals physical pain, they behave in ways suggestive of pain, and the change in behavior may last several hours. (It is a myth that fish have short memories.) Fish learn to avoid unpleasant experiences, like electric shocks. And painkillers reduce the symptoms of pain that they would otherwise show...

> Last year, a scientific panel to the European Union concluded that the preponderance of the evidence indicates that fish do feel pain.

> Why are fish the forgotten victims on our plates? Is it because they are cold-blooded and covered in scales? Is it because they cannot give voice to their pain? Whatever the explanation, the evidence is now accumulating that commercial fishing inflicts an unimaginable amount of pain and suffering.[5]

Scientists have mapped over twenty "nociceptors" in fish. Unlike pain receptors, as these are misidentified in PETA's article "Fish Feel Pain,"[6] *nociceptors* detect "noxious tissue-damaging stimulus and [the detection] is sometimes accompanied by a reflex response, such as withdrawal."[7] So while the existence of these nociceptors may not prove that fish feel *pain* as we understand it, they nevertheless detect harmful substances in their vicinity, and this detection often results in signs of distress and discomfort. The majority of these receptors are found in a fish's head and mouth.

Despite its misidentification of nociceptors, PETA's article shares a valuable insight, courtesy of Scottish scientist Dr. Ian Duncan: while fish do not possess a neocortex, "we have to look at behavior and physiology. It's possible for a brain to evolve in different ways. That's what is happening in the fish line. It's evolved in some other ways in [other] parts of the brain to receive pain."

Another notable tidbit from the article:

> A study in the journal Applied Animal Behaviour Science found that fish who are exposed to painful heat later show signs of fear and wariness— illustrating that fish both experience pain and can remember it.

It's tough to know whether we should be using the word *pain* or *discomfort* here, as that which we believe to be necessary for pain in mammals is not present in fish, but as Dr. Duncan pointed out, we know enough just by observing their behavior in various circumstances to understand that fish are definitely capable of *suffering*. Whether their suffering is comparable to that of mammals or not is irrelevant; that they are capable of experiencing any form of suffering or discomfort at all is reason enough for us to leave them alone.

Now let's take a look at some non-fish members of the ocean community. Lobsters, unlike mammals, do not possess a centralized brain area; however, they do possess ganglia throughout their bodies. *Ganglia* are clusters of nerve cells; in lobsters, the largest of these clusters can be found both above and below the mouth. Invertebrate zoologist Dr. Jaren Horsley asserts that lobsters "have a sophisticated nervous system that, among other things, allows them to sense actions that will cause harm…[Lobsters] can, I am sure, sense pain."[8]

A *Washington Post* article titled "Do Lobsters and Other Invertebrates Feel Pain?" explains that a team of researchers at Queen's University in Belfast, led by Dr. Robert Elwood, tackled the question of whether oceanic invertebrates such as lobsters, crabs, and prawns could feel pain by first taking a look at their behavior. As noted by both Braithwaite and Singer with respect to fish, the Queen's U team noted that shelled ocean life exhibits responses similar to pain when exposed to noxious stimuli; however, some scientists argue that these responses are mere reflexes and not sufficient evidence to prove that lobsters and the like truly feel pain.

Washington Post correspondent Tamar Stelling described the difference between a pain response and a reflex as follows:

> …when an animal responds to something we would consider painful, it does not necessarily mean the animal is in pain. The response might be a simple reflex, where signals do not travel all the way to the brain, bypassing the parts of the nervous system connected with the conscious perception of pain. When we scald our hand, for example, we immediately—and involuntarily—pull it away. Pain is the conscious experience that follows, once the signals have reached the brain. The key for Elwood was to look for responses that

went beyond reflex, the crustacean equivalents of limping or nursing a wound.[9]

Elwood's team did just that. While the details of his study are admittedly depressing, I for one believe that ultimately, if this study can prove once and for all that these animals *do* suffer and thus lead to the end of their suffering (at least, that which is imposed upon them by humans), perhaps it was worth it. This was not a case of animal testing for humans' sake but rather a rare instance of animal testing for animals' sake. Dr. Elwood and his team applied brief electric shocks to various parts of the bodies of crabs, and brushed a small amount of acetic acid on the antennae of prawns. In both cases, the resulting observable behaviors proved to be more complex and prolonged than any reflex could be.

Reflexes are characterized primarily by their **immediate** and **involuntary** nature. The crabs who were exposed to the brief shocks rubbed the affected area for long periods of time, while the prawns employed complex, prolonged movements with their front legs in an effort to groom their antennae and remove the irritant. When anesthetic (*pain suppressant*) was applied to some prawns prior to the acetic acid treatment, this grooming behavior greatly diminished—a strong indication that the prawns who engaged in this grooming behavior did so as a direct result of pain and/or discomfort, from which the latter group of prawns was spared. As these behaviors were neither immediate (they were observed over long periods of time, rather than only upon initial application of the shock or irritant) nor involuntary (due to both their complexity and longevity), they do not qualify as reflexes.

Both the prawns and the crabs would also, every so often, contract and contort their limbs in complex and unusual ways after their respective treatments. "This is prolonged and complicated behavior, which clearly involved the central nervous system," Elwood declared.

Evolutionary neurobiologist Robyn Crook at the University of Texas has been studying the question of pain in cephalopods, such as squids and octopi. Her team has determined that these creatures, like fish, possess nociceptors; and an octopus demonstrates pain in a manner very similar to that of mammals, grooming and favoring injured body parts while reacting violently and/or fearfully (by, say, squirting ink or swimming hurriedly away) should they be poked or prodded in an injured area. Squids, while also possessing nociceptors, demonstrate pain in a manner distinct from both that of mammals and that of their close cousins, octopi. When a squid is injured, nociceptors do not become active solely at the site of injury, but, rather, are activated throughout the squid's body. This suggests that when a squid feels pain, regardless of the location of the source, he or she feels pain *everywhere*.

Can Fish Feel Fear?

Issue 11 (Spring/Summer 2004) of *CCSAW News*, produced by The Colonel K.L. Campbell Centre for the Study of Animal Welfare at the University of Guelph in Ontario, Canada, speaks directly and thoroughly on this issue (whereas many other sources confound the assessment of fear in fish with discussions of *pain* in fish, rather than regarding these as two distinct capabilities). Stephanie Yue, a U-Guelph PhD student at the time, alongside professors Richard Moccia and Ian Duncan, studied various characteristics of sentience among domesticated rainbow trout. The team was primarily interested in both the learning and memory capacity of fish—both of which form strong indications of fear, as it is through learning that one comes to understand whether something should be feared or not in the first place, and through memory that one is able to exhibit the same fear-responses upon exposure to a fearful element a second, third, or eighth time. One must have both reasons learned for fearing an entity and memories retained of encountering said entity (or a similarly fearsome entity) in order to exhibit fear responses (*That's fire, and I'm scared to touch it because it is very hot; I remember that the last time I touched fire it burned me, and I didn't like it—so this time I will avoid it*).

The U-Guelph team's first experiment focused on proving capacity for fear in fish more generally:

> The fish were shown a frightening stimulus (a fish net was plunged into the tank) and were given the opportunity to escape through a door to an adjacent tank. The fish quickly escaped. They were then shown a light 10 seconds before the net came into the water. Over a 5-day period, all the fish learned to avoid the plunging net by escaping when the lamp was illuminated. Interestingly, after a 7-day period without testing, the fish responded to the light in the same way, suggesting the capacity for longer-term memory. Rather than being immediate and reflexive-like, these responses were more deliberate in nature, which may indicate that trout's avoidance responses are motivated by fear.[10]

Already this experiment tells us a lot about fish's capacity for learning and memory, ultimately revealing that they are in fact capable of experiencing fear. For starters, the fact that the trout reacted negatively at all to the presence of the net implies that they had already *learned to fear nets*, as the net was not used to cause the fish any physical harm whatsoever and was merely plunged into their environment. Secondly, the last two sentences of the above excerpt reaffirm what was said of reflex versus deliberate action in our discussion of pain in fish: fish not only have the capacity for pain—and fear—but also the ability to *remember it* and *deliberately avoid it*. These are not thoughtless, automated reflexes but rather *conscious decisions made by fish to promote their own survival.*

Our poor, shocked crustaceans were responding to memories of pain; our domesticated trout, while never hurt by the net being used in the experiment, may have been doing the same. Perhaps they remember that fateful day on which they were caught from wild waters and thrown into tanks; or perhaps they recall, while in captivity, a net having been used to remove a deceased member of their community, and have come to associate nets with death as well as imprisonment. In any case, never having been caused *pain* by the nets, their responses indicate a greater depth of critical thinking than that of crabs who know better than to get shocked twice. Who knew that fish could even *think*, let alone *think critically?*

In response to these findings, skeptics argued that the fish were merely swimming away instinctively, due to a disruption in their environment—not responding specifically to the net itself but rather to the plunging motion and ripping of the water. Further exploration was therefore necessary to quell such critiques.

In 2008, the *Journal of Applied Animal Welfare Science* published the results of the second study conducted at U-Guelph with the trout back in 2004.[11] In this study, the fish were first trained to press a pendulum for a food reward, thus creating a new positive association between the pendulum and food. They were then, as in the first study, trained to accept a light source as a prelude to a plunging net. Finally, this light was shined on the fish *when they pressed the pendulum.* The U-Guelph team was eager to see whether or not the introduction of the light upon pressing the pendulum would deter fish from pressing it, thus confirming their ability to associate a fearful stimulus with a new situation. The trout's ability to remember what the light signifies even after having been trained to think that the pendulum is a "good thing" would speak highly of both the endurance of their memories and the *deliberate* (non-reflexive) nature of their actions.

It worked. The mean rate at which the pendulum was pressed dropped from 3.6 to 2.9 upon the introduction of the light; and when the light was left on after an extended period of pendulum-pressing, no other fish pressed the pendulum until the light was turned off. In three-minute periods prior to turning the light on, the pendulum was pressed an average of 14.3 times; once the light was turned on after a press and remained lit, the average rate dropped to 0.1 time (meaning that over several such three-minute periods, no fish pressed the pendulum and during some of these occasions, perhaps one fish pressed it).

Granted, not all fish were intelligent enough to even participate in the study; of the ten initially selected for study, four remained unable to learn the pendulum-pressing task after five or more training sessions. These fish were then omitted from the study, and the successful six remained. Thus, it appears that—as is the case with humans, dogs, pigs, and all other sentient beings—intelligence in fish varies according to the individual. Still, over half of the selected fish were able to learn the task—some in as few as two training sessions.

I definitely know several humans who have been taught not once, but twice, how to do something—and still can't do it. Me and bike riding, for instance. Yes, I went to an Ivy League school and I run my own business, and here I am writing a book, but I can't ride a bike to save my life. Two different people, at different times in my life, have tried to teach me. Both failed. Judging distances by sight alone just isn't my wheelhouse, and I lack the coordination with which to respond physically to visual stimuli in a quick and efficient manner (I'm also a pretty bad catcher, and I'm doing the world a HUGE favor by not seeking a driver's license).

So, to sum up: The U-Guelph studies confirm that a) fish are capable of learning to fear something and, therefore, to avoid it; and b) fish are capable of retaining this knowledge over the span of days, as well as in spite of the introduction of conflicting knowledge (being "told" that the light means snack time after having learned that the light means net time). In other words, not only can fish *fear*, but also they can *learn* and *remember*—for far longer than just a few seconds.

Do Fish Have Social Lives?

In a 2003 issue of the journal *Fish and Fisheries*, biologists Calum Brown, Kevin Laland, and Jens Krause asserted that there had been huge changes in science's understanding of the psychological and mental abilities of fish at the turn of the century, and that fish were in fact highly intelligent—and highly social—creatures. The experts hail from the universities of Edinburgh, St. Andrews, and Leeds in Europe.[12]

> Now, fish are regarded as steeped in social intelligence, pursuing Machiavellian strategies of manipulation, punishment and reconciliation, exhibiting stable cultural traditions, and co-operating to inspect predators and catch food.

These biologists published a collection of essays written in the nineties and early 2000s regarding intelligence, socialization, and overall sentience in fish. They then proceeded to summarize important points about fish, using these studies to support their claims. Among the points for which this tremendous trio was able to find ample justification in recent research are:

- That fish are able to **identify individual shoal-mates** and **monitor the social prestige of others.** (Yes, apparently it is possible to be a prestigious fish.)

- That fish **use tools.**

- That fish **build complex nests and bowers,** similar to the bowerbird discussed in Chapter Two.

Lee Alan Dugatkin's 1997 book, *Cooperation Among Animals,* explores various social behaviors observed in fish. Among these are cooperative foraging, intraspecific cleaning, schreckstoff, and mobbing behavior.[13]

Cooperative foraging is typically the result of territorial defense, in fish as well as in many other species. A good example in the fish community is the relationship between sergeant major damselfish and those who prey upon them—members of the Labridae and Serranidae families, such as cleaner wrasses, sea basses, and groupers. Male sergeant major damselfish become hyper-aggressive when tending eggs, changing color from white to dark blue or indigo. They defend their territory by nipping at fish and divers who invade their space. While these activities do not require cooperation, foragers of damselfish eggs (such as sea basses) must cooperate in order to succeed against these formidable foes.

What this boils down to is that fish are not only capable of cooperating with one another—proof positive that their lives are not solitary, but social—but also possess sufficient intelligence to discern when cooperation is necessary for success. Fish do not always cooperate in order to forage, but when confronted with a daunting obstacle between themselves and a desirable resource, they will team up for the sake of achieving a common goal. Humans behave in much the same way; on a daily basis, we typically do things by ourselves, with minimal cooperation amongst our friends, relatives, and coworkers. When trying to achieve something too difficult for just one person, such as curing a disease or constructing a building, we form large teams—organizations, companies, committees, and so forth.

Intraspecific cleaning refers to the practice of cleaning the bodies of others. Many mammals, for instance (such as monkeys), remove parasites from each other's bodies. This behavior has been observed among carp, guppies, Panamic sergeant majors, bluegill sunfish, and other species of fish.

Schreckstoff was originally observed by Austrian ethologist Karl von Frisch in 1938, as a chemical alarm signal emitted by minnows. R. J. F. Smith defined this chemical signal in a 1992 study as, "A response produced by an individual—the 'sender'—reacting to a hazard that warns other animals—the 'receivers'—that there is danger."[14] Since von Frisch's original discovery, schreckstoff has been detected in other fish species besides the minnow, as well as among sea anemones, sea urchins, tadpoles, and even rats. Whether or not this is a social behavior is debatable, as it remains unclear whether fish actually *choose* to sound the alarm or it occurs naturally when a fish is under duress. Still, Smith argues that aside from chemical signals there exist certain auditory, tactile, and visual forms of schreckstoff that require intent to produce.

Mobbing behavior refers to the act of multiple potential prey coming together to attack or harass a potential predator. Dugatkin cites numerous studies in which this behavior has been observed among members of at least five groups of fish: bluegill, butterfly, threespot damsel, blue and gold damsel, and whitebar gregory (yet another subspecies of damselfish). A simple, individually minded creature would merely flee from a predator as quickly as possible, once he or she has determined that a physical confrontation would be unwise; these guys stick together, teaming up against an individual bully. Their concern is not limited to their own safety but extends to that of their *community*.

Critique of Muddled Reason: How the Media Threatens the Movement

While perhaps the least respected victims of the Animal Holocaust, fish have previously been spared from murder in the quantities other animals face due to concerns over whether or not fish consumption is healthy. While misinformation about protein has thoroughly convinced most of the world that humans need land meat for nutritional reasons, concerns about the mercury content of fish flesh in particular has steered many people away from eating fish—without any moral or ethical eyebrows needing to be raised. The question of whether or not it was "okay" to eat fish was irrelevant, because the prevailing attitude of the medical community was to avoid fish consumption *for your own safety*. In 2004, the Environmental Protection Agency released a "seafood advisory" that set upper—but no lower—limits to the amount of fish that various segments of the population should consume.

Some celebrities touted high-fish diets for a while, beginning around the turn of the century, apparently undeterred by the EPA's advisory in 2004, but these were merely desperate weight-loss attempts intended not to improve one's health, but simply to minimize one's daily caloric intake (for some, cholesterol was an additional concern—although some fish, like salmon, are high in cholesterol).

On June 10, 2014, I was shocked to discover that the *New York Times* had published an article entitled, "Health Officials Call for More Fish in Diets of Children and Pregnant Women." I'm ashamed to say I have actually grown accustomed to the Meat Myth at this point, and am never shocked to see an article about how important it is to eat enough land animal flesh—even though scores of doctors and nutritionists (not to mention vegan bodybuilders and professional athletes) have already proven this false. Angry? Sure. Shocked? No. But at least fish were (largely) safe, I thought, because even people who were not compassionate toward animals were at least compassionate toward *themselves* and typically (though not always) avoided that which could hurt them.

Now here's our nation's flagship newspaper telling everyone that it's not only *okay* to eat fish *(cuz they don't have any feelings…)*, but that you *should*—indeed, *need to*—eat fish. Perhaps fish sales have been on the decline, and someone up the food chain (so to speak) is trying to turn that around? Or could there really, actually be a concrete reason that we—especially the young and the pregnant among us—should forgo empathy and feast on the flesh of innocent sea creatures?

From the article:

Dr. Stephen Ostroff, the F.D.A.'s acting chief scientist, said the agency was concerned that pregnant and nursing women were missing out on the benefits of eating fish. He cited studies showing that children born to women who consume fish have higher I.Q.s and better cognitive development than children born to women who do not.

"A large percentage of women are simply not eating enough fish, and as a result they are not getting the developmental and health benefits that fish can provide," he said. "Studies very consistently demonstrate that among women who consumed more fish during pregnancy—or at least the amounts we're currently recommending—that there were improvements in children."[15]

Before we go any further, I'd like to remind everyone that the FDA receives roughly half of its funding from pharmaceutical companies, as the 1992 Prescription Drug User Fee Act requires that any company seeking drug approval pay user fees. Therefore, half of the FDA's funding comes from companies that sell treatments for illnesses and conditions such as Haff disease, high cholesterol, impaired memory, and scombroid poisoning—all of which can be traced back to the salmon, tuna, and other low-mercury sea creatures now being touted as beneficial for children and expectant mothers.

I'm going to go out on a huge, rather precarious limb here and endeavor to illustrate how and why the *New York Times* is dead wrong on this one:

- **PCBs found in fish—including low-mercury fish, such as salmon and tuna—cause memory loss (i.e., mild brain damage) and vertigo, as well as contribute to such devastating conditions as cancer and infertility.**

Comically enough, a *New York Times* article published on July 22, 1984 asserted:

> Predatory fish like lake trout and salmon can have especially high concentrations of PCBs. Because of the cancer risk, pregnant women, nursing mothers, women of childbearing age and young children have been advised in the past to limit their consumption of fish species likely to have high accumulations of PCBs...
>
> "I would advise women of childbearing age not to eat fatty fish like salmon and lake trout at all," said Joseph L. Jacobson, one of the researchers... [of a study published in the journal Developmental Psychology in 1984.][16]

Soooooo I guess we're all just supposed to forget about that now? PCBs don't matter all of a sudden, and mercury is now the only enemy with which fish-eaters must contend? How convenient. Way to flip-flop, *NYT*.

- **Even mild/minimal exposure to mercury can result in both heart and brain damage among fetuses, babies and children.**

Scientists at the Harvard School of Public Health have found that fish consumption can cause heart damage, as well as *irreversible* impairment to brain function in children, both in the womb and as they grow. Professor of environmental health at HSPH and co-editor of the journal *Environmental Health* Philippe Grandjean asserts: "If something happens in the brain at development, you don't get a second chance."[17]

Environmental Protection Agency biochemist Kathryn R. Mahaffey reported in 2004 that *mercury levels in a fetus's umbilical cord blood are roughly 70% higher than those in his or her mother's blood*; therefore, even if an expectant mother's mercury consumption is minimal, the impact it will have on her baby can be severely detrimental.[18]

• **Fish flesh is not the only source of omega-3 fatty acids on the planet.**

In researching this portion of the book, I came across site after site, institution after institution, and publication after publication bowing to the FDA's recent decree by asserting the fact that fish are rich in omega-3 fatty acids—which are indeed a necessary part of a healthy diet. However, fish are not the only source of these essential nutrients, and there are ample sources of omega-3 fatty acids that do not present one with the risk of brain damage, high cholesterol, impaired motor skills, and the like. Such sources include, but are not limited to: *flax seeds, chia seeds, seaweed, winter squash, spinach, broccoli rabe, kale, blueberries, mangoes, honeydew melons, Brussels sprouts, and cauliflower.*

This is why morality must trump all. Whether or not something is "good" for you seems to change every year, every month—sometimes even *every day*. I first heard the question bandied about when I was about five, "Is milk good or bad for you?"—and today, it is still being bandied about.

One cornerstone of the Animal Liberation Movement that will never change is the fact that *these bodies do not belong to us. They are not our property.* When we consume them, we violate them. We disrespect them, and ultimately, we hurt ourselves, our children, and our planet by threatening the endurance of the biological diversity on which our planet so heavily relies. Nutritional hair-splitting can only go so far; it is ultimately the Moral Imperative—rather than any claims made by those pursuing the nutritional sciences—that wields sufficient power to see all animals liberated in our lifetime.

Pets: Captivity or Mercy?

People often ask me at demonstrations if I have any pets. While I do not at the moment, I grew up in a house full of various animals. We always had at least three pets—sometimes as many as seven or eight! When I tell people I do not currently own a pet, the next question is often along the lines of, *Would you own a pet? Do you think people SHOULD own pets?*

The response I give to this line of questioning mirrors that which I had in mind when a gentleman asked PALS at a circus protest, "What do you *do* with a horse?" It's not an ideal solution, but the world is not ideal; all any of us can do is the very best we can with what we know.

Here's what I know: There are hundreds of thousands of dogs, cats, and other domesticated animals currently in shelters or on the street. These animals, having been domesticated over eons, would not survive if thrown into what were once their natural habitats—in the case of a dog, for instance, the wilderness. A domesticated dog would not survive in a forest full of wolves; a domesticated cat would not survive in a jungle or desert populated by wild tigers and lions. These guys would not be able to compete for food, and would maybe become food themselves. They would not be anyone's first choice for mating, and so would gradually die out as a species while their bigger, stronger counterparts continue to mate with one another—and their road to extinction would inevitably be a lonely one, as they would be excluded not only from the sexual, but also from the social activities of their counterparts. They would be outcasts.

Shelters can't afford to feed and house infinite animals indefinitely. Ultimately, thousands of would-be pets are "put down" (murdered) day after day simply because shelters cannot afford to care for them any longer and no one has stepped forward to adopt them.

Based on what I know, here's what I believe: Yes, people should have pets—and they should *adopt* them. The aesthetic preference for particular breeds over other breeds is a vanity paid for in murder and rape. Animals who are "bred" are condemned to a fate similar to that of the dairy cow—constant pregnancy, no baby. They produce litter after litter, watch helplessly as a box full of their children grows emptier and emptier; then, as soon as their bodies are capable of it, they are impregnated once again. Breeding also results in an overabundance of strays, as it is tough to control the size of a litter, and breeders who cannot sell off an entire litter often simply release the "leftover" creatures so as not to pay for feeding and housing them.

There are more than enough nonhuman animals out there *right now* who need homes, without anyone needing to pay top dollar for a puppy or kitten who looks a certain way but who is the product of the immense suffering and exploitation of his or her mother—both of which will continue for as long as you're willing to hand breeders your hard-earned cash. Not only is pet adoption the ethical choice, but it is also the more affordable choice, so if you're looking for a nonhuman companion, I implore you to visit your local animal shelter and adopt someone who needs you most—someone whose life quite literally depends on it. I promise you, a mutt is every bit as capable of exuding love, fun, and friendship as an expensive purebred.

Chapter Six

A Family to Feed: The Slaughterhouse Laborer, and Other Human Victims of the Animal Holocaust.

Pigs on the kill floor have come up and nuzzled me like a puppy. Two minutes later, I had to kill them—beat them to death with a pipe.

— Ed Van Winkle, hog-sticker at Morrell slaughterhouse plant,

Sioux City, Iowa

In this chapter, we will explore some of the more obvious human victims of animal agriculture; but, before we do so, I want to remind everyone of what is meant by *Animal Liberation is Human Liberation*. The examples below make this clear in specific cases, but there are two generalities worth noting here. The first is that *all* humans are victims of the commodification of nonhuman animals. Not only are those who work in the industry, or who are raised by those who do, negatively impacted, but also our *society as a whole* is negatively impacted by the mantra of animal agriculture: suppress your empathy for nonhumans, because We are more important than They are. Encouraging this disconnect between product and process, as well as both cognitive and emotional distance between us and our fellow sentient beings, hardens us and prevents us from reaching our true potential as compassionate, responsible inhabitants of Earth.

Secondly, their needs are our needs, too. The wealthiest human on Earth still requires clean air to breathe, clean water to drink, and healthy land on which to exist and grow food. Without these, anyone—male or female, of any sexual orientation, of any race, and with any amount of income—will inevitably perish. All of these basic necessities are jeopardized by animal agriculture; therefore, increasingly, we humans find ourselves victims of air, land, and water pollution that could be at best eliminated, and at the very least limited.

The Slaughterhouse Laborer

The Food Empowerment Project (FEP), a nonprofit organization committed to creating "a more just and sustainable world by recognizing the power of one's food choices," cites numerous facts concerning both slaughterhouse laborers and factory farm workers in the US on its website, among which are:

- The vast majority of both are minorities, with workers from Mexico and other parts of Latin America working full-time on factory farms while approximately 40% of all slaughterhouse laborers are born outside of the US.

- In both cases, many employers knowingly hire undocumented workers "in an effort to satisfy the extremely high turnover rate of the industry, which often exceeds 100% annually." Fear or exposure decreases the likelihood that an undocumented worker will complain about hazardous work conditions or low pay.

- In both cases, most workers are "at-will" workers, meaning that employers can fire them at any time, without due cause. The threat of unemployment pressures those who are fully aware of the hazardous conditions in which they are working, the pain and suffering they are inflicting, and/or the unjust pay they are receiving to keep silent. In factory farms, many laborers are not even fully aware of the many dangers they encounter daily.

- The vast majority of these individuals lack an education. Some were lucky enough to at least attend some high school; others, not so much. Many slaughterhouses and factory farms also neglect to institute an age requirement, and will readily hire teens and pre-teens to do their dirty work—feeding off the desperation of young, uninformed immigrants to survive in a strange new land.[1]

It is clear from the information above that many slaughterhouse laborers and factory farm workers face limited employment options, and may work at animal-abusive institutions regardless of any moral or ethical qualms because, at the end of the day, we all gotta eat and we've all got rent to pay. Already, it is apparent that these individuals are victims of Limited Choice.

They are also victimized *physically*:

- **Factory farms are full of harmful chemicals, such as ammonia and hydrogen sulfide.** Ammonia is known to cause eye irritation and respiratory problems in levels as low as 6 parts per million (ppm); still, the Occupational Safety and Health Administration permits ammonia levels up to 50 ppm in the workplace. Kelly wasn't kidding about her black nose-gunk at the chicken farm; not only was it a serious health hazard to her and others, but it was also perfectly legal. Fancy that.

Repeated exposure to low volumes of hydrogen sulfide, a gas released from liquid manure, can cause symptoms such as dry skin, eye irritation, nausea, low blood pressure, headaches, and chronic coughs. Approximately 20,000 US farm workers are diagnosed with agricultural-chemicals poisoning every year—and that's just the number of *reported* cases.[2]

- Many slaughterhouses operate nearly twenty-four hours a day, seven days a week; and the speed with which they send animals down the line for slaughter is, to put it mildly, demanding. A Human Rights Watch report in 2004 entitled, "Blood, Sweat and Fear: Workers' Rights in U.S. Meat and Poultry Plants," quotes one slaughterhouse laborer: **"The line is so fast there is no time to sharpen the knife. The knife gets dull and you have to cut harder. That's when it really starts to hurt, and that's when you cut yourself."**[3]

- **Due to long hours combined with repetitive motions, many laborers at both factory farms and slaughterhouses develop chronic pain in their limbs, joints, and backs.**

- **Most of the women interviewed for a 2010 study by the Southern Poverty Law Center, a nonprofit civil rights organization, reported enduring harassment that rose to the level of sexual assault while working in agricultural fields or slaughterhouses.** Sexual predators regard undocumented women as "perfect victims" because they are isolated, often do not know their rights, and lack legal status.[4]

and *mentally*:

- "Most workers become deadened to the fact that they are working with live animals," says Gail Eisnitz, author of the 1997 book *Slaughterhouse: The Shocking Story of Greed, Neglect, and Inhumane Treatment Inside the US Meat Industry.* **"Many of the individuals I interviewed described suffering from alcoholism, while others explained that they had taken out their frustrations through physical violence directed at their wives and children."**[5]

- **Structural Discrimination:** Due to their low income, in spite of long hours (averaging $23,000 annually, working ten-plus-hour days)[6], as well as their often questionable legal status in this country, factory farm workers and slaughterhouse laborers are repeatedly, generationally disenfranchised from accessing affordable healthcare, education, social security, and other advantageous programs. Not only is lack of access to education a form of mental victimization, but the compound stress of knowing that one can't have any of these things (or provide them for one's family) and spending over ten hours a day hurting and killing sentient beings—hearing their screams, looking into eyes wide with fright—is mentally and emotionally torturous.

- **Development of Psychosis:** From Jennifer Dillard's "A Slaughterhouse Nightmare: Psychological Harm Suffered by Slaughterhouse Employees and the Possibility of Redress through Legal Reform":

In this country, we have a common understanding that taking pleasure in the cruel death of a helpless animal is an antisocial and potentially psychotic characteristic. The countless stories of slaughterhouse employees inflicting pain on animals "just for fun" indicate that the nature of slaughterhouse work may have caused psychological damage to the employees, because the employees' actions certainly rise to the level of abnormal cruelty that would cause concern among the general population.[7]

One of the biggest "red flag" behaviors among children is cruelty to animals. Conventional wisdom asserts that, while a degree of initial animosity or jealousy extended from a child to a nonhuman animal is natural, a child who deliberately abuses or torments an animal in any way is psychologically unstable and perhaps even dangerous to humans.

What is it about adulthood that suddenly makes this behavior okay? I'm reminded of our discussion of children and family entertainment in *Cruelty Isn't Fun*. At what point do we as a culture shift from addressing such behavior with, "I can't believe you did that, you must be psychotic; let's go get you some help," to, "Ah well, you work in a slaughterhouse—you're just blowing off some steam; you're still a stable person, and this is still a normal institution"?

What am I missing here?

The Farmer's Son

The amount of courage it takes to examine the basic assumptions that you've carried since childhood, and to question those—and then find that there is another way to be in the world...And then to follow that vision, that dream...It's really a joyous thing. It's going home.

—Harold Brown, Peaceable Kingdom

In 2009, the socially responsible film production company Tribe of Heart released an award-winning documentary entitled

Peaceable Kingdom: The Journey Home. This documentary was ripe with inspirational interviews, among the most poignant of which featured Harold Brown, a farmer's son. Harold, like most farm boys, was taught at an early age to shut his empathy switch *Off;* nevertheless, he found his way toward the Animal Liberation Movement in adulthood, and is now an outspoken animal advocate.[8]

Harold gives us a peek into how children raised on farms are taught to accept the violence inherent in the family business:

> I was taught as a child what I suppose every farm kid gets, which is that they're there for our use; it's part of a natural cycle of birth and death, and they sustain us through that cycle. But there was something in the back of my mind that didn't...make sense...that didn't feel right about it. Because we had pets, too; we had dogs and cats. And I was very attached to my dogs. It was like we were best buddies, did everything together. But the farm animals were different.

> It was okay to feel bad about it—my mom taught me that; it was okay to feel bad about animals...you know, killing animals to eat...but don't let it show. You don't let it show. You keep it inside...

> The last thing you want to be is weak. Weak farmers don't survive.

I was particularly moved by this last statement. It resonated with not only the travails of children on farms of which I already knew, since both of my parents were raised on farms, but also with those of American men in general who empathize with animals.

I was surprised upon moving to the Bay Area at how many male animal liberationists I encountered. In New York, being vegan—at least from the perspective of the small community with which I engaged—was considered very much a "chick thing," while the phrase "animal liberation" was not employed at all (though I understand it is now commonly used there). Here we see yet another instance of sexism and speciesism walking hand-in-hand. It is weak to love animals, and it is weak to be female; therefore, only females should love animals. "Real men" eat meat—and they certainly don't cry about it.

Upon moving to Cleveland, Ohio from Michigan in his thirties, Harold first heard the word *vegetarian:*

> I was actually working as a mechanic and the very first car I worked on had this bumper sticker and I could not figure out that bumper sticker. I fixed her car. I delivered the car to her and I said, "Do you mind if I ask you about your bumper sticker?"
>
> And she said, "Sure."
>
> I said, "It says, 'I don't eat my friends.'" I said, "Is that a joke that you're not a carnivore?"
>
> And she said, "No, I am vegetarian."
>
> I said, "What's that?" And she looked at me with astonishment, and said, "You don't know what a vegetarian is?"
>
> I said, "No I'm 31 years old, and I have never heard that word."

This experience prompted Harold and his wife to seek other vegetarians and vegans and learn more about the plight of nonhumans. A subtle shift took place in his brain with respect to how he regarded nonhumans, coming from a background in which nonhuman animals are food and commodities—not individuals with rich emotional lives and a strong desire to be free. Harold eventually adopted a cow named Snickers at Farm Sanctuary in New York. He visited him two or three times before an absence of several months.

Upon returning, Harold wondered whether or not Snickers would remember him, but he needn't have worried. As soon as Harold, arms outstretched, called his name, Snickers came running—or as close to "running" as a cow can get.

As a result of this experience, Harold became determined to re-integrate into his character and his life the love and compassion for animals that he had once felt but that had been suppressed for so long. Harold connected with other former farmers and children of farmers, and ultimately founded Farm Kind: a community and resource center for farmers who endeavor to make the switch from animal-based to plant-based agriculture.

Harold Brown shared the following words of wisdom on the television program *Animal World*, on Supreme Master Television:

> People will look at environmental and social justice, animals' rights, and veganism; they look at all these different things as different issues. They're actually not different issues. They're all part of the same problem; there is systemic problem in human culture. I really feel it's our ego that keeps us tied up to these things and it's those attachments that keeps us from seeing that how we treat the animals is how we treat each other, and how we treat the environment.
>
> If we are able to easily look at animals as being a commodity, an economic unit, then we will always look at the other human beings as the same.

It is this kind of worldview that we developed and then it becomes this kind of destructive cycle of not looking beyond our own self and what we want. We have to open our eyes and open our hearts to what we all need—what the Earth needs and what all of creation needs and not just what we want.[9]

The Reformed Businessman

I loved being around the animals, and I really felt that I was doing the best for them. I was doing the new modern agriculture: using the chemicals, bringing Mother Nature to heel.

—Howard Lyman, Peaceable Kingdom

Peaceable Kingdom: The Journey Home also interviewed Howard Lyman, a self-identified Fourth-Generation Farmer/Rancher/Feedlot Operator. Lyman attended Montana State University in the 1970s to become an "agribusinessman." After meeting his wife, Willow Jeane, in college, the two graduated, got married, and proceeded to run Howard's farm together. Within a few years' time, they had over 7,000 cows in their charge.

Because the cows came from so many different places across the US, the Lymans were encouraged by their education to lace the cows' feed with antibiotics so as to prevent the acquisition or spread of bacteria. In spite of this precaution, the Lymans found themselves eventually administering as many as seven to twenty-one vaccines, including hormones, daily. They also participated in de-horning, castration, and the branding of calves with a hot iron.

As new issues began to arise on the farm, Howard continued to follow his MSU training to the letter and attempted to embrace the "new modern agriculture." He found himself spending roughly a million dollars a year on chemicals, and told McSpotlight.org that he "...ended up eliminating the birds, killing the trees—turned the soil into something that looked like we had imported it from Mars."

In *Peaceable Kingdom*, Lyman laments:

> On our feedlot, I've seen the flies so bad that you could reach out and grab 'em and end up with a handful of them. So we would get up early in the morning when there was dew in the air, and we'd take a fogger with insecticides and drive up and down the feed allies with a great fog of insecticide that would go out and it would drift over the cattle and over the water troughs and over the bunks. Two hours later, we would fill those feed bunks up, cattle would eat 'em, lick the water troughs, and drink 'em.

Meanwhile, the Lymans—Howard in particular—became enamored of one industrious pig in their charge, whom they called Piggo. Piggo had the ability to stand on his hind legs while using his mouth to open the screen door, and took to coming and going as he pleased. Howard especially appreciated that whenever Piggo showed up, Howard's mother-in-law, if present, immediately left. "I never let anything happen to that hog. I had a very soft spot in my heart about that hog."

Willow Jeane, on the other hand, developed a more profound affection for Piggo, beyond his ability to make her mother disappear:

> That pig would come over and play with the kids, and I thought, "Well, this is unusual. It's not like the other hogs, but it's still a hog..." And that sparked a thought

in my mind about animals that was coming back—
that I'd had as a child, but I'd lost.

Presumably, the thought was akin to: *animals are individuals.*

Getting to know Piggo, coupled with a near-death experience in which Howard was sent to the hospital to undergo what he describes as a "one-in-a-million operation," inspired Howard and Willow Jeane to shut down their agribusiness in 1983. Since then, they have sold most of their farmland and preserved what remains as a wildlife sanctuary. Howard also runs the website MadCowboy.com and engages in interviews regularly to spread the word about the atrocity of industrialized farming.

The J Word: How Animal Liberation Would Impact Employment

Now for the stuff liberationists loathe to talk about (myself included), the dreaded J word: JOBS. Since the economic recession starting around 2007 in the US, the banner of *job creation* coupled with the looming threat of *job loss* have dominated discussions on everything from immigration reform to environmental policy to investments in construction and even the War Machine. Nowadays, anything that promises to bring jobs into an area suffering from high unemployment rates is, at least initially, perceived as *Good*, while anything that threatens to put Americans out of work is immediately labeled *Evil*.

Of everyone in my family, my sister Denise is by far the most likely to ever embark on the path of animal liberation. She has admitted to me on more than one occasion that I've "almost converted" her—yet there are two large cinderblocks preventing her from fully entering my animal-friendly universe. The first is her children, which was part of my impetus for devoting a portion of the *Resources* section at the end of this book to works concerning how to raise healthy, happy vegan children—as well as the works of various medical experts confirming that veganism is the healthiest diet humans can have, at any age.

The second cinderblock, one to which she did not introduce me but of which she has reminded me, is the plight of the small farmer. She, too, has immense sympathy for these particular human victims of the Animal Holocaust; unfortunately, she once positioned them to me not as victims of the Animal Holocaust, but as victims of the Animal Liberation Movement! By cutting out meat and dairy altogether, she argued, rather than simply being more selective about where I purchase it, I was threatening the ability of small, "humane" farmers to survive and feed their families in these tough times.

While I sympathize with the notion, I think it is ultimately the cruel practice into which they've been manipulated that victimizes these farmers—not those who try to end said practice. There are other crops they can grow; in fact, many do. Very rarely nowadays does one encounter a small-time farmer who *only* sells eggs or *only* sells milk; typically, these individuals also have fruits and/or vegetables to sell. Moreover, the Big Guys in the industry are already swallowing the Little Guys in droves; a small-time farmer cannot possibly compete, neither pricewise nor with respect to volume of product (which, naturally, go hand-in-hand), with his or her larger, wealthier, industrialized counterparts.

So in my mind, rather than threatening their business—which the Big Guys are already doing—animal liberationists are presenting small-time farmers with an opportunity to **distinguish themselves from their counterparts by taking the ethical high ground.** As small farmers opt to specialize more and more in vegan produce and eschew animal exploitation, scores of animal advocates will flock to them for their nutritional needs while frequenting meat-and-dairy-selling grocers less and less. This may well also enable small-time farmers to decrease their annual expenses, as raising animals for slaughter is indeed a costly as well as malicious enterprise.

That said, let's talk about the Big Guys. Just how big are they? How many US citizens do they employ? Surprisingly, not that many; according to the Bureau of Labor Statistics, "Farming, Fishing, and Forestry" occupations employed 435,250 people in May 2013—only 0.1% of the US population from April–July of that year. Not one percent of the population; one *tenth* of a percent of the population.[10]

Taking into account persons under 18 or over 65 (37.4% of total population),[11] who were most likely not working in May 2013, we are still left with 197,896,654 employable parties in the US at that time. This adjustment yields a new percentage of 0.2% (two tenths, or one fifth, of a percent) of employable persons employed by one of the Three Fs in the US in May 2013. In other words, these three industries barely make a dent when looking at the larger picture of American employment.

This data also suggests a dip from 2010, the year in which William Kandel and Ashok Mishra estimated the employment figure for the meat-processing industry alone to be 500,000 workers.[12]

One must also bear in mind that "Farming Occupations" are not divided into the subgroups *animal-based* (meat and dairy) and *produce-based* (actual food); as a result, the true figures describing how many people are employed by Meat and Dairy in the US are even smaller than they appear at first glance. Similarly, "Forestry Occupations" include both cutting down trees to create space for cattle (Meat and Dairy) and doing so to create space for schools, houses, and other human facilities (falling under the umbrellas of Construction and City Planning).

The ugly, immediate truth from which liberationists shy away and to which many a speciesist clings is that *the permanent shut-down of the meat and dairy industries in America would result in an initial loss of roughly 500,000 jobs*—not as many as I'd anticipated, but still 500,000 jobs too many for those who would be affected.

I'm reminded of the quote from the anti-suffrage pamphlet, mentioned in Chapter Two: "It can be of no benefit commensurate with the additional expense involved." This certainly appears to be the case at first glance, but as we've seen with women's suffrage, it *is* indeed worth the initial expense. The contribution of women to American politics, culture, and society since the suffrage movement of the 1920s has been astronomical. We have so much to thank so many women for, none of whom would have had a voice if a group of devoted do-gooders hadn't decided back in the twenties, "Women deserve a public voice—at all costs."

So, what do we do with 500,000 unemployed Americans? For starters, it is important to understand that these industries will not shut down overnight, which gives us the advantage of time—time in which to *plan*. To put programs in place that will support these people and their families. Ultimately, we must treat these victims like the victims they are.

Treating Victims like the Victims They Are

The traditional profile of the slaughterhouse laborer, as previously discussed in this chapter, is: racial minority, limited English language abilities, minimal to no education, and often though not exclusively, in this country illegally. So, in treating these victims like victims, we need to be strategic about what their needs are with respect to seeking nonviolent employment.

The first and perhaps most obvious need would be to improve English language skills for non-native speakers. Free ESL classes already abound; this wouldn't be a "new thing" we would have to implement, but rather an existing institution that liberationists would have to commit to further publicizing (so that the people who need these programs know that they exist, and where to find them) as well as contribute to staffing (to ensure that these free programs remain available—and free—in the long term). Many colleges and universities across the US host these programs, with flexible hours—making them convenient for those who must continue to work to feed their families while enrolled, as well as for those with small children who cannot afford childcare and must wait for a friend or relative to become available before departing for class.

One way liberationists can expand upon these programs, beyond simply publicizing those already in existence, is to start hosting such programs in their own meeting spaces and/or in public spaces (such as parks). If you want to contribute to empowering reluctant slaughterhouse laborers to find new employment, but don't live close enough to an existing ESL program to volunteer at one, roll up your sleeves, learn Spanish, and start your own. This is also an example of why the Animal Liberation Movement, like any other movement for social justice, needs people of color—people who can not only speak the language of these victims, but who are also familiar with both the cultural biases they may have developed in their youth *and* those by which factory farm laborers have been systematically oppressed (such as racism and classism). While seeking to empower minorities living on a limited budget, one must be careful to avoid the common "outreach" pitfall of "white people teaching brown people how to live."

With respect to empowering slaughterhouse laborers academically, the Open Educational Resources (OER) Movement aims to do just that—not only for slaughterhouse laborers, but also for anyone who seeks to improve himself or herself by increasing knowledge without paying today's sky-high tuition costs. OER are resources, lectures, and courses that established universities, such as MIT, Stanford, and Berkeley, provide for free online. These courses do not provide credit—they represent the free dissemination of knowledge for the betterment of humankind.

The University of the People is one exception, providing fully developed, tuition-free degree programs to the public. Their website describes their mission as follows:

The tuition-free, nonprofit, online academic institution, University of the People (UoPeople), is part of the Open Educational Resources movement and utilizes open educational content in all courses. The nonprofit UoPeople was created in order to provide quality collegiate education at low expense, so individuals in need around the world can overcome financial, geographic, or societal constraints and attain higher education. Its mission is straightforward in purpose— to assist in the democratization and global advancement of higher education worldwide.[13]

Where the target audience comes into play is with respect to the word "online." Not every low-income-earning individual, regardless of race or any other sociocultural factor, has consistent, reliable access to the Internet; and those who do have said access do not always know how to most effectively utilize it. So a challenge for liberationists in the long run will be to educate these communities about online resources while contributing to the dissemination of online access.

Supporting your local library is perhaps the easiest way to go about this; I have often seen, as a frequenter of public libraries in both New York and California, low-income individuals—including the homeless—using the Internet for free. On more than on occasion, I've allowed curiosity to get the better of me and peeked over the shoulders of these individuals; and in every instance save one, these individuals were using the Internet either to seek employment or to seek educational benefits.

Libraries are grossly underfunded, and I've frequently encountered petitions at various branches seeking to prevent them from closing. Our libraries are in danger, and for so many reasons beyond liberation (as if liberation itself weren't a strong enough reason), we simply cannot allow this to happen.

Another way we can improve Internet access and competence among these communities is by using our liberationist meeting spaces toward these ends. As with the ESL programs, liberationist spaces at which more than one computer is available can be used to regularly host basic training sessions on Internet use (or even computer use more generally, such as how to make spreadsheets or how to use design programs like Photoshop) as well as to allow those enrolled in online courses to complete their coursework. Opening our spaces up to not only fight for the rights of nonhuman animals, but also to empower the humans currently caught in the speciesist machine is one surefire way to ensure *true* animal liberation for humans and nonhumans alike.

The Robin Hood Foundation, based in New York City, is just one of many examples of existing organizations that teach career and trade skills to underprivileged individuals. Some of this foundation's programs include:

- *Bill Michelson Home Care Education Fund:* Trains low-income women to become certified nursing assistants, patient care associates, and licensed practical nurses.

- *Coalition for Queens' Access Code:* Provides tech training to individuals from underserved and underrepresented communities.

- *Edith and Carl Marks Jewish Community House of Bensonhurst:* Teaches recent immigrants English, and places them in new jobs.

- *Grace Institute:* Trains 300 low-income women annually for administrative assistant positions and provides them post-training services to help trainees get and keep work.

- *LIFT:* Uses an innovative, low-cost model that relies

on college student volunteers to work one-on-one with low-income individuals to help them solve housing, employment, and public-benefits problems.[14]

These are precisely the types of services our slaughterhouse laborers will need in order to walk away from their speciesist professions without starving to death. Animal liberationists have a wide variety of skill sets. Some have technical training; others are good with computers; many know how to cook, sew, garden, and so forth. We should be sharing our skills with individuals who can then benefit from using our skills in the workplace. *LIFT* is a particularly strong model for this, as it is entirely volunteer-based and therefore low-cost. We don't need to be heavily funded to make these things happen; we just have to be committed. We need to prioritize these matters as much as we prioritize the release of nonhumans from captivity and exploitation; the latter cannot happen without the former.

The former cannot happen unless we also remain committed to *coming from a place of love, not hatred.* As long as we continue to lump everyone currently employed by speciesist industries into the category "evil," and ourselves into the category "good," we cannot expect true animal liberation to ever be realized. Not only do I personally feel it is morally corrupt to call people with good intentions (feeding their families) "evil" because you don't approve of how they're doing it, but in a completely objective, practical sense, this attitude can only hurt the movement, as these people will be less inclined to change their ways if we are approaching them hatefully and/or condescendingly. They are victims, not perpetrators. The true perpetrators are the industries themselves—industries that will ultimately collapse if we are successful at robbing them of the fuel on which they run: the desperation of poorly educated, limited-English-speaking immigrants to take care of themselves and their families in a strange new world that is not always welcoming to them.

Chapter Seven

Liberation as Autonomy

The deepest and most comprehensive question for our social movement is why and how modern human society has developed through patterns of domination; and the greatest challenge we face is imagining humanity without the master role.

–Lee Hall
On Their Own Terms: Bringing Animal Rights Philosophy Down to Earth

Domestication and Breeding: Ancient Barriers

Central to the liberationist mentality is the notion that all sentient beings have a right to autonomy over their own bodies. What some modern animal rights advocates fail to realize is that true, full-fledged bodily autonomy is a privilege reserved solely for wild animals. Through years of domestication, humans have regrettably disabled countless nonhumans from ever experiencing true autonomy.

How can that be possible? Even if, say, dogs, cows, and chickens have all been domesticated for thousands of years, wouldn't simply letting them go—allowing them to live freely, without being exploited—mend the broken fence? Can we not return this stolen autonomy to its rightful owners?

Not quite. Truth be told, many of today's domesticated animals exist specifically because of domestication; in other words, they were bred. Therefore, they were born into a system of domination from which they cannot escape; from their very first breath, they were not autonomous beings but rather property. Abandoning this notion of animals as property is by no means a new idea; however, our movement has, in an uncharacteristic display of optimism, so far focused far more heavily on *freeing the domesticated* than it has on *ending domestication once and for all.*

Consider our horseman's question from earlier: "*What do you do with a horse?*" A fundamental point of the ideal reply is that he should not only allow the horses he lives with to live as freely as possible, given prior domestication, but also that the caretaker should not breed them. He himself, in an effort to adhere to the ideals of animal liberation, would have to reject domestication as an option, and central to rejecting domestication is halting the breeding process.

The victims of companion animal breeding, to use another example of how autonomy impacts liberation, are not only the mothers, whose bodies are exploited and thus who are never allowed to experience autonomy, but also the pups who are treated as commodities from the very moment of their births. Their position upon entering the world is immediately one of *dependence.*

While countless loving and lovable dogs exist in shelters around the world, some people still pay top dollar for a young "purebred"—a dog who was *designed prior to birth* to maintain certain attributes considered desirable by "pet owners" who regard their companions as status symbols or showpieces rather than friends. The closest moral equivalent from a human perspective that I can surmise is for a family to mate exclusively with blue-eyed people to ensure the eventual birth of an exclusively blue-eyed generation.

(This does, of course, happen by accident from time to time, according to region; some regions just host a higher percentage of certain physical traits than others. That said, to engage in this behavior intentionally—to exclude all other potential partners in favor of blue-eyed partners because it has been culturally dictated that blue eyes are somehow "better" than brown or hazel eyes—is evocative of a fascist, sci-fi nightmare.)

Does this mean we shouldn't bother to free the already domesticated? Certainly not. We owe it to them to try, but if we truly want to see a liberated world for all animals, domestication—and its primary method, breeding—must be eradicated. The liberationist community must prioritize this as much as it prioritizes dispelling the Humane Myth; in fact, the two are inextricably linked. The Humane Myth encourages the uninterrupted perpetuation of domestication by implying that there is a "good life" to be had for animals who are domesticated—a life good enough to justify permanent removal from their natural state and irreparable loss of autonomy.

Depending on what you choose to compare it to, anything could be labeled "good" or "bad," but these animals deserve to enjoy the same natural state of autonomy into which we humans are born (or those of us lucky enough to live in "free" societies, where human slavery is illegal)—to be born as creatures out in the world, exploring and learning from life itself. Not confined, not trained, and not used. Even those who have been rescued, and will live out their remaining days at animal sanctuaries, will never be truly free, as they are ever-reliant on their caregivers for basic needs, which, in the wild, they would have learned to fulfill on their own. These animals do not have autonomy over when or what they eat, how far they can travel, and a host of other life choices we free beings habitually take for granted.

In an interview published on the animal-centric blog *AR Zone*, Lee Hall—lawyer, animal advocate, and author of the book, ***On Their Own Terms: Bringing Animal Rights Philosophy Down to Earth***—highlights another of many means through which the Humane Myth perpetuates human domination: "...expanded cages and pastures take habitat from free-living animals."[1] In other words, by framing larger cages as a "right" for domesticated animals, humans not only allow them to remain caged—maintaining their status as "property" and denying them any true autonomy—but also actively *strip even more nonhumans of autonomy by appropriating their space and resources for industrial purposes.*

How can we hasten the abolition of domestication? In ***On Their Own Terms,*** Hall makes several promising suggestions. One of these is for the Animal Liberation Movement to become further involved with environmental legislation.[2] Owing to our horrendous destruction of habitats worldwide, even animals currently in The Wild are being crushed under Human's heel. Aside from looking inward at the animals we exploit in more obvious ways, such as pigs and chickens (and standing on the platform of their "rights" to strip wild animals of autonomy by widening jail cells), we need to also look outward and ensure that those who were born free have the ability to *stay* free and don't wind up trapped in our ever-expanding territory.

One intriguing possibility for a future in which we humans take up less space and ruin less land lies in the emergence of "tiny houses"—houses measuring under 200 square feet. Popularized as an economic measure for young couples and those looking to downsize, some proponents of the "Tiny House Movement" chose—and continue to choose—to build and live in tiny houses for the sake of environmental protection. The documentary *TINY: A Story about Living Small* (2013) follows a couple striving to build a tiny house from scratch, with no construction experience whatsoever. As their story unfolds, it is interlaced with the stories of others who have engaged in this process as well—each with limited budgets and limited, or often no, experience.[3]

Many of those interviewed in the film spoke of how we humans take up such a gargantuan amount of space given our relatively small size, and with more of us springing up every day there simply isn't enough room—nor is there any real need or advantage—for all of us to aspire to the McMansions of which the American Dream was once comprised. The Tiny House Movement is revolutionizing the status quo, spinning the pitying expression, "It's 'okay' to live modestly," into a more encouraging and prideful message: "It is responsible and ethical to live modestly."

Whereas the Mansion has for ages served as a status symbol—the symbol that one has "made it," i.e., that one has money to waste—living small offers us a new, more significant status symbol: an emblem of our respect and consideration for other creatures, as well as our planet. It can no longer be taken for granted that people who live small do so out of necessity; rather, it is becoming more and more socially acceptable for people to do so *by choice*.

Veganism is also fundamental to the elimination of domestication. Many vegans talk about the lives they are personally saving by abstaining from animal byproducts and eschewing forms of entertainment and fashion that exploit animals, but there is a larger endgame here even than these countless lives "saved." That endgame, that highest priority, is that the vegan lifestyle has the potential to *end* animal domestication by depleting the demand for anything for which domestication is a prerequisite. The fewer animals used, the fewer animals "needed"—ergo, the fewer animals bred. It is important to acknowledge the full breadth and scope of veganism. While on the surface it may seem like a dietary choice, and after some digging one deduces that it also has fashion and entertainment consequences, one aspect of daily living that might not immediately sound "vegan"—but is— is rejecting domestication and breeding.

The deeper one digs into the core concepts of veganism, the more apparent it becomes that this way of life is about promoting *life itself*—not just about eating or dressing or researching or partying a certain way. There is no manual, no list of instructions. The instructions are easily intuited once one grasps the core message: that all sentient beings have a right to autonomy over their bodies and lives. It is from this message that the "rules" are derived, not the opposite. That adhering to the tenets of veganism yields changes in one's choices as a consumer does not make veganism itself consumerist. That abstaining from animal flesh, milk, and cheese naturally causes many humans to lose weight does not reduce the totality of veganism to a diet. The vegan ethos is as much about how we treat one another—humans and nonhumans alike—and how we perceive our place and purpose in the universe, as any other philosophical or religious tradition is. It is a deep-seated, unwavering commitment to walking the path of least harm.

Genetic Mutation and Cloning: Modern Barriers

Aside of the issue of strategic breeding, in which animals are paired with specific partners and bred to promote the expression of particular traits, there is also the matter of genetic mutation—how we humans have systematically rendered some nonhuman animals incapable of autonomy by changing the very structure of the bodies over which said autonomy would be granted. In an effort to increase production of milk, meat, wool, and other animal byproducts, as well as to promote disease resistance, advanced growth rates, and other desired traits, biotech companies fund scientific research to genetically manipulate the animals we enslave. In other words, we violate their bodies on a structural level in order to create genetically superior slaves.

Leave aside, for a moment, the many horrific instances in which this fails—in which, say, genes from a spider injected into a goat yield results that greatly hinder the quality of life of the goat while failing to produce the results desired by the powers that be. (Countless animals also die on the operating table, and between 85 and 90% of genetically modified embryos die before they are born.)[4] Even in instances where this "works," it is still the utmost violation, and we must bear in mind that what is desirable for the powers that be may not be in the best interests of the animals or our environment. Increased egg production in hens, for instance, leads to infections of the vent, as footage of rescued hens shows us. Increased milk production in cows leads to a condition known as udder edema—fluid accumulation in the udders that causes painful swelling.

Frighteningly, genetic mutation is, on occasion, purported to be employed for the purpose of *protecting* animals. In 2005, a team of US researchers turned to genetic mutation in order to make dairy cows resistant to mastitis, a condition caused by the introduction of harmful bacteria to the cow's genital region, which involves swelling of the udders. Rather than end the introduction of such bacteria by ending the use of the rape rack and all other forms of artificial insemination, society has chosen to address this problem by injecting a gene from one offensive bacterium into a bunch of New Jersey cows. The result was that "only 14%" of mammary glands infused with the bacteria cultures became infected, as opposed to the 71% of said glands in non-genetically-manipulated cows.[5] A massive reduction, to be sure, but the number should be 0%. This is something that rarely, if ever, occurs in nature. The 14% is not something to celebrate, as the scientists responsible (and those funding them) would have us believe. Our addiction to approaching animal-abusive problems with animal-abusive solutions is a snake eating his own tail.

It may not be immediately apparent how cloning is, or can lead to, animal abuse—aside from the necessity of artificial insemination, that is, which violates the autonomy of the mother-to-be. To further clarify the cruelty potential of cloning, consider the dangerous cliff that is de-extinction—the practice of bringing previously extinct animal species back. In February 2014, the *New York Times* released an article called, "The Mammoth Cometh," addressing the very real possibility of bringing back extinct species via new genomic technologies developed by Harvard molecular biologist George Church. Nathaniel Rich begins the article with a romantic ode to the passenger pigeon, a species that existed in abundance as recently as the 1860s but whose last known representative—a captive pigeon named Martha at the Cincinnati Zoo—passed away in 1914:

The fact that we can pinpoint the death of the last known passenger pigeon is one of many peculiarities that distinguish the species. Many thousands of species go extinct every year, but we tend to be unaware of their passing, because we're unaware of the existence of most species. The passenger pigeon's decline was impossible to ignore, because as recently as the 1880s, it was the most populous vertebrate in North America. It made up as much as 40 percent of the continent's bird population. In "A Feathered River Across the Sky," Joel Greenberg suggests that the species' population "may have exceeded that of every other bird on earth." In 1860, a naturalist observed a single flock that he estimated to contain 3,717,120,000 pigeons. By comparison, there are currently 260 million rock pigeons in existence. A single passenger-pigeon nesting ground once occupied an area as large as 850 square miles, or 37 Manhattans.[6]

Stewart Brand, founder and former editor of the *Whole Earth Catalog*, learned of the aforementioned technologies and got to work on a campaign to resurrect the passenger pigeon. Brand hoped that the pigeon project would provide "a beacon of hope for conservation," and conference attendees at both Harvard Medical School and the National Geographic Society tended to agree. The prevailing voice at these conferences was one of support, *and Church saw, it was good, it was good.*

That the scientific community raised its banner for de-extinction last year should come as no surprise, given that these efforts have been underway for years. Dr. Alberto Fernández-Arias and his team of scientists in Spain conducted the first de-extinction over a decade ago, of the bucardo, a subspecies of mountain goat also known as the Pyrenean ibex, that went extinct in 2000. Unfortunately, the cloned kid died just a few minutes after its birth in 2003.[7]

Here's where it gets interesting for liberationists. On the surface, this may sound like a great thing. We've caused so much damage to the earth that we've sacrificed many of its previous occupants. If we can bring them back, perhaps we can treat them better this time around; perhaps they, and the earth, will forgive us our past transgressions. The world naturally aims at genetic diversity. Wouldn't bringing back old species only contribute to Earth's natural intention? Reinstate Mama Nature as the true decider of who lives and dies—instead of us?

Not so much. For starters, many extinct animals lived in conditions that can no longer be replicated—or at least, cannot be replicated without a lot of time, money, and planning. In short, they can't be replicated *naturally*. Nathaniel Rich in the *Times* article argues:

> Just as the loss of a species decreases the richness of an ecosystem, the addition of new animals could achieve the opposite effect. The grazing habits of mammoths, for instance, might encourage the growth of a variety of grasses, which could help to protect the Arctic permafrost from melting—a benefit with global significance, as the Arctic permafrost contains two to three times as much carbon as the world's rain forests.

How exactly would the fact that mammoths require certain grasses to feed naturally result in an abundance of said grasses? Wouldn't they just look for the grasses, not find them, and starve? I thought it worked the other way around—that the presence of grasses would increase the mammoth population, rather than an abundance of mammoths resulting in a magical increase in food supply.

An alternative would be to unnaturally plant these grasses again, in places where we want mammoths to live, which means we humans would have to decide in advance where we will allow these creatures to live and where we will *not* allow them to live. Is this any different from keeping an animal at a zoo? Are we to bring back all these glorious creatures we prematurely sentenced to death (okay, so maybe we didn't kill the mammoth, but that's one of precious few exceptions), only to sentence them to imprisonment instead? Can any such creature be said to truly have autonomy, when said creature cannot choose where to live?

If we decide, "Okay, so these pastures here, these will be for the mammoths," what will happen to the people who are doubtlessly already living on or otherwise utilizing said pastures? What of the nonhuman animals living in this area; are we to strip them of autonomy in order to make way for the new guys, just as welfarist initiatives to make room for slaves threaten the free? What would happen when the mammoth population inevitably outgrew the area we had allocated to it?

This is not reinstating Mama Nature; it's mocking her.

The term "de-extinction" is a misnomer. We're not really talking about bringing extinct pigeons back from the dead; we are talking about *altering the genetic makeup of currently existing pigeons* (band-tailed pigeons, specifically—thus stripping them of bodily autonomy) in an effort to *replicate* the departed. The "de-extincted" bucardo, for instance, was not a resurrected bucardo but rather the offspring of a goat who had been artificially inseminated with genetic material from Celia, the last living bucardo. For this to take place, both Celia and the inseminated mother were taken hostage, and, ultimately, the poor offspring died after just a few minutes of life—not life as an animal in nature would experience it but an entirely human-dominated, human-constructed life.

Ed Green, a biomolecular engineer who works on genome-sequencing technology in the UC Santa Cruz paleogenomics lab, said, "There are a million things that you cannot predict about an organism just from having its genome sequence." Would "de-extincted" passenger pigeons truly behave as their ancestors did? Would they be mutated band-tailed pigeons who can no longer mate with, or perhaps even peacefully coexist with, unaltered band-tailed pigeons? Or would they form a new species entirely—one that would, doubtlessly, upset the balance of our fragile ecosystem?

Finally, consider the effect this might have on human societal behavior. If we knew we could bring back any extinct species whenever we wanted to, what would be the impetus to halt species-destroying activities such as meat consumption and deforestation? Might humans begin to act even *less* ecologically responsibly than we do presently, armed with the presumption that we can simply "undo" any harm we cause down the road?

Chapter Eight

Their Stories

What follows are just three of the many stories that abound concerning rescued and/or adopted animals who are typically used for food, fashion, or other purposes by our society. These individuals have names, likes, dislikes, and personalities all their own, and if it weren't for the compassionate humans who took an interest in them, their lives would have been cut short. These stories are a testament to the nonhuman animal spirit, and the overwhelming good that results when we reach across speciesist barriers to share our lives with others.

Frankie, By Gwen and Peter Jakubisin[1]
(from *The Liberationist*, slightly modified)

Three potbellied pigs stand in the corner of a ten-by-twenty-foot pen lined with pea gravel (no shelter), near a dirty, plastic swimming pool, old bits of dog kibble scattered on the ground. The smallest of the three is covered in a fine layer of dust. Her ribs are showing, and she's as bald as a newborn. The man who put the ad on Craigslist explains to us nonchalantly how lucrative breeding potbellied pigs can be. He feeds them scraps from a fast food restaurant down the street to keep his costs low. His three-year-old daughter is walking around the enclosure, aggressively waving a large tree branch as the terrified family of pigs struggles to find a way out of her path.

We've come prepared with peanut butter and jelly tortilla roll-ups, and the sight of snacks inspires the smallest pig to brave toward us, stretching from her back legs and preparing to run in case our offer is a trap. The man calls her "Frankenstein" because he thinks she looks odd for a pig. Her "odd" appearance turns out to be her saving grace. The man can't find anyone to buy her as a pet, and we've talked him into letting us give her a good home instead of selling her body to be turned into "meat." We resolve to call her Frankie—a much more suitable name for a beautiful pig embarking on a new life. We reach out slowly to pet her and she nips at our hands, attempting to bite them, but hoping for more peanut butter-filled tortillas.

Frankie. We're in love.

We bring her home with us that day, even though we don't really have a plan. We've both collectively spent years volunteering at farm sanctuaries, but we don't have a clue as to how we're going to integrate Frankie into our current family of four dogs and two bunnies. All we know is that she needed out of her current situation. She needed to be rescued.

Frankie's story is not uncommon. Every day there are animals in need of rescue— at auction houses, in the backyards of breeders, sometimes even in the homes of well-intentioned folks who don't have the time, money, or space to care for them. We've seen the atrocious conditions of "humane" farms and slaughterhouses. We've watched the rescue of Mei Hua [referring to DxE's Truth Matters video] and the countless others who have been given salvation by those of us willing and able to open our hearts and homes. For us, part of being an activist is adjusting our lives so that we have space and time to offer animals in need. Understandably, not every activist can provide these things, but almost all of us can support farm sanctuaries in one way or another.

Farm sanctuaries are such an incredibly important part of the animal rights movement. While we fight diligently for the right of every animal to be happy, safe, and free, there are folks across the country and world making sure those who are rescued enjoy the very freedoms for which we fight. They provide an education to the public that protests and demonstrations can't: an opportunity to bond and establish a real friendship with a nonhuman animal. Most people, when given the chance to experience the individual personality of an animal they traditionally see as "food," have a really hard time justifying their continued participation in the exploitation of that animal.

Sanctuaries offer a refuge to activists as well. Once we open ourselves up to the world's many injustices against animals, we are inundated with them every day. We become overwhelmed with Facebook posts, news articles, and graphic videos. They are all essential to our activism because they help keep us motivated and aware, but they take a huge emotional (and sometimes physical) toll. Volunteering at a farm sanctuary can balance out all of that pain and anxiety. Witnessing an animal's freedom, connecting with them, taking part in their wellbeing, and knowing that these few will forever be excluded from the torment that their brothers and sisters will endure can have powerful and positive influences on our activism.

This is why it is so necessary for activists to support farm sanctuaries. Owning and operating a farm sanctuary is incredibly hard work. Long days filled with endless tasks and the constant heartbreak of not being able to save everyone or losing the ones you have saved because their bodies were just too broken. It is also expensive work, requiring continuous funds for vet care, proper shelter, and nutritious food. Every form of support we can offer is immensely appreciated and needed, and there are many ways to get involved:

- **Volunteer.** Find a sanctuary close to you and volunteer your time as much as possible.

- **Donate** and encourage your family and friends to donate.

- **Organize fundraisers**, like bake sales or movie screenings.

- **Support sanctuaries on social media.** Acknowledging the hard work these folks put in can go a long way.

- **Share the stories of rescued animals** like Mei Hua, Frankie, and those you meet at sanctuaries. By passing along their histories, including their recoveries, we help foster a culture in which their stories are of moral significance.

As for us, along with volunteering at our local farm sanctuary (Lighthouse Farm Sanctuary in Scio, Oregon), we are also working toward finding a home with additional land so we can offer a loving refuge to more animals that so desperately need it— just like Frankie.

Frankie is still unsure of humans, and we do our best to make her feel safe and happy. Sometimes we talk about how Frankie may never be the kind of pig that wants a belly rub or a back scratch. We occasionally forget her fear of suddenness and inadvertently reach to pet her head, only to be reminded by a quick, startling bark that she is still not okay with being touched. We've learned to show our affection and love for one another in different ways. We can't imagine our lives without her, and every day we get to spend with her makes the knowledge of people eating her kind so much less comprehensible. She isn't here to entertain us or to make us laugh, and she most *certainly* isn't here to be abused or eaten. She's here to live her life, and we're here to make her life as amazing as we can while she is with us.

Frankie: our family.

Luv, Kush, and Gandalf, By Mukul Banbihari and Madhulika Singh
(told to me over email)

Luv, Kush, and Gandalf are three lovable goats currently living with us at PreetiRang Sanctuary in California. Luv and Kush were 4H "projects" who were slated for auction at the Pleasanton Fairgrounds last summer (2014). Jenna Nilbert, a twenty-year-old college student, worked at the fairgrounds during the summer. She spent $550 to buy these twin brothers pre-auction. She had contacted us with her plan months before. These are Boer goats, or "meat goats." Their future was slaughter. We picked them up at the fairgrounds last 4th of July.

Gandalf was a pet goat also in danger of being sold for slaughter after being confiscated as a zoning violation in Richmond, CA. A friend of the original caretaker took him as a favor, and tied him up behind his house in a grassy area for the past one and a half years. We picked him up about two weeks ago.

***

[Having met Luv, Kush and Gandalf recently myself, I can attest to their distinct, vibrant characters. Poor Gandalf was a little standoffish, having undergone surgery the day before I met him, but both Luv and Kush were playful, excited little treasures who clearly loved attention. The dynamic between the two of them was also reminiscent of young twin human boys; they often butted one another out of the way, competing for head rubs, yet at the same time they were inseparable. Where one went, the other followed. Adorable. I am ever so grateful that they will not be exploited as "meat goats," but knowing that so many others *just like them* will be breaks my heart.

Remember, these are the lucky ones. They have suffered previously, but thanks to human intervention that was, for once, positive, they are now safe and happy. All nonhuman animals deserve this same fate.]

Frost, By Lisa Zorn[2]
(from *The Liberationist*, slightly modified)

I met Frost in 2003. We had just adopted our first rabbit, Fury, and we thought he needed a friend. We naively assumed that we could just find one for him, so we stopped at a fair and encountered a man with stacks of cages—multiple sections to a cage, each section the size of a rabbit. The rabbits inside the cages couldn't move. It was upsetting, but we asked him what he was doing with them and if we could have one. He said he was selling them to someone there and sure, we could have one for $5. (Note: Please adopt from shelters or rescues like SaveABunny. I was ignorant in 2003.) He took out a few and we looked at their teeth, then went home with Frost: a little tortoiseshell Netherland Dwarf with the letters "A39" tattooed in her ear.

I don't know what happened to the others, but it was probably something terrible. Frost came from a bad place.

On the car ride home, I held Frost in a towel, and she didn't move much. She must have been terrified. When we got home, we introduced her to Fury, and he loved her at first sight (or sniff). (Side note: rabbits can be very picky about other rabbits, so this is no little thing.) Once Frost realized she was safe, everything changed.

Frost was an adventurous rabbit. She was the opposite of Fury—she liked to leap before considering, to hurl her body through time and space and worry about the consequences afterwards. She was the kind of rabbit who would bump into walls in her enthusiasm, who would chew a hole through the screen door to the balcony and go exploring, who would climb the shelves I put up for her so she could gaze out the window at the world.

Frost told us, in no uncertain terms, that being caged at night was completely unacceptable. She would rattle the cage bars all night long, so we got rid of the cage. Frost loved all greens, especially broccoli. Frost loved Fury (and Fury loved her). Eventually, Frost grew to love me too, sitting next to me in bed at the crack of dawn and demanding that I pet her by pushing her head underneath my hand whenever I started to fall asleep.

Frost was a Netherland Dwarf, which is a tiny breed of rabbit with a blunt nose and little ears; they are typically bred for show and for the pet trade (and sometimes used as food for snakes). The blunt nose of the Netherland Dwarf means they often have teeth problems (rabbits' teeth constantly grow, and need to be worn down by chewing on hay), and Frost eventually developed a tooth infection. We had several of her teeth pulled, but the infection kept spreading, and none of the antibiotics we tried worked. Eventually we decided to euthanize Frost because she was in so much pain, and she couldn't eat anything on her own. My heart broke that day, and I will always miss her and always love her.

We gave her the best life we could, and she was happy. In return, she and Fury transformed me. They taught me the meaning of unconditional love. They woke me up; I realized that everyone is Frost—that every cow, every chicken, every turkey, every pig, every fish… They are Frost in the ways that matter: in their desire for bodily autonomy, in their feelings of joy and fear and love.

That's why when Whole Foods started selling the flesh of rabbits last year, it felt to me like a punch in the gut. Not because rabbits deserve to live more than any of the other animals slaughtered by Whole Foods, but because rabbit meat is a fairly small market in the US, and Whole Foods is a large grocery chain with a lot of influence. This step just made the world a lot worse for rabbits. Already, rabbits tread a sort of middle ground; though many of us love them as family members, they are also exploited by almost every industry: fur, meat, medical, and cosmetic testing. The battle for personhood is often in the foreground for rabbits, and those of us who have rabbit companions are often at the receiving end of "jokes" about violence against our loved ones.

When rabbit advocates contacted Whole Foods expressing our dismay about their decision to start selling rabbit meat, Whole Foods routinely responded by saying:

> Whole Foods Market is sensitive to the companion animal issue and we understand this

product won't appeal to everyone. However, for those customers who have been asking us to carry rabbit, it's our job to make sure we offer the highest-quality product from responsible sources. A number of shoppers have been asking Whole Foods Market to carry rabbit for years but conventional raising practices do not meet our rigorous animal welfare standards. To meet our customers' requests for rabbit we needed our own set of animal welfare standards, and these rabbit welfare standards are a direct result of a rigorous four-year process to address the welfare issues in rabbit production. As we have done in the past, our hope is that our high standards will be a model for industry change.

Whole Foods is breeding and killing New Zealand White rabbits, a domestic breed of rabbit that many of us know and love as companions. Whole Foods suppliers take rabbits from their families and kill them at eight weeks of age, when they are barely weaned babies. Spayed and neutered house rabbits typically live for eight to twelve years. Digging further into the "rigorous animal welfare standards" provided by Whole Foods, one finds: "Stocking density must not exceed 2lbs/square foot." This means that an eight-pound adult New Zealand rabbit could be housed his whole life in a two-foot by two-foot space. A mother and her eight babies could be housed in a two-and-one-eighth-foot square space. These "rigorous animal welfare standards" are actually just routine. Further, the standards make points about keeping the rabbits in groups, but doesn't require it for males or females. Whole Foods sources their rabbits from Iowa and Missouri, both of which have passed ag-gag laws.

None of this really matters, though, because *even if* companies that sell rabbit flesh kept rabbit families intact, *even if* the rabbits were given lots of room to run and jump and play and binky (that's the rabbit happy dance), *even if* they were fed strawberry treats every night and workers gave them good morning kisses, it would not be ok. At the end of the day, a young rabbit is taken from her family and her throat is cut. She will never love or be loved again, just so restaurants and grocery stores can make a few bucks.

I will fight for Frost, and all of her sisters and brothers, and all of the beautiful beings who are exploited and killed by Whole Foods and other businesses. Until every animal is free.

Chapter Nine

Final Words from the Author

Until we extend our circle of compassion to all living things, humanity will not find peace.

—Albert Schweitzer, *The Philosophy of Civilization*

Your Liberationist Friends, Your Liberationist Family

Presumably, if you are reading this book and are not yourself an animal liberationist (yet?), someone you love is. First of all, on behalf of the entire liberationist community, *thank you*. Thank you for taking the time to read at least one book in an effort to understand your friend or relative's position, rather than prejudging it or dismissing it. Thank you for caring enough about the liberationist in your life to devote time and energy to learning about a cause that may not immediately resonate with you.

Secondly, an excellent resource I'd like to recommend to you is Casey Taft's e-book, ***Mom, Dad, I'm Vegan: A Guide for Understanding Your Vegan Family Member***. The book is available via Vegan Publisher's website, and explores the matters discussed here more in depth from your perspective as a non-vegan.

Lastly, please bear in mind that, whether the vegan in your life chooses to tell you so or not, it is incredibly painful for us to see people we love consuming animal byproducts. While we cannot force anyone to stop doing so, I hope this book has encouraged you to give veganism a try; if not, at the very least, please consider refraining from consuming meat, dairy, eggs, and other exploitative products in the presence of the vegan in your life. If that vegan has been spending less time with you, please try to understand that this is a result of the pain caused by your actions and not at all an indication that this person doesn't love *you* anymore. It is precisely because they love you that it hurts them all the more to see you do these things than it does to witness strangers doing these things.

I do not mean to support this decision to avoid non-vegans; my concerns about this approach will follow shortly. I mean only to clarify that while their actions may be hurtful to you, that is not their intention—just as you do not intend to hurt them when you eat a hamburger in front of them. Please forgive them, as they must also forgive you.

Your Speciesist Friends, Your Speciesist Family

When you first open your eyes to the violence inherent in meat, dairy, and so many other industries supported by our current culture, the world can be a very painful place in which to live. You see violence in places you never saw it before, or where it might have been easier to ignore in the past—in the refrigerator at your best friend's house, on your mother's dining room table at Thanksgiving, in the leather handbag your colleague rests casually on your desk while she chats you up in the morning. You may also find it difficult to talk to people with whom you previously spoke with ease; you can't help yourself—you get on the topic of animal liberation, and others just don't agree with you. They say hurtful things, make tasteless jokes. Your comfort level drops dramatically.

Many activists I've encountered have dealt with this problem by elimination; they've ended years-long friendships, refused to visit their families. Some not only engage in this behavior themselves, but also actively endorse it to others, claiming that to sit at a speciesist table is to be speciesist oneself. The reasons for excluding speciesists from one's social circle abound, ranging from philosophical (*To be with this person is to support speciesism, and since I don't support speciesism, I can't be with this person.*) to emotional (*It's just too painful to watch people eat meat now; I'd rather not ever have to see that again.)* to purely coincidental (*I just spend so much time engaged in activism that the only people I see regularly are other activists!*).

While I empathize completely with those who choose, or submit to, this way of life, I must issue to them a word of warning (several, actually). For starters, as I mentioned in Chapter Two with respect to reaching out to people who come from cultural backgrounds different from our own, we cannot hope to ever change the minds of a community with which we do not engage. Therefore, while some may view abstaining from attending a speciesist dinner as a point of pride—a demonstration of their personal commitment to the cause—I see it as a missed opportunity. How can we open the eyes of our speciesist friends and family if we stop spending time with them? How can we understand why they're doing what they're doing, and therefore effectively convince them to do otherwise, when we won't even talk to them?

Some have argued that by being absent, they are attempting to change minds. They hope that their presence will be missed and, therefore, those who miss them will stop engaging in speciesist behaviors in order to get them to come back. If you've found this to be effective in your own community, then, bully for you; unfortunately, for many of us, this simply would not work. For many, the people whom they actively exclude from their lives will simply adjust to being without them. They will consider it the missing person's choice not to be present rather than a result of their actions (both of which, by the way, are true; but while the liberationist would prioritize the latter, many non-liberationist friends and relatives may prioritize the former), and absence will enable them to continue engaging in speciesist behaviors without anyone there to call them out on doing so—to remind them that what they are doing is not "normal," but *cruel.*

Not only do we forfeit an opportunity to change minds in the moment, by not attending a particular function, but we also miss out on countless opportunities in the long run by *limiting our sphere of influence.* We fall into the trap of preaching to the converted, spouting arguments our new friends have already heard and with which they already agree, because they have already rejected speciesism. Our ability to *spread the message*—as opposed to reiterating it to those by whom it has already been received—greatly diminishes.

Isolating yourself from everyone who doesn't agree with you is one surefire way to push people out, rather than *draw people in*, to the movement. Jealousy is inevitable. Rather than considering the Animal Liberation Movement as a necessary step on the path of social justice—which they might if you continued to engage with them on the subject—rejected friends and family may start to think, "The Animal Liberation Movement stole my [daughter/best friend/boyfriend]." They may become resentful of the movement, and regard it, rather than their own behavior, as the reason for your absence.

(It is worth noting that this behavior also leaves one open to more outlandish criticisms, such as that one has joined a cult. One of the most commonly known indicators that someone has joined a cult, gang, or other such brainwashing enclave is that the person *stops spending time with people to whom they were once close.*)

If our goal is for every animal to be free, we need to speak to as many people as possible about it—not just people who are already on board. We need to keep a stiff upper lip, and continue to attend the same social functions we did before, but whereas before we may have sat by idly as an animal was served, now we must take it upon ourselves to *speak up for the animals on the table.* We must be wary of how our newfound passion is perceived by others and be sensitive to their jealousies. Activism is very much about stepping outside of one's comfort zone—not just with respect to public demonstrations, but even in one's own home. It starts with *you*—and the fewer liberationists who your friends and family know, the more thoroughly you become an emblem of the movement in their eyes. If they can find fault with your behavior, and they have no other liberationists in their lives as examples, they will attribute those faults to the movement—and reject it.

I know it's easier said than done, but social justice is not about doing what is easy or what is comfortable. It's about fighting for the rights of others, whatever the emotional cost. To abstain from engaging with speciesists, while perhaps making your own life more enjoyable in some ways, is to allow the speciesist machine to continue to operate on them, uninterrupted.

Nutrition

By far the most common argument I am confronted with against veganism is the nutrition angle. Many a concerned mother and scientifically inclined friend have bombarded me with questions about how vegans get their protein, how to raise healthy vegan babies once they're off the breast milk, and so forth. At the Conscious Eating Conference in Berkeley, CA on April 4, 2015, an audience member did not mince words when addressing a panel of activists: "I know many people who believe—I mean strongly, firmly *believe*—that they *need* meat to survive. They *really* think they *need* it. What do you say to them?"

That's just one of many examples of why this (aside from the less factually-challengeable matters of *apathy* and *selfishness*—"I don't care" and "It tastes good") is a *fundamental issue* to address when trying to convince someone to go vegan. Whether you like it or not, you *will* be asked about this, and if you cannot provide a sufficient answer, you will lose the opportunity to change that person's mind. Yes, there are scores of activists who are willing to forgo something their body might need in order to not harm others—but just because a few people are willing to do something doesn't mean you can expect everyone on the planet to follow suit.

In April 2015, The Dietary Guidelines Advisory Committee, a federally appointed panel of nutritionists, declared that a "diet lower in animal-based foods"—political code for the vegan diet—is healthier for humans, in addition to being better for our planet.[1] Little by little, those in the know about human health are coming out of the closet with respect to declaring veganism as not just safe, but as *healthier than non-veganism*. While they continue to avoid using the term "vegan," just as scientists habitually avoid using the term "language" when discussing nonhuman communication, the end result is the same. The diet lowest in animal-based foods is a vegan diet.

Independent of research, the proof is in the coconut-based pudding; if humans required meat and/or dairy in order to survive, how could there be any vegan community of which to speak? Wouldn't we all be dead by now? You don't need to read a book or take a class to know that it is possible to be vegan and healthy; just Google "vegan bodybuilders," "vegan wrestlers," "vegan marathon runners," etc. You'll be bombarded with images of and articles about strong, healthy, physically active vegans. They're not all scrawny little nerds, like me.

If you have any specific concerns about the ins and outs of vegan living (i.e. the infamous Protein Question with which every vegan is inundated), I strongly encourage you to reach out to any of the numerous vegan-friendly doctors that exist, spend some time online, or even reach out to me directly if you wish. I am not a doctor, but I'm someone who has had numerous vegan nutrition discussions in the past decade, and being thus compelled to keep up with all of the latest research, I would love to share this information with anyone still struggling with this aspect of the movement.

Chapter Ten of this book includes a list of books about the plant-based diet. One such book is called *Rethink Food: 100+ Doctors Can't Be Wrong*. That's right, over a hundred doctors—and those are just the ones authors Castle and Goodman chose to include! My heart goes out especially to those scores of animal-loving parents out there who are afraid that putting their children on a vegan diet will somehow cause them harm; for that reason, you will find a list of resources in Chapter Ten for just such parents. These resources include not only nutrition-based titles, but also wonderful children's books designed to explain veganism to young minds.

Survival

I have said in several places throughout this text that every species is hardwired to promote its own survival. It occurs to me that this may sound a hell of a lot like, "Every species is hardwired to be speciesist." If that were the case, why fight speciesism? Well, for starters, that is not the case, in my view; to promote one's own survival over that of others' is not the same as thinking that one is *superior to* or *more important than* another. It is a biological instinct that has nothing whatsoever to do with evaluating the intelligence, sentience, or emotional capabilities of others.

It is not par for the course for humans to kill nonhumans under this banner. Killing nonhumans does *not* promote our own survival; it in fact hinders it by polluting our air and water, as well as by making us more susceptible to a host of ailments, such as heart disease from clogged arteries. So while prioritizing one's own life, or even the life of one's own kind, is innate, *speciesism*— the unwavering belief that one's own species is superior to all others—is not. The latter is a culturally developed illness, like racism and sexism. To prioritize the wellbeing of one's own human tribe over another human tribe is innate; to decide that one's own tribe is superior to another human tribe, and therefore choose to enslave or otherwise oppress the other human tribe, is not.

It's a fine line, and I struggle with it myself often. For instance, one question I always ask myself is: If a human baby and a kitten were both in the same kind of trouble, and you could only save one of them, whom would you save? My answer is, and has always been, *the baby*. Now, is this because I am speciesist? Or because the survival of the baby ensures the survival of my species? I'd like to think the latter, but realistically, the death of one human baby would not result in the extinction of humanity; other humans would continue to breed and produce more babies. So, why am I so inclined to save the human baby over the kitten? They're both cute. They're both conscious. Neither has offended or harmed me in any way.

I don't know, ultimately, why I answer that question the way I do, with such certainty; what I do know is, being prepared to save a baby at the risk of a kitten does not mean I should habitually engage in animal cruelty in perpetuity. These tough questions— *would you save a human baby over a kitten, would you steal a human's liver to save your own life*—are compelling mental exercises for any philosopher or social justice advocate, but with respect to enacting positive social change, they are irrelevant. The most effective way forward, in my view, is to own up to our instinct to promote our own survival and to keep that instinct in perspective—not to give it too much weight.

Survival, in short, is not the same as *dominion*. It is our insistence on *dominion* over the planet and its inhabitance, rather than our drive to promote the survival of humanity, that causes so much undue suffering in the world.

Safety in Numbers

Protesters of any sort in the Bay Area have it easy. At every demonstration I've engaged in or witnessed here, whether the cause was animal rights, opposition to police brutality, or either side of the abortion debate, *hoards* of people showed up to speak their minds. With DxE East Bay, perhaps the smallest demonstration I attended consisted of roughly ten people other than myself.

In Arizona, by contrast, as a PALS member, I often attended demonstrations at which there were only three or four other people. To say that it was nerve-racking is an understatement. It was, at times, *terrifying*. I didn't speak. I chanted with the group, but I did not perform any speak-outs, in English or in Spanish (the latter of which would certainly have been useful). The culture of Phoenix, Arizona is arguably also less vegan-friendly than that of the East Bay. To enter a place of violence with just a few other individuals and speak to a community you know will be patently—yes, at times even *violently*—unreceptive to your message is no small feat. The elephant march in Phoenix in the summer of 2013 would not have been canceled if Eddie James and Kelsey Mosher hadn't challenged Ringling Brothers as a pair, undeterred by the fact that no one else could make it that day.

Aishwarrya Prakash discovered DxE online and wanted to participate; at the time, there was no DxE presence in her hometown of Chennai, India. So, she started one; near the end of 2014, she participated in one of our International Days of Action alone, entering a restaurant and delivering a beautiful speech before standing outside with her sign for several hours. By the time she engaged in her third Day of Action, she had approximately eight other people at her side, but she could not possibly have known that would happen on that very first day. She took a huge risk, and it's people like her who have made the movement what it is today and will contribute to its growth and inevitable success.

I have never demonstrated all by my lonesome, and truthfully, I probably never will. I admire such courage, and want to thank every participant in the Animal Liberation Movement who has dared to demonstrate alone or with a small group. The bravery of people like PALS organizers Zubair Hussaini, Eddie James and Ioana Samartinean, and DxE Chennai's founder Aishwarrya Prakash, is paramount to any social justice movement.

Braving the Elements

Another consideration with respect to the ease of public demonstrations is weather. None of us can control the climate where we live, and it is undoubtedly harder to sustain an outdoor demonstration in places where there is extreme cold, consistent storms, or heavy snowfall. While the culture of the Bay Area is conducive to activism in a lot of ways—and there are ample historical precedents for this—one way in which West Coast and Southwestern activists are extremely privileged is that it is warm and sunny for them more often than it is not. Having spent most of my adult life in New York City, I can honestly say that I've come to many, many more protests since moving West than I ever did in New York, particularly in the winter. My activism in those days consisted mostly of writing, and attending indoor demonstrations and indoor meetings.

So, in keeping with the spirit of giving credit to those whose tasks are more challenging than our own, I want to offer a special thanks to activists in places like New York, Chicago, Canada, and Russia for braving the elements over and over again to spread the message of animal compassion. By keeping their suffering in perspective and prioritizing the needs of nonhumans they have never met above their own, they truly lead by example and embody the spirit of the self-sacrifice necessary to push the movement forward.

The Role of Sanctuaries

As for the scores, hundreds, thousands of currently farmed animals that would become homeless should the meat and dairy industries shut down, they, too, deserve to be treated like victims. Here is where the role of **farm sanctuaries** becomes fundamental. These are places where previously abused and/or exploited pigs, chickens, cows, and other "non-pets" or "farmed animals" are cared for while they are simultaneously granted autonomy over their bodies. Here, the employees are not *owners* of the animals in their charge; they are simply *caregivers*.

Currently, animal sanctuaries across the US and around the globe attain the animals in their charge in a variety of ways. In

some cases, the animals are found abandoned; in others, industrialized farms that go under call to have their animals picked up
because they can no longer afford to feed or house them. There
are also cases in which people adopt a non-traditional pet (most
commonly, small pigs), wholly unaware of the animal's needs or
what to expect from his or her behavior. In any case, donating
to and volunteering at animal sanctuaries should be a top-tier
priority among animal liberationists. In sharing Frankie's story,
Gwen and Peter provided us with a great list of other ways to
contribute, such as hosting fundraisers and promoting sanctuaries on social media.

Not only is free labor and funding necessary to keep
these places operational, but sanctuary work also puts all of the
other forms of activism in which we engage into perspective. It
adds a face, a name, and a story to our values; rather than just
fighting for "chickens," for instance, members of Direct Action
Everywhere who have encountered Errol now fight with his face,
his demeanor, his silky feathers, and taloned feet in mind. Kelly Atlas has her two recently adopted hens, Snow and Duala,
to consider when she speaks out about animal liberation, while
Gwen and Peter will undoubtedly continue to be both inspired
and motivated by Frankie. I am completely in love with Luv,
Kush, Gandalf, Harvey (a young bull), Brahma (a cow), and all of
the other creatures I met at PreetiRang, as well as the many hens
I've encountered at both Hen Harbor and Animal Place whose
names I regrettably can't remember. It is an incredibly rewarding
experience to work hands-on with the beings about whom activists spend so much time talking, writing, and reading.

Many sanctuaries have a Wish List on their websites (or
in their newsletters, for which you can sign up online) of basic,
often inexpensive supplies; if you're not close enough to one to
volunteer regularly, see if you have any of these items to spare
(common items include towels, blankets, snacks, and animal
grooming products) and, if so, ship them. Most sanctuaries also

allow you to sponsor an animal, meaning that for a small monthly fee you will contribute to the needs of a specific nonhuman of your choosing.

A Cultural Shift

I used to think that animal sanctuaries were the one and only answer, that once the animals were freed, they would all go to sanctuaries and live happily ever after. DxE Bay Area organizer Chris Van Breen—the same gentleman who shares with me the Parable of the Liver—has since enlightened me to the reality that there simply isn't enough room at existing sanctuaries for *all* of the animals that need to be freed. Perhaps if these places were better funded, and could therefore purchase more land, that would ultimately change; in the meantime, Chris suggested that what might help speed our movement along is a cultural shift in which humans agree to adopt previously farmed nonhumans— animals such as pigs and chickens.

Many groups and individuals are currently working toward this shift by partaking in a new movement dubbed The Microsanctuary Movement. The idea here is that you don't need tons of space or resources to raise nonhumans; if you limit the number of those you take in, you can provide a wonderful home for someone other than a cat or a dog—someone who really, truly needs it and might otherwise end up on a human's plate or wrapped around a human's waist. Justin Van Kleeck wrote an amazing article for *Our Hen House* on the issue, entitled "The Sanctuary in Your Backyard: A New Model for Rescuing Farmed Animals."

In the article, Justin details how shortly after he and his wife, Rosemary, founded Triangle Chance for All, they used their three-acre property outside of Chapel Hill, North Carolina to start a microsanctuary. While there are no specifications as to what "microsanctuary" means, it's inherent in the word itself—a sanctuary much smaller than the better-known ones like Farm Sanctuary in

New York and Animal Place in California, with fewer residents and a much smaller budget. According to Justin, however, the primary distinction has nothing to do with dimensions or dollars: "I think that microsanctuary is as much a state of mind—a perspective on the world and our place as rescuers and caregivers—as it is about property lines and resident numbers."[2]

In other words, microsanctuaries are one means of promoting one of many necessary cultural shifts required for animal liberation to become a reality: a shift from living *next to* or *around* animals to living *amongst* them. The one obvious downside that I can see is that it doesn't seem possible for the millions of Americans who live in apartments. Can any farmed animal live happily without regular outdoor access? I don't think so, so in order to undertake this, yes, you will need some land—but not much. More importantly, what you'll need is the ability to refrain from regarding farmed animals as property, and consider them instead your housemates—or even, to an extent, your children, as you will not only be living alongside of them, but also providing for basic needs such as food. (Most people don't supply their human roommates with food on a daily basis—at least, not willingly.)

Other proud microsanctuary operators include Ren and Brandy Hurst-Setzer in California (raising horses and other farmed animals); Amy Dye, who is currently raising two sheep in her (yarded) home in Maine; and Rachel Waite, who raises chickens, ducks, and goats in Michigan.

Such a massive cultural shift as movements like this one promote would force us to truly respect these nonhumans—not just feel sorry for them. We would have to learn to *coexist* with them in the deepest sense of the word, in a manner that has been unknown to most of the Western world, or at least to the United Stated, for centuries. We would have to move beyond simply allowing them the live, and embrace them as part of our world, sharing our world with them as naturally and readily as we do with our fellow humans.

Before we could even attempt this, however, we would first have to *learn more about them*. In an interview with sanctuary founder Mary Schanz at Ironwood Pig Sanctuary in Marana, Arizona, I was surprised to learn that the majority of pigs in her charge was not rescued from the clutches of factory farming, but, rather, from the living rooms of naïve adopters:

> So many are now being released because people bought these poor pigs after being told lies that they were "teacup" pigs and would only reach thirty to forty pounds. Many of these people know nothing about pigs or their needs, and very soon after buying them they try to dump them...

> Most unwanted potbelly pigs end up at auction, where they are sold for about fifty cents a pound to be slaughtered and rendered. Most animal control facilities do not take them; and when they do, some send them to the action anyway when they are not adopted. Arizona shelters will often call us because pigs they have are not being adopted, so the only out is euthanasia...

> These animals have become fad pets... They are affectionate, smart, wonderful animals, but they are not easy to manage. They bulldoze backyards, destroy household items, and often become aggressive beginning at about age one to three. They are driven to become the head of the herd, which is natural for them amongst their own but is not well received in the human household. Of the hundreds of pigs we have picked up over the years, very few have come from a good home for a pig. Not that many of the people did not care for

their pig; they just didn't understand what a pig needs. One of the most important needs for any pig, for instance, is a companion pig—and most people only want one pig.

So before we all race to the nearest animal sanctuary in our pickup trucks and load the beds with our new roommates, we need to educate ourselves on what our potential roomies would need from us as well as what we would need from them. If you live in a tiny urban apartment, a cow probably isn't the best choice for you, and you're probably not the best choice for a cow. If you have a fondness for pigs, that's great, but be prepared to adopt at least two of them, because these guys just aren't the loner types.

Time to Get to Work!

So there you have it, folks; this is where the movement stands presently. All of the old excuses for not participating—that we need meat and dairy to survive, that we need to test on animals to treat illnesses and cure diseases, that animals aren't conscious/cannot think/cannot feel—have been blown out of the water. For every excuse meat-eaters, rodeo enthusiasts, and the like throw out into the world for perpetuating animal abuse, scores of leading sociologists, psychologists, doctors, lawyers, and other top-tier professionals in our society have come out with myriad rebuttals.

No more excuses; it's time to get to work!

This book has provided only a light framework of some of the ways you can contribute to the Animal Liberation Movement. My primary intention here, beyond disseminating knowledge, was to *inspire*, so please, let your creative juices flow and feel free to develop your own actions, your own institutions, your own networks through which to fight for animal liberation. There are infinite ways you can contribute, pretty much all of which fall under the umbrella of *nonviolent direct action*.

Volunteering at animal sanctuaries is nonviolent direct action. Hosting public demonstrations at institutions of violence is nonviolent direct action. Writing books, articles, or blog entries about animal liberation is nonviolent direct action. Distributing publications by others about the movement is nonviolent direct action. Shooting, editing, or promoting documentaries and other videos concerning animal liberation is nonviolent direct action. Developing visual art installations conveying the message of animal liberation is nonviolent direct action. Composing songs about animal liberation is nonviolent direct action. Empowering slaughterhouse laborers and other human victims to escape the speciesist machine and find peaceful employment is nonviolent direct action.

In short, there is room in the Animal Liberation Movement for everyone—not just the extroverts.

External threats to the movement abound, but perhaps the singular largest threat to the movement comes to us not from without, but from within. I am referring to the tendency toward *welfarism* rather than liberation.

In 1991, Ronald Duchin, an Army War College graduate and former special assistant to the Secretary of Defense, gave a speech to the Cattlemen's Association in which he outlined three critical steps in eliminating the threat animal liberationists pose to their business:

1. Isolate the radicals.

2. Cultivate the idealists and educate them into becoming realists.

3. Co-opt the opportunists into agreeing with the industry.[3]

Humanewashing—welfarist bread and butter—fires on all of these cylinders. It makes it seem "weird" or "extreme" to demonstrate at humanewashers like Whole Foods and Chipotle—even though they sells meat and dairy (Step 1). It convinces many who would otherwise become liberationists to focus on a more practical, easily obtainable goal: improved animal welfare (Step 2). Finally, it co-opts opportunists by convincing them that their supporters, readers, and viewers will be jeopardized if they take what is perceived as the "extreme" course of action, and to celebrate "victories" of industry-nonprofit compromise (Step 3).

There are, regrettably, some people in this world who genuinely just "don't care" about animals, but this is a miniscule minority. The vast majority *does* care about the plight of nonhumans. Humanewashing, while itself an external threat, has given birth to (or, perhaps more accurately, has accelerated the growth of) the internal threat of welfarism—resting on one's laurels because bullhooks are no longer being used on elephants, because the horse-drawn carriages in Central Park are being abolished, or because chickens have "access" to the outdoors.

I do not mean to impugn these indications of social progress. I'm as grateful for them as anyone ever could be, but we can't stop there. True animal liberation is about saving lives—not making them more comfortable for the limited time we allot them. Going vegan isn't enough, either—unless you use this term in its fullest sense, meaning that you not only *eat* vegan, but that you *live* vegan. The elephants and tigers at the circus don't care what you eat. Neither do the horses and bulls at rodeos.

Please join me and countless others all over the world at the frontier of global justice—until every animal is free.

Chapter Ten

Resources and Suggestions for Further Reading

Disclaimer: While I've done my best to ensure that the sanctuaries below are vegan-friendly, I strongly recommend that you call in advance to determine whether a sanctuary is vegan or not before you visit it! Online representations are not always accurate, and information changes over time. I have not personally visited each and every one of these sanctuaries.

Animal Sanctuaries: Coast-to-Coast
(Note: This list is not exhaustive.)

West Coast/Pacific Northwest:

Animal Place
Grass Valley, CA: animalplace.org
Animal Place Farm Rescue
Vacaville, CA: animalplace.org
Farm Sanctuary's Animal Acres
Los Angeles, CA: farmsanctuary.org/the-sanctuaries/los-angeles-ca/
Farm Sanctuary's Northern California Shelter
Orland, CA:farmsanctuary.org/the-sanctuaries/orland-ca/
Harvest Home Animal Sanctuary
French Camp, CA: harvesthomesanctuary.org

Howling Acres Wolf Sanctuary
Grants Pass, OR: trekaroo.com/activities/howling-acres-wolf-sanctuary-grants-pass-oregon
Lighthouse Farm Sanctuary
Scio, OR: greenpeople.org/listing/Lighthouse-Farm-37863.cfm

Out to Pasture Animal Sanctuary

Estacada, OR: outtopasturesanctuary.org

Sanctuary One

Jacksonville, OR: greenpeople.org/listing/Sanctuary-One-65087.cfm

Wildwood Farm Sanctuary

Newberg, OR: wildwoodfarmsanctuary.org

Pigs Peace Sanctuary

Stanwood, WA: pigspeace.org/main/index.html

Precious Life Animal Sanctuary

Edmonds, WA: preciouslifeanimalsanctuary.org

River's Wish Animal Sanctuary

Spokane, WA: riverswishanimalsanctuary.org

Idaho Farm Animal Sanctuary

Boise, ID: asensorylife.com/idaho-farm-animal-sanctuary.html

Idaho Humane Society Rescue Ranch

Boise, ID: idahohumanesociety.org/programs/rescue-ranch/

Snowdon Wildlife Sanctuary

McCall, ID: snowdonwildlife.org

Rolling Dog Ranch Animal Sanctuary

Ovando, MT: rollingdogranch.com

United in Light, Inc.

Livingston, MT: draftrescue.com

Kindness Ranch

Hartville, WY: kindnessranch.org

Southwest:

Cockadoodle Moo

Reno, NV: cockadoodlemoo.org

Desert Rescue Animal Sanctuary

Las Vegas, NV: desertrescue.org

Safe Haven Rescue Zoo

Imlay, NV: safehavenwildlife.com

Healing Hearts Animal Rescue and Refuge
Phoenix and Willcox, AZ: healingheartsaz.org

HoofsnHorns Farm Inc.
Tucson, AZ: hoofsnhorns.com

Ironwood Pig Sanctuary
Marana, AZ: ironwoodpigsanctuary.org

Tranquility Trail Animal Sanctuary
Scottsdale, AZ: tranquilitytrail.org

Whisper's Sanctuary
Elgin, AZ: rrheartranch.com/Sanctuary.html

Best Friends Animal Society
Kanab, UT: bestfriends.org

Ching Farm Rescue and Sanctuary
Riverton, UT: chingsanctuary.org

Denkai Sanctuary
Weld County, CO: denkaisanctuary.org/Animals.html

Moyer Animal Farm Rescue
Bennett, CO: moyeranimalrescue.com

Peaceful Prairie Sanctuary
Deer Trail, CO: peacefulprairie.org

Rooster Sanctuary at Danzig's Roost
Bennett, CO: danzigtherooster.com

Heart and Soul Animal Sanctuary
Santa Fe, NM: animal-sanctuary.org

Olde Windmill Trail Farm Animal Sanctuary
Cerrillos Hills, NM: oldewindmillfarmanimalsanctuary.org

Midwest/Central United States:

E.T. Farms Animal Rescue
Delmont, SD: animalshelter.org/shelters/et_farms_animal_rescue_rid9038_rs_pc.html

Spirit of the Hills Wildlife Sanctuary
Spearfish, SD: spiritofthehillssanctuary.org

Nebraska Wildlife Rehab, Inc.
Louisville, NE: nebraskawildliferehab.org
The Old Poor Farm
Elkhorn River Valley, NE: theoldpoorfarm.com

Safari's Sanctuary
Broken Arrow, OK: safarizoo.com

Chicken Run Rescue
Minneapolis, MN: brittonclouse.com/chickenrunrescue/
Wildcat Sanctuary
Sandstone, MN: wildcatsanctuary.org
Wildlife Rehabilitation Center of Minnesota
St. Paul, MN: wrcmn.org/index.php

Iowa Wildlife Center
Ames, IA: iowawildlifecenter.org/mission.aspx
Lusco Farms Rescue
Malvern, IA: luscofarmsrescue.org/Pages/default.aspx

DD Farm Animal Sanctuary
Columbia, MO: ddfarmanimalsanctuary.wordpress.com
Missouri Forget-Me-Not Horse Rescue and Sanctuary
Linn Creek, MO: missouriforgetmenot.org

Amazing Grace Equine Sanctuary
Elkhart Lake, WI: rescuehorses.org
Heartland Farm Sanctuary
Madison, WI: heartlandfarmsanctuary.org

Have a Heart Farm
Glenview, IL: haveaheartfarm.org
Wedrose Acres
Gridley, IL: wedroseacres.org

Black Sheep Crossing Farm Animal Sanctuary

Northport, MI: blacksheepcrossing.org

It's Meow or Never

Michigan Center, MI: itsmeowornever.org

Sasha Farm Animal Sanctuary

Manchester, MI: sashafarm.org

A Critter's Chance

Greenfield, IN: acritterschance.org/About.html

Black Pine Animal Sanctuary

Albion, IN: blackpine.org

Uplands PEAK Sanctuary

Salem, IN: uplandspeaksanctuary.org

Forever Safe Farm

Salem, OH: foreversafefarm.org

Happy Trails Farm Animal Sanctuary

Ravenna, OH: happytrailsfarm.org

Sunrise Sanctuary

Marysville, OH: sunrisesanctuary.org

South:

Dreamtime Sanctuary

Elgin, TX: dreamtimesanctuary.org

Potbellied Pig Haven Rescue

Cedar Park, TX: animalshelter.org/shelters/Potbellied_Pig_Haven_Rescue_rId5172_rS_pC.html

Saint Francis Wolf Sanctuary

Montgomery, TX: saintfrancissanctuary.org

Sunny Day Farms

La Coste, TX: sunnydayfarms.wix.com/texas#!__index

Enoch J. Donaldson Animal Sanctuary

Mount Hermon, LA: humanela.org/news.htm

Wings of Hope Wildlife Sanctuary

Livingston, LA: wingsofhoperehab.org/home.html

Riddle's Elephant and Wildlife Sanctuary

Greenbrier, AR: elephantsanctuary.org/default2.asp

Cedar Hill Animal Sanctuary

Caledonia, MS: cedarhillanimalsanctuary.org

Hope Animal Sanctuary

Grenada, MS: idausa.org/hope/

Halls Farm Animal Sanctuary

Vance, AL: animalshelter.org/shelters/Halls_Farm__Animal_Sanctuary_rId6706_rS_pC.html

Red Gate Farm Rescue

Tuscaloosa, AL: redgatefarmrescue.org/cms/

Sampson's Sanctuary

Blountsville, AL: sampsons-sanctuary.org

Noah's Ark Animal Sanctuary

Locust Grove, GA: noahs-ark.org

Sunkissed Acres Equine Rescue

Summerville, GA: sunkissedacres.org

Englewood Animal Rescue Sanctuary (EARS)

Englewood, FL: earsanimalrescue.com

Forest Animal Rescue at Peace River Rescue and Ranch

Silver Springs, FL: forestanimalrescue.org

Kindred Spirits Sanctuary

Ocala, FL: kindredspiritssanctuary.org

Sanctuary Animal Refuge

Clewiston, FL: sanctuaryanimalrefuge.thegivingeffect.com

Full Circle Farm Sanctuary

Burnsville, NC: fullcirclefarmsanctuary.org

Goat Mountain Ranch Sanctuary

Leicester, NC: goatmountainsanctuary.org

Piedmont Farm Animal Refuge

Pittsboro, NC: piedmontrefuge.org/about-us

Big Oaks Rescue Farm

Greenwood, SC: bigoaksrescuefarm.org

Cotton Branch Farm Animal Sanctuary

Leesville, SC: cottonbranch.org

Paws Animal Wildlife Sanctuary

Waterloo, SC: paws-sc.com

Forever Farm Animal Rescue and Sanctuary

Shelbyville, TN: americantowns.com/tn/shelbyville/organization/forever-farm-animal-rescue-and-sanctuary

Horse Creek Wildlife Sanctuary and Animal Refuge

Savannah, TN: horsecreekwildlife.org

Watertown Farm Animal Sanctuary

Watertown, TN: watertown-animal-sanctuary.org

Home at Last Animal Sanctuary

Salvisa, KY: homeatlastanimals.org

PIGS Animal Sanctuary

Shepherdstown, WV: pigs.org

The White Pig Bed and Breakfast and Animal Sanctuary at Briar Creek Farm

Schuyler, WV: thewhitepig.com

Angels of Assisi Harmony Farm Sanctuary

Roanoke, VA: angelsofassisi.org/programs/harmony-farm/

Rugby Creek Animal Rescue

Mouth of Wilson, VA: rugbycreekanimalrescue.org

United Poultry Concerns

Machipongo, VA: upc-online.org

East Coast/New England:

Burleigh Manor Animal Sanctuary
Ellicott City, MD: burleighmanorretreat.org
Star Gazing Farm Animal Sanctuary
Boyds, MD: stargazingfarm.org
Whispering Rise Farm and Animal Sanctuary
Freeland, MD: wrfas.org

Bonniedale Farm Animal Sanctuary
North Scituate, RI: bonniedalefarmanimalsanctuary.com/home
West Place Animal Sanctuary
South Tiverton, RI: westplace.org

Blue Chip Farm Animal Refuge
Dallas, PA: bcfanimalrefuge.org/default.aspx
Chenoa Manor
Avondale, PA: chenoamanor.org
Hog Heaven Rescue Farm Inc.
Cochrantown, PA: hogheavenrescue.org/home.html
Hope Haven Farm Sanctuary
Pittsburg, PA: hopehavenfarm.org
Indraloka Animal Sanctuary
Mehoopany, PA: indraloka.org

Finally Home Farm Animal Rescue
Williamstown, NJ: finallyhomefarm.org
For the Animals Sanctuary
Blairstown, NJ: fortheanimalssanctuary.org
Oasis Animal Sanctuary Inc.
Williamstown, NJ: oasisanimalsanctuary.org
The Barnyard Sanctuary
Columbia, NJ: barnyardsanctuary.org

Catskill Animal Sanctuary
Saugerties, NY: casanctuary.org

Farm Sanctuary

Watkins Glen, NY: farmsanctuary.org/the-sanctuaries/watkins-glen-ny/

Hudson Valley Animal Rescue and Sanctuary

Poughkeepsie, NY: hvars.org

Spring Farm Cares

Clinton, NY: springfarmcares.org

Woodstock Farm Animal Sanctuary

Woodstock, NY: woodstocksanctuary.org

Binn Animal Rescue and Sanctuary

Ridgefild, CT: binnanimalrescue.org/about.html

Out to Pasture Farm and Rescue, Inc.

Newington, CT: outtopasture.org

Maple Farm Sanctuary

Mendon, MA: maplefarmsanctuary.org

Promising Hope Animal Sanctuary

Middleboro, MA: promisinghope.com

Sunny Meadow Sanctuary

Holden, MA: sunnymeadowsanctuary.org

Mountain View Farm Animal Sanctuary

East Burke, VT: mvfas.org

Spring Hill Horse Rescue

Clarendon, VT: springhillrescue.com

Turtle Hill Farm Animal Sanctuary

Reading, VT: turtlehillfarm.net

VINE Sanctuary

Springfield, VT: vine.bravebirds.org

Live and Let Live Farm, Inc.

Chichester, NH: liveandletlivefarm.org/index.htm

Rolling Dog Farm

Lancaster, NH: rollingdogfarm.org

Maine State Society for the Protection of Animals Farm
Windham, ME: msspa.org/visit-our-farm

Peace Ridge Sanctuary
Penobscot, ME: peaceridgesanctuary.org

Non-Continental US:

Meadow Gates Farm Sanctuary
Wasilla, AK: jollyrogersranch.com/meadowgates

Leilani Farm Sanctuary
Haiku, Maui, HI: leilanifarmsanctuary.org

Books about the Plant-Based Diet

The China Study by Dr. T. Colin Campbell and Thomas Campbell
Comfortably Unaware: What We Choose to Eat is Killing Us and Our Planet by
    Dr. Richard Oppenlander
The Food Revolution by John Robbins and Dr. Dean Ornish
Forks over Knives: The Plant-Based Way to Health by Gene Stone and Dr. T.
    Colin Campbell
*The Plant-Powered Diet: The Lifelong Eating Plan for Achieving Optimal
    Health, Beginning Today* by Sharon Palmer and Dr. David Katz
*The Power of Your Plate: Eating Well for Better Health—20 Experts Tell You
    How* by Dr. Neal Barnard
Rethink Food: 100+ Doctors Can't Be Wrong by Shushana Castle and Amy-Lee
    Goodman

Kick-Ass Plant-Based Cookbooks

The Candle Cafe Cookbook by Joy Pierson and Bart Potenza
Chloe's Kitchen by Chloe Coscarelli
Chloe's Vegan Desserts by Chloe Coscarelli
The Vegan Bible by Publications International, Ltd.
Veganize This! by Jenn Shagrin
Veganomicon by Isa Chandra Moskowitz and Terry Hope Romero *(For the
    fancier, more adventurous at-home chef!)*
Vegan Soul Kitchen by Bryant Terry

Raising Vegan Kids

The Complete Idiot's Guide to Vegan Eating for Kids by Dana Villamagna and
Dr. Andrew Villamagna

Dave Loves Chickens by Carlos Patino

*The Everything Vegan Pregnancy Book: All you need to know for a healthy
pregnancy that fits your lifestyle* by Reed Mangels

Feeding Your Vegan Infant with Confidence by Sandra Hood

Lena of Vegitopia and the Mystery of the Missing Animals by Sybil Severin

Plant-Powered Families: Over 100 Kid-Tested, Whole-Foods Vegan Recipes by
Dreena Burton

Raising Vegan Children in a Non-Vegan World: A Complete Guide for Parents by
Erin Pavlina

Steven the Vegan by Dan Bodenstein

That's Why We Don't Eat Animals by Ruby Roth

Vegan is Love: Having Heart and Taking Action by Ruby Roth

*Vegan Lunch Box: 130 Amazing, Animal-Free Lunches Kids and Grown-Ups
Will Love!* by Jennifer McCann

*Vegan Lunch Box Around the World: 125 Easy, International Lunches Kids and
Grown-Ups Will Love!* by Jennifer McCann

V is for Vegan: The ABCs of Being Kind by Ruby Roth

*The Vegan Pregnancy Cookbook: Over 200 Recipes to Keep You and Baby Happy
and Healthy for All Three Trimesters (and Beyond!)* by Lorena Novak Bull
and Jolinda Hackett

The Vegan Pregnancy Survival Guide by Sayward Rebhal

Acknowledgements

First and foremost, I'd like to thank my mother, Iris Rodriguez, for all of the love and support she has provided me with throughout my lifetime. It was through her that I learned the values of perseverance, honesty, and compassion that have both motivated and empowered me in everything that I do.

I would also like to thank my current partner, Alex Ludlum, for his endless patience as I worked on this book, supporting me both financially and emotionally throughout this process in spite of the fact that he does not share my views on animal liberation. Hopefully, this book will light a spark.

My former colleague and de facto mentor, Joy Tutela, taught me almost everything that I know about the world of publishing, and her insights have been invaluable to me in creating a work that not only conveyed the views about which I am so passionate, but one that is also accessible and marketable. My good friend from college and another publishing dynamo, Donna Loffredo at Simon and Schuster, also lent a hand in finalizing this book—between Christmas and New Year's 2014, a time when most people aren't even engaged in the work assigned to them, let alone volunteering to take on additional tasks, gratis, for a friend.

My PALS, Phoenix Animal Liberation Squad, made me feel at home in the brief time I spent living in Arizona, and inspired me to stop talking and start doing. I found my voice as a member of this group, stepping further and further out of the closet with respect to my commitment to animal liberation. Various members of Direct Action Everywhere's East Bay branch, including founder Wayne Hsiung and organizers Priya Sawhney, Kelly Atlas, Brian Burns, and Chris Van Breen, lent their experience and expertise to this work; I simply could not have done this without them.

John Sanbonmatsu, Matthew Liebman, Jessica Blome, Mary Schanz, and others lent invaluable insights to this work via interview. Renowned scholar Peter Singer paved the way for this book by writing *Animal Liberation* and defining speciesism for us all. I would also like to thank the scores of doctors and nonhuman animal behaviorists who wrote the works from which material found herein was derived. The Animal Liberation Movement as a whole owes a debt of gratitude to the various underpaid and unpaid staff members at animal sanctuaries without whom the animals we liberate would have no place to go.

Finally, I would like to thank my publisher, Casey Taft; editors Justin Van Kleeck and Breanna Locke; friend and fellow activist Christopher-Sebastian McJetters; and the entire team at Vegan Publishers for their support and enhancement of this book. Everyone's feedback made the book so much stronger, and their work on this and other projects (such as their *awesome* blog) makes each and every one of them truly inspirational.

Endnotes

Chapter One: How This Became My Life

1. Neal Barnard, *Breaking the Food Seduction* (New York: St. Martin's Griffin, 2004).
2. Rafael Brown, trans., *The Little Flowers of Saint Francis* (Colorado: Image Books, 1971).
3. Paul Rogers, "California: New Mandatory Water Conservation Rules for Lawns, Hotels, Restaurants," *Mercury News*, March 18, 2015, http://www.mercurynews. com/drought/ci_27729990/california-drought-state-passes-mandatory-new-water-conservation.
4. Donny Moss, "Media Coverage of California Water Shortage Omits Biggest Culprit— Animal Agriculture," *Their Turn*, April 7, 2015, http://theirturn. net/2015/04/07/animal-agriculture-water-shortage.
5. Martin Luther King, Jr., "Letter from a Birmingham Jail," University of Pennsylvania website, Accessed April 22, 2015, http://www.africa.upenn.edu/ Articles_Gen/Letter_Birmingham.html.

Chapter Two: Speciesism: The Final Frontier

1. Peter Singer, *Animal Liberation* (New York: Avon, 1975), 6.
2. "Race and Justice Shadow Report," *The Sentencing Project*, October 2013, http:// sentencingproject.org/doc/publications/rd_ICCPR%20Race%20and%20Justice%20 Shadow%20Report.pdf.
3. "Table 6: Public high school number of dropouts and event dropout rate for grades 9–12, by race/ethnicity and state or jurisdiction: School year 2009–10," *National Center for Education Statistics*, Accessed January 2015, http://nces.ed.gov/ pubs2013/2013309/tables/table_06.asp.
4. Christina Huffington, "Women and Equal Pay: Wage Gap Still Intact, Studies Show," *The Huffington Post*, April 9, 2013, http://www.huffingtonpost. com/2013/04/09/women-and-equal-pay-wage-gap_n_3038806.html.
5. Jenika McCrayer, "My Feminism is Black, Intersectional, and Womanist—and I Refuse to be Left Out of the Movement," *Everyday Feminism*, May 6, 2015, http:// everydayfeminism.com/2015/05/black-womanist-feminism/.
6. George Dvorsky, "Prominent Scientists Sign Declaration that Animals Have Conscious Awareness, Just Like Us," *Io9.Com*, August 23, 2012, http://io9. com/5937356/prominent-scientists-sign-declaration-that-animals-have-conscious-awareness-just-like-us.
7. J.M Coetzee, *The Lives of Animals* (New Jersey: Princeton University Press, 1999), 44–45.
8. "The Real Price of Dairy," YouTube video, posted by EVOLVE Campaigns, December 1, 2012, https://www.youtube.com/watch?v=Q4qQNi3WZdQ.
9. *Blackfish*, directed by Gabriela Cowperthwaite (2013; Los Angeles, CA: Magnolia Pictures), Film.
10. Karl Von Frisch, *The Dance Language and Orientation of Bees,* (Cambridge, MA: Harvard University Press, 1967).

11. Sarah Graham, "Birds Share 'Language' Gene with Humans," *Scientific American,* March 31, 2004, http://www.scientificamerican.com/article.cfm?id=birds-share-language-gene.

12. Constance Scharff and Jana Petri, "Evo-devo, deep homology and FoxP2: implications for the evolution of speech and language," *Philosophical Transactions of the Royal Society B* 366, no. 1574 (July 27, 2011), http://rstb.royalsocietypublishing.org/content/366/1574/2124.full.

13. John Endler, "Bowerbirds, Art and Aesthetics," *Communicative and Integrative Biology* 5, no. 3 (May 1, 2012), http://www.ncbi.nlm.nih.gov/pmc/articles/PMC3419115/.

14. "Aesthetic," *Oxford Dictionary Online*, 2015, http://www.oxforddictionaries.com/us/definition/american_english/aesthetic.

15. Haruka Wada, "The Development of Birdsong," *Nature Education Knowledge* 3, no. 10 (2010), http://www.nature.com/scitable/knowledge/library/the-development-of-birdsong-16133266.

16. "Strictly Animals Dancing," *Discover Wildlife*, December 23, 2010, http://www.discoverwildlife.com/animals/strictly-animals-dancing.

17. Don Wilmeth and Christopher Bigsby, *The Cambridge History of American Theatre*, Volume One, (Cambridge, England: Cambridge University Press, 1998).

18. Eleanor Barkhorn, "'Vote No on Women's Suffrage:' Bizarre Reasons for Not Letting Women Vote," *The Atlantic*, November 6, 2012, http://www.theatlantic.com/sexes/archive/2012/11/vote-no-on-womens-suffrage-bizarre-reasons-for-not-letting-women-vote/264639/.

19. "1800s," *Quotes on Slavery*, Accessed June 2014, http://quotesonslavery.org/category/decades/1800s/.

20. Ibid.

21. Wayne Hsiung, "Is there a place in animal rights for a kid from China? Part I: Performing Whiteness," *The Liberationist*, November 4, 2014, http://directactioneverywhere.com/theliberationist/2014/11/3/is-there-a-place-in-animal-rights-for-a-kid-from-china-part-i-performing-whiteness.

22. Direct Action Everywhere Forum: "The Color of a Movement," *The Liberationist* (blog), March 21, 2014, http://directactioneverywhere.com/theliberationist/2014/3/21/the-color-of-a-movement-the-curious-story-of-race-and-animal-rights-and-why-it-matters.

23. Jennifer Eberhardt, Phillip Atiba Groff, Melissa J. Williams, and Matthew C. Jackson, "Not Yet Human: Implicit Knowledge, Historical Dehumanization, and Contemporary Consequences," *Journal of Personality and Social Psychology* 94, no. 2 (2008): 293-306, http://www-psych.stanford.edu/~mcslab/PublicationPDFs/Not%20yet%20human.pdf.

24. Carol J. Adams. *Animals and Women: Feminist Theoretical Explorations* (Durham, NC: Duke University Press, 1995).

25. Marilyn French, *Beyond Power* (Minnetonka, MN: Olympic Marketing Corps, 1985), 341.

26. David Kirk, "The Intersectional Web of Oppression," chart, 2015, https://www.facebook.com/groups/world.intersectional.liberation/.

27. Saryta Rodriguez, "On Cooperative Learning," *The Liberationist*, April 3, 2015, http://directactioneverywhere.com/theliberationist/2015/4/3/on-cooperative-learning.

28. Ngọc Loan Trần, "Calling In: A Less Disposable Way of Holding Each Other Accountable." *Black Girl Dangerous*, December 18, 2013, http://www.blackgirldangerous.org/2013/12/calling-less-disposable-way-holding-accountable/.

29. Ahmad, Asad. "A Note on Call-Out Culture." *Briarpatch Magazine*, March 2, 2015. http://briarpatchmagazine.com/articles/view/a-note-on-call-out-culture.

Chapter Three: Lifting the Veil

1. Dan Shapley, "Nine Food Label Lies," *Good Housekeeping*, Accessed January 2015, http://www.goodhousekeeping.com/home/green-living/reading-food-labels-470201.

2. "Truth Matters: DxE Investigators Expose 'Humane' Fraud at Whole Foods," YouTube video, posted by Direct Action Everywhere, January 7, 2015, https://www.youtube.com/watch?v=yU4PJCuslD0.

3. Karina Ioffee, "Petaluma Farms Sued over 'Cage Free' Labeling," *PetalumaPatch*, October 3, 2012, http://petaluma.patch.com/groups/business-news/p/petaluma-farms-sued-over-cage-free-labeling.

4. Matt Brown, "Animal Rights Activists Target Petaluma Slaughterhouse," *Press Democrat*, April 7, 2014, http://www.pressdemocrat.com/article/20140407/articles/140409655.

5. Dana Liebelson, "Behind the Burrito: 5 Things Chipotle's Ads Don't Tell You," *Mother Jones*, September 25, 2013, http://www.motherjones.com/politics/2013/09/chipotle-commercial-sustainable-food-truth.

6. David Sirota, "Chipotle's Self-Serving Deception: A 'Vegetarian' Bait-and-Switch," *Salon*.com, September 19, 2013, http://www.salon.com/2013/09/19/chipotles_self_serving_deception_a_vegetarian_bait_and_switch/.

7. Rich McManus, "Ex-Director Zerhouni Surveys Value of NIH Research," *NIH Record*, June 21, 2013, http://nihrecord.nih.gov/newsletters/2013/06_21_2013/story1.htm.

8. Aysha Akhtar, "Want to Improve Medical Research? Cut Out the Animals!" *Huffington Post*, July 11, 2013, http://www.huffingtonpost.com/aysha-akhtar/want-to-improve-medical-r_b_3576080.html.

9. "Genomic Responses in Mouse Models Poorly Mimic Human Inflammatory Diseases." *Proceedings of the National Academy of Sciences*, January 7, 2013, http://www.pnas.org/content/early/2013/02/07/1222878110.

10. "Researchers Find Striking Differences between Human and Animal Insulin-Producing Islet Cells," *Diabetes Research Institute* (Press Release), 2006, http://www.diabetesresearch.org/page.aspx?pid=409.

11. Aysha Akhtar, "Why Animal Experimentation Doesn't Work— Reason 1: Stressed Animals Yield Poor Data," *Huffington Post*, July 31, 2013, http://www.huffingtonpost.com/aysha-akhtar/animal-experimentation_b_3676678.html.

12. Ann Baldwin and Marc Bekoff, "Too Stressed to Work," *New Scientist* 194, no. 2606 (June 2, 2007), http://www.sciencedirect.com/science/article/pii/S026240790761358X.

13. "Alternatives to Animal Testing," *PETA*, Accessed July 2014, http://www.peta.org/issues/animals-used-for-experimentation/alternatives-animal-testing/.

14. Dylan Walsh, "Of Mice and Micro-Organs," *New Yorker*, November 1, 2013, http://www.newyorker.com/online/blogs/elements/2013/11/of-mice-and-microorgans.html.

15. "Alternatives," *PETA*.

16. Visala Kantamneni, "These Eight Countries Have Banned Wild Animals in Circuses…Why Can't We Do It?" *OneGreenPlanet.Org*, March 19, 2014, http://www.onegreenplanet.org/animalsandnature/10-countries-that-have-banned-wild-animals-in-circuses/.

17. Charisse Jones, "Ringling Brothers Eliminating Elephant Acts," *USAToday.com*, March 5, 2015, http://www.usatoday.com/story/money/business/2015/03/05/ringling-brothers-elephants/24423553/.

18. Richard Pérez-Peña, "Elephants to Retire from Ringling Brothers Stage," *NYTimes.com*, March 5, 2015, http://www.nytimes.com/2015/03/06/us/ringling-brothers-circus-dropping-elephants-from-act.html?_r=0.

19. "About the CEC," Center for Elephant Conservation website, accessed March 7, 2015, http://www.elephantcenter.com/about-us/about-cec/.

20. Samuel Dewitt Haddock Jr., "Declaration of Samuel Dewitt Haddock Jr.," August 28, 2009, http://www.ringlingbeatsanimals.com/pdfs/haddockDeclarationRedacted.pdf.

21. "SeaWorld Stock Gets Soaked, Plunges 33%," *CNNMoney New York*, August 19, 2014, http://money.cnn.com/2014/08/13/investing/seaworld-earnings/.

Chapter Four: Putting Animal Liberation on the Public Agenda

1. "Statement of Purposes," *Animal Liberation Victoria*, Accessed March 2015, http://www.alv.org.au/about.php.

2. "Campaigns," *Animal Liberation Victoria*, Accessed February 2015, http://www.alv.org.au/campaigns.php.

3. Beau Donelly, "'They've Upset the Hens': Charged Activists in Second Chook Break," *The Sydney Morning Herald*, April 5, 2012, http://www.smh.com.au/environment/animals/theyve-upset-the-hens-charged-activists-in-second-chook-break-20120404-1wdvn.html.

4. "Egg Factory Lockdown - Animal Liberation Victoria," Vimeo video, posted by Animal Liberation Victoria, 2013, http://vimeo.com/40568491.

5. Mark Hawthorne, "Chicken Rescuers Share Their Stories," *Striking at the Roots*, June 3, 2009, https://strikingattheroots.wordpress.com/tag/virtual-battery-cage/.

6. Patty Mark and Erik Gorton, "What's Wrong with the RSPCA?" *RSPCA Watchdog*, Accessed February 2015, http://www.rspcawatchdog.org/articles/whatswrong.htm.

7. "RSPCA Free Range Fraud Exposed," *Animal Liberation Victoria* (Press Release), August 28, 2013, http://www.humanemyth.org/alvexposesthemyth.htm.

8. James LaVeck and Jenny Stein, "An Open Letter to Animal Advocates," *Humanemyth.org*, August 2013, http://www.humanemyth.org/alvexposesthemyth. htm.

9. Claudette Vaughan, "Interview with Patty Mark. Abolitionist-Online," *Kara*, Accessed February 2015, http://animalrightskorea.org/essays/interview-with-petty-mark-of-animal-liberation-victoria.html.

10. "KFC Cruelty Demo- You Animal Liberation Youth," YouTube video, posted by alvopenrescue, May 11, 2009, https://www.youtube.com/watch?v=2_-_oMWc33E.

11. "Animal Liberation Youth," *Animal Liberation Victoria*, Accessed February 2015, http://www.alv.org.au/youth.php.

12. "Patty Mark and Animal Liberation Victoria Sued by Animal Industry," *Animal Liberation Victoria*, Accessed February 2015, http://www.alv.org.au/storyarchive/0835ALV-Sued/Patty-Mark-and-Animal-Liberation-Victoria-Sued. php.

13. Karen Barlow, "From Farm to Fork" (transcript), *Australian Broadcasting Corporation*, March 25, 2010, http://www.abc.net.au/lateline/content/2010/s2856547.htm.

14. "Organizing Principles," *Direct Action Everywhere*, Accessed February 2014, http://directactioneverywhere.com/organizing-principles/.

15. Daniel Quinn, *Ishmael: An Adventure of the Mind and Spirit* (New York: Bantam, 1995), *The Story of B* (New York: Bantam, 1997).

16. "Chipotle Investor Relations – SEC Filings," *Chipotle.com*, Accessed May 2014, http://ir.chipotle.com/phoenix.zhtml?c=194775&p=irol-SECText&TEXT=aH R0cDovL2FwaS50ZW5rd2l6YXJkLmNvbS9maWxpbmcueG1sP2lwYWdlP TkzNjIzNTImRFNFUT0wJlNFUT0wJlNRREVTQz1TRUNUSU9OX0VO VElSRSZzdWJzaWQ9NTc%3d.

17. Kevin McCoy, "Chipotle Shares Chill 6% on Lower-than-Expected Earnings," *USA Today*, April 17, 2014, http://www.usatoday.com/story/money/business/2014/04/17/chipotle-q1-earnings/7814821/.

18. Stephanie Strom, "After Suspending Supplier, Chipotle Takes Pork Off Menu in 600 Stores," *The New York Times*, January 14, 2015, http://www.nytimes. com/2015/01/15/business/after-suspending-supplier-chipotle-takes-pork-off-menu-in-600-stores.html.

19. "Chipotle to Test 'Sofritas' in Seven San Francisco Bay Area Restaurants," Chipotle website, Accessed April 22, 2015, http://ir.chipotle.com/phoenix. zhtml?c=194775&p=irol-newsArticle&ID=1778960.

20. "Mission, Goals & Values," *Nonhuman Rights Project*, Accessed February 2015: http://www.nonhumanrightsproject.org/mission-goals-values/.

21. Charles Siebert, "Should a Chimp be Able to Sue its Owner?" *The New York Times*, April 23, 2014, http://www.nytimes.com/2014/04/27/magazine/the-rights-of-man-and-beast.html.

22. Saryta Rodriguez, "On Redefining Personhood," *The Liberationist*, April 27, 2015, http://www.directactioneverywhere.com/theliberationist/2015/4/27/on-redefining-personhood.

23. "NhRP Files Motion for Leave to Appeal to Court of Appeals in Tommy's Case," *Nonhuman Rights Project*, February 25, 2015, http://www.nonhumanrightsproject.org/2015/02/25/nhrp-files-motion-for-leave-to-appeal-to-court-of-appeals-in-tommys-case/.

24. Jesse McKinley, "Judge Orders Stony Brook University to Defend Its Custody of 2 Chimps" *The New York Times*, April 21, 2015, http://www.nytimes.com/2015/04/22/nyregion/judge-orders-hearing-for-2-chimps-said-to-be-unlawfully-detained.html?_r=2.

25. Animal Legal Defense Fund Facebook Page, Accessed March 12, 2015, https://www.facebook.com/AnimalLegalDefenseFund?fref=ts.

26. Michael Grynbaum, "Mayor de Blasio Unveiling Bill to Ban Horse-Drawn Carriages," *The New York Times*, December 1, 2014, http://www.nytimes.com/2014/12/02/nyregion/mayor-de-blasio-unveiling-bill-to-ban-horse-drawn-carriages.html.

27. Mark Bittman, "Christie's Pig-Crate Politics," *The New York Times*, December 2, 2014, http://www.nytimes.com/2014/12/03/opinion/christies-pig-crate-politics.html.

28. Kelly Atlas, "Allies and Images: The Importance of Communicating The Victim's Personhood," *The Liberationist*, October 28, 2014, http://directactioneverywhere.com/theliberationist/2014/10/28/allies-and-images-the-importance-of-communicating-the-victims-personhood.

29. Wilson, "This Woman Really, Really Loves Her Chicken," GlennBeck.com, October 7, 2014, http://www.glennbeck.com/2014/10/07/this-woman-really-really-loves-her-chicken/.

30. Donald Watson, *The Vegan News* 1, November 1944, PDF, http://ukveggie.com/vegan_news/.

31. Will Tuttle, editor, *Circles of Compassion* (Danvers, MA: Vegan Publishers, 2014).

32. J.M. Coetzee, *The Lives of Animals* (New Jersey: Princeton University Press, 1999), 21.

Chapter Five: Where to Draw the Line?

1. Action for Animals, "What about Fish?" *All-Creatures.org*, Accessed August 2014, http://www.all-creatures.org/alert/WhatsFishyAboutSeafood.pdf.

2. Jeanette Bradley, "The Eight Most Common Food Allergies," *About Health*, December 16, 2014, http://foodallergies.about.com/od/foodallergybasics/a/big_eight_fa.htm.

3. Forschungsverbund Berlin e.V. (FVB), "Do fish feel pain? Not as humans do, study suggests," *ScienceDaily*, Accessed April 22, 2015, www.sciencedaily.com/releases/2013/08/130808123719.htm.

4. Victoria Braithwaite, *Do Fish Feel Pain?* (New York, NY: Oxford University Press, 2010).

5. Peter Singer, "Fish: The Forgotten Victims on Our Plate," *The Guardian*, September 14, 2010, http://www.theguardian.com/commentisfree/cif-green/2010/sep/14/fish-forgotten-victims.

6. "Fish Feel Pain," *PETA*, Accessed August 2014, http://www.peta.org/issues/animals-used-for-food/factory-farming/fish/fish-feel-pain/.

7. L.U. Sneddon, V.A. Braithwaite, M.J. Gentle, "Do fishes have nociceptors? Evidence for the evolution of a vertebrate sensory system," *Royal Society Publishing*, June 7, 2003, Abstract, http://rspb.royalsocietypublishing.org/content/270/1520/1115.

8. "The Silent Suffering of Lobsters," *Animal Aid*, Accessed August 2014, http://www.animalaid.org.uk/images/pdf/factfiles/lobsters.pdf.

9. Tamar Stelling, "Do Lobsters and Other Invertebrates Feel Pain? New Research Has Some Answers," *The Washington Post*, March 10, 2014, http://www.washingtonpost.com/national/health-science/do-lobsters-and-other-invertebrates-feel-pain-new-research-has-some-answers/2014/03/07/f026ea9e-9e59-11e3-b8d8-94577ff66b28_story.html.

10. Campbell Centre for the Study of Animal Welfare, "Do Fish Experience Fear?" *CCSAW News* 11 (Spring/Summer 2004): 1–2.

11. Stephanie Yue, Ian J.H. Duncan, and Richard D. Moccia, "Investigating Fear in Rainbow Trout (Oncorhynchus mykiss) Using the Conditioned-Suppression Paradigm," *Journal of Applied Animal Welfare Science* 11, no. 1 (January 1, 2008): 14–27, http://www.animalsandsociety.org/assets/library/715_investigatingfearinrainbo.pdf.

12. Keven N. Laland, Culum Brown, and Jens Krause, "Learning in Fishes: From Three-Second Memory to Culture," *Fish and Fisheries* 4, no. 3 (August 12, 2003): 199–202.

13. L.A. Dugatkin, *Cooperation Amongst Animals* (New York, NY: Oxford University Press, 1997).

14. R. J. F. Smith, "Alarm signals in fishes," *Reviews in Fish Biology and Fisheries* 2 (1992): 33–63.

15. Anahad O'Connor, "Health Officials Call for More Fish in Diets of Children and Pregnant Women," *The New York Times*, June 10, 2014, http://well.blogs.nytimes.com/2014/06/10/updated-advice-on-eating-fish-during-pregnancy/?_php=true&_type=blogs&_r=0.

16. Daniel Goleman, "Peril is Seen for Babies Whose Mothers Ate Fish with PCBs," *The New York Times*, July 22, 1984, http://www.nytimes.com/1984/07/22/us/peril-is-seen-for-babies-whose-mothers-ate-fish-with-pcb-s.html.

17. Elizabeth Weiss, "Mercury Damage 'Irreversible,'" *USA Today*, February 8, 2004, http://usatoday30.usatoday.com/news/health/2004-02-08-mercury-usat_x.htm.

18. "Fish: Toxic for Mothers, Poisonous to Babies," *PETA*, Accessed November 2014, http://www.peta.org/living/food/fish-toxic-mothers-poisonous-babies/.

Chapter Six: A Family to Feed: The Slaughterhouse Laborer, and Other Human Victims of the Animal Holocaust

1. "Slaughterhouse Workers," *Food Empowerment Project*, Accessed January 2015, http://www.foodispower.org/slaughterhouse-workers/.

2. "Factory Farm Workers," *Food Empowerment Project*, Accessed January 2015, http://www.foodispower.org/factory-farm-workers/.

3. "Blood, Sweat and Fear: Workers' Rights in U.S. Meat and Poultry Plants," *Human Rights Watch*, 2004, http://www.hrw.org/reports/2005/usa0105/.

4. "Injustice on Our Plates: Immigrant Women in the U.S. Food Industry," *Southern Poverty Law Center*, 2010, http://www.splcenter.org/sites/default/files/downloads/publication/Injustice_on_Our_Plates.pdf.

5. Mark Hawthorne, "Inside the Life of a Factory Farm Worker," *VegNews*, May 1, 2013, http://vegnews.com/articles/page.do?pageId=5732&catId=1.

6. Lucas Spangher, "The Overlooked Plight of Factory Farm Workers," *The Huffington Post*, August 18, 2014, http://www.huffingtonpost.com/lucas-spangher/plight-of-factory-farm-workers_b_5662261.html.

7. Jennifer Dillard, "A Slaughterhouse Nightmare: Psychological Harm Suffered by Slaughterhouse Employees and the Possibility of Redress through Legal Reform," *Georgetown Journal on Poverty Law & Policy, Forthcoming*, July 5, 2010, http://papers.ssrn.com/sol3/papers.cfm?abstract_id=1016401.

8. *Peaceable Kingdom: The Journey Home*, directed by Jenny Stein (2009; Ithaca, NY: Tribe of Heart Films), Film.

9. Supreme Master Television, "Harold Brown: From Cattle Farmer to Animal Advocate, Part I," *Animal World*, March 19, 2010, http://suprememastertv.com/aw/?wr_id=425.

10. "May 2013 National Occupational Employment and Wage Estimates United States," *Bureau of Labor Statistics*, May 2013, http://www.bls.gov/oes/current/oes_nat.htm#45-0000.

11. "State and County Quick Facts," *United States Census Bureau*, 2013, http://quickfacts.census.gov/qfd/states/00000.html.

12. William Kandel and Ashok Mishra, "Immigration Reform and Agriculture," *U.S. Department of Agriculture*, March 1, 2007, http://ageconsearch.umn.edu/bitstream/8099/1/fo07ka01.pdf.

13. "Free Online Education Without Credit or Full University Degree Programs, Tuition-Free," *University of the People*, Accessed February 2015, http://uopeople.edu/articles/free_online_education.

14. "Programs," *Robin Hood Foundation*, Accessed February 2015, https://www.robinhood.org/programs.

Chapter Seven: Liberation as Autonomy

1. "Lee Hall Interview," *Animal Rights Zone*, August 21, 2010, https://arzonetranscripts.wordpress.com/2010/08/21/lee-hall-guest-chat-transcript/.

2. Lee Hall, *On Their Own Terms: Bringing Animal Rights Philosophy Down to Earth* (Darien, CT: Nectar Bat Press, 2010).

3. *Tiny: A Story about Living Small*, directed by Merete Mueller and Christopher Smith (2013; New York, NY: First Run Features), Film.

4. Toby Koberle, "Animals and Genetic Engineering: Unlimited Cruelty," *AllCreatures.Org*, July 2005, http://www.all-creatures.org/articles/ar-animalsandge.html.

5. Roxanne Khamsi, "Transgenic Cows have Udder Success," *Nature.Com*, April 2005, http://www.nature.com/news/2005/050328/full/news050328-14.html.
6. Nathaniel Rich, "The Mammoth Cometh," *The New York Times*, February 27, 2014, http://www.nytimes.com/2014/03/02/magazine/the-mammoth-cometh.html?hp&_r=0.
7. Paul Rincon, "Fresh Effort to Clone Extinct Animal," *BBC*, November 22, 2013, http://www.bbc.com/news/science-environment-25052233.

Chapter Eight: Their Stories

1. Gwen and Peter Jakubisin. "On The Importance of Sanctuaries," *The Liberationist*, March 25, 2015, http://directactioneverywhere.com/theliberationist/2015/3/25/on-the-importance-of-sanctuaries.
2. Lisa Zorn, "Would Whole Foods Kill My Family?" *The Liberationist*, February 10, 2015, http://directactioneverywhere.com/theliberationist/2015/2/10/would-whole-foods-kill-my-family.

Chapter Nine: Final Words from the Author

1. Lydia Wheeler, "Vegan diet best for planet," *The Hill*, April 5, 2015, http://thehill.com/regulation/237767-vegan-diet-best-for-planet-federal-report-says.
2. Justin Van Kleeck, "The Sanctuary in Your Backyard: A New Model for Rescuing Farmed Animals," *Our Hen House*, June 24, 2014, http://www.ourhenhouse.org/2014/06/the-sanctuary-in-your-backyard-a-new-model-for-rescuing-farmed-animals/.
3. James LaVeck, "Invasion of the Movement Snatchers: A Social Justice Cause Falls Prey to the Doctrine of 'Necessary Evil," *Humane Myth*, October 2006, http://www.humanemyth.org/invasion.htm.